THE BATTLE OF NÖRDLINGEN 1634

The Bloody Fight between Tercios and Brigades

Alberto Raúl Esteban Ribas

'This is the Century of the Soldier', Fulvio Testi, Poet, 1641

Helion & Company

Helion & Company Limited
Unit 8 Amherst Business Centre
Budbrooke Road
Warwick
CV34 5WE
England
Tel. 01926 499 619
Email: info@helion.co.uk
Website: www.helion.co.uk
Twitter: @helionbooks
Visit our blog http://blog.helion.co.uk/

Published by Helion & Company 2021
Designed and typeset by Mach 3 Solutions Ltd (www.mach3solutions.co.uk)
Cover designed by Paul Hewitt, Battlefield Design (www.battlefield-design.co.uk)

Text © Alberto Raúl Esteban Ribas 2021
Illustrations © as individually credited
Colour artwork by Serge Shamenkov © Helion & Company 2021
Maps drawn by George Anderson © Helion & Company 2021

Every reasonable effort has been made to trace copyright holders and to obtain their permission for the use of copyright material. The author and publisher apologise for any errors or omissions in this work and would be grateful if notified of any corrections that should be incorporated in future reprints or editions of this book.

ISBN 978-1-914059-73-5

British Library Cataloguing-in-Publication Data.
A catalogue record for this book is available from the British Library.

All rights reserved. No part of this publication may be reproduced, stored in a retrieval system, or transmitted, in any form, or by any means, electronic, mechanical, photocopying, recording or otherwise, without the express written consent of Helion & Company Limited.

For details of other military history titles published by Helion & Company Limited contact the above address or visit our website: http://www.helion.co.uk.

We always welcome receiving book proposals from prospective authors.

Contents

Introduction   iv

1   The Armies   7
2   The Leaders   50
3   The War in Germany   61
4   Fate Beats a Path to Nördlingen   86
5   The Path of the Cardinal-Infante   92
6   Movements around Nördlingen   102
7   The Battle   106
8   The Aftermath   160
9   The Consequences   164
10   Conclusion   167

Colour Plates   180

Appendices
I   Battlefield Photograph locations by Daniel Staberg   184
II   Battle Maps Key and Phases   188

Bibliography   191

Introduction

The long conflict of the Thirty Years' War is a decisive and fascinating stage in European history. The reasons for the escalation of war that led to all-out war in Germany were diverse.[1] The localised revolt starting with the defenestration of Prague revealed the political and religious tensions that existed in the Habsburg Empire. But soon the revolt was rapidly transformed into a pan-European conflict: in 1625, with the Danish intervention; in 1630, with the Swedish intervention; and in 1635, the entry of France into the war.

Many books have been written to study and understand the reasons that led to such bloodshed across Europe. In the words of Peter Wilson, it became a European tragedy. This book focuses on a study of the Battle of Nördlingen, on 5 and 6 September 1634 where a Swedish-German army faced an army from the Holy Roman Empire, the Catholic League and Spain.

Firstly, I would like to clarify that for practical and literary reasons I use the words 'Protestant' and 'Swedish-German' as synonyms. With them, I refer to the troops of the Generals Gustav Horn and Bernard of Saxe-Weimar. Similarly, I use the word 'Catholic' to designate Spanish troops, but also imperial soldiers, those of the Catholic League and of Bavaria. I do this a literary simplification, but the reality was more complex as in both sides fought Catholics and Protestants. This was not a war for religious reasons, but a war for political interests.

Throughout the book I use the expression 'Hispanic Monarchy' as a synonym for Spain. The word 'Spain' was used by foreigners to refer to most of the territory of the Iberian Peninsula. The Kingdom of Portugal was considered a part of Spain as it was ruled by the King of Spain between 1580 and 1640. On the other hand, the so-called 'Spaniards', when they spoke to each other, were designated as by the name of their regions: Castilian, Catalan, Valencian. This also happens with Italy or Germany in the seventeenth

---

1 To understand the general situation, the following books are essential: Guthrie, William P.: *Batallas de la Guerra de los Treinta Años. De la Montaña Blanca a Nördlingen, 1618–1635*. Ediciones Platea, Malaga, 2016; Livet, Georges: *La Guerra de los treinta años*. Davinci Continental, Barcelona, 2008; Parker, Geoffrey: *La Guerra de los Treinta Años*. Editorial Antonio Machado, Madrid, 2004; Polišenský, Josef V.: *The Thirty Years' War*. New English Library, London, 1974; Schiller, Friedrich: *The history of the thirty years' war in Germany*. A. L. Burt, New York, 1897 and Wilson, Peter H.: *Europe's Tragedy: A History of the Thirty Years War*. London, Penguin UK, 2010.

century and later: for example, the people of Venice, Rome or Naples, where all were known as 'Italians'.

The 'Hispanic Monarchy' refers to all the territories governed by the King of Spain, each with its own administration and laws. The King of Spain was also the sovereign of each of these countries. The Hispanic Monarchy included the Crowns of Castile, with Navarre and the territories of America, the East Indies and Africa, Aragon, with Sicily, Naples and Sardinia; Portugal and its overseas territories of Brazil, Africa and India, the territories of the Circle of Burgundy, Franche-Comté, the Spanish Netherlands, Charolais, the Duchy of Milan and the Marquisate of Finale.

Since the King of Spain could not travel to all countries, the King met with representatives of these countries in assemblies called *Consejos* (Royal Councils). The King of Spain did not have unlimited powers. In fact, his power was different in each territory, because the laws were different. The King ruled in all countries with the common strategy of fighting the Turks, the French and the English, but since there were different laws in each country, he could not always get the money and soldiers, that as King of Spain, he needed.

The author and Series Editor would like to thank Daniel Staberg for his generous support in the making of this book.

1

The Armies

The Swedish Army

King Gustavus II Adolphus (1594–1632) ascended the throne of Sweden in 1611. His country was engaged in three simultaneous wars at that time; against the Principality of Moscow (called the Ingrian War), Denmark (War of Kalmar) and Poland (the Polish-Swedish War). During the first 10 years of his reign, he devoted himself to consolidating Swedish power against the Danes and Poles. In order to maintain its independence, Sweden had mobilised its human and economic resources extremely well and efficiently, and had achieved a system capable of defending itself against so many external threats.

The new Swedish king was immersed in very serious conflicts. But his intelligence and military skills he managed to win, especially thanks to the military reforms that he introduced throughout his army. He made his army a sophisticated machine in its tactical and technological aspects. He also made it a true national militia and it had a feeling of unity ('esprit de corps'). But he also made great use of diplomacy, and he negotiated an end to hostilities with his enemies in order to obtain peace and the time needed to improve his army.

After many years of war, in 1630 the Swedish army had a powerful nucleus of veteran soldiers and officers. They were experts in the handling of weapons and the deployment of units on the battlefield. In addition, the Swedish army was characterised by severe discipline, applied to both the native and the mercenary units. Religion was used as a factor of cohesion and all the soldiers were forced to go to religious services.[1]

In the first decades of the seventeenth century the Swedish army consisted of some eight *storregement* (big regiments) of 3,000 men, raised on a regional basis and often referred to as *landsregiment* (provincial regiments). Gustavus had studied the tactics and organisation of the Spanish, Dutch, Imperial, Polish and Russian armies. He changed his army, from a semi-feudal levy into a professional army. His ill-trained peasants, recruited locally, turned into well-trained

---
1   Negredo, *Guerra*, p.152.

THE BATTLE OF NÖRDLINGEN 1634

Gustavus Adolphus, King of Sweden, attributed to Jacob Hoefnagele (circa 1624), where this Flemish painter came to Sweden in the 1620s. The young king appeared in full armour, with a white ribbon with decoration. It also highlights the exquisite collar that falls over the breastplate, a symbol of wealth. The beginning of his reign was not easy, with wars against Russia, Denmark and Poland, but he was going to successfully overcome these difficulties. (Livrustkammaren, LSH_T2467)

regular soldiers, raised through conscription. To reorganise the army, it was partially based on the German system of *landesdefension*. Sweden was divided into several military regions, depending on wealth and population and each region would have to recruit one or two regiments. For his part, the King had the obligation to pay and train them. In order to motivate the soldiers, the King handed over new flags, assigning a characteristic colour – black, green, red-[2] that coincided with the colour of their uniforms.[3] This ceremony helped reinforce the army's very high morale.

For the defence of Sweden, the King always had six of these powerful regiments in his country; and in addition, there were two more regiments on the eastern border. As such, Sweden was the first country to equip itself with a permanent national army.[4]

Gustavus emphasised drill, military discipline, and volley fire, by regiments freed from the old formation of infantry squares and reorganised instead into flexible linear formations. As with Maurice of Nassau, Gustavus Adolphus opted to organise his infantry in smaller companies, making orders easier to convey, and the officers had more direct control over their men. Small units were more manoeuvrable on any terrain, and they were more versatile and independent, and could be sent to help other units or to defend a remote position.

Swedish companies were initially 150 men: 16 officers and eight staff, 72 musketeers (divided into three sections of 24 men) and 54 pikemen (three sections of 18). The ratio of pikemen to musketeers was altered and actually increased so that every sub-unit of 24 musketeers in the company had a designated number of 18 pikemen to support them.

Four companies formed a battalion or *demi-regiment*; two battalions formed a regiment; between two and four regiments formed a brigade.[5] The regiment's senior command consisted of 23 officers and staff.

The combat unit was the the infantry squadron (Swedish: *skvadron*), following Continental terminology and well-knowed as a battalion, which consisted of four companies, although often during campaigns, the units had lost part of their strength through casualties in combat, disease and desertion

---

2   This habit, initially Swedish, was adopted also when they disembarked in Pomerania and their new German allies raised several regiments in its support (Brzezinski, *Gustavus Adolphus Infantry*, pp.11–14).

3   With this practice of assigning a dominant colour to each regiment, which served as guide for the colours of its uniforms, it was believed that the Swedish king was the inventor of the 'military uniform'. However, he adopted a practice that had already been used in other armies. (Brzezinski, *Gustavus Adolphus Infantry*, p.33).

4   Brzezinski, *Gustavus Adolphus Infantry*, p. 6–10.

5   Fredholm Von Essen, Michael: *The Lion from the North*. 2 vol. Helion, Warwick, 2020.

THE ARMIES

so had less than one hundred of men. The battalion were formed with six or more companies. Like the Spanish Tercios' *Escuadrones*, the Swedish brigades were not permanent structures, but their composition fluctuated to maintain the nucleus of 648 pikemen for which there were brigades with three battalions, or sometimes with four or more.[6]

In battle, a Swedish battalion usually formed with a front line consisting of pikemen (216), a second line with their musketeers (192) and a third line with reserve musketeers (96). The second line musketeers could be deployed on the flanks of the pikemen to support them. The musketeers of the third line were usually used as a reserve, or also to support cavalry or guard the camp.

Dutch, Imperial and Spanish companies deployed 10 ranks deep, but Swedish units deployed in only 6 ranks. Gustavus Adolphus shifted from dense infantry squares to linear formations, wherein three or four brigades formed a flexible, articulated and extended battle line. The Swedish companies were thus wider and smaller than their opponents and they occupied a larger, but shallower, front, giving them an advantage in flanking their enemies and conducting crossfire. In addition, when a Swedish unit was defeated, the impact of this defeat was less, as the rest of the units were barely affected. However, with a larger formation, the moral and tactical impact on the other units was greater.

The Swedish brigades often deployed in a T-shape: a squadron at the forefront, with their pikemen at the front and musketeers behind; then came two *demi-regiments*, side by side, with the pikemen on the inside and the musketeers on the outer flanks. Finally, the reserve musketeers of the three units marching together, in the rear of the brigade.[7]

At the battle of Lutzen, the Swedish infantry was deployed in the centre of the battle line, in eight brigades formed into two battle lines. The cavalry was located on both wings, in several squadrons of between 100 to 400 riders. In addition, a detachment of 200 musketeers with two regimental guns was placed between each cavalry squadron. The heavy artillery was placed in front of the four leading infantry brigades.[8]

At Nördlingen, the Swedes used the theorical infantry brigade of three squadrons, with between 500 and 750 soldiers per unit. The soldiers deployed in five or six ranks, as at the battles of Breitenfeld and Lutzen.[9]

The Swedish monarch, like other great generals, recognised that firepower was already an essential element of the 'Art of War' in the seventeenth century. Gustavus also understood the role of shock in combat, and that is

Pikeman's cuirass, period 1600–1650. It is completely painted black. It has the following dimensions: height 48cm; width 65cm; diameter 36cm; weight 10kg. Both the belt fabric as well as the belt buckle mounts are modifications, so it follows that the armour assembly contains unrelated parts when manufactured and assembled at later times. The three straps internally supporting the right and left arms were broken and replaced with wire. (Armémuseum, AM.056982)

---

6   Brzezinski, *Gustavus Adolphus Infantry*, p.34.
7   Brzezinski, *Gustavus Adolphus Infantry*, p.35.
8   Brzezinski, *Gustavus Adolphus Cavalry*, p.25.
9   Guthrie, *Battles*, p.376.

THE BATTLE OF NÖRDLINGEN 1634

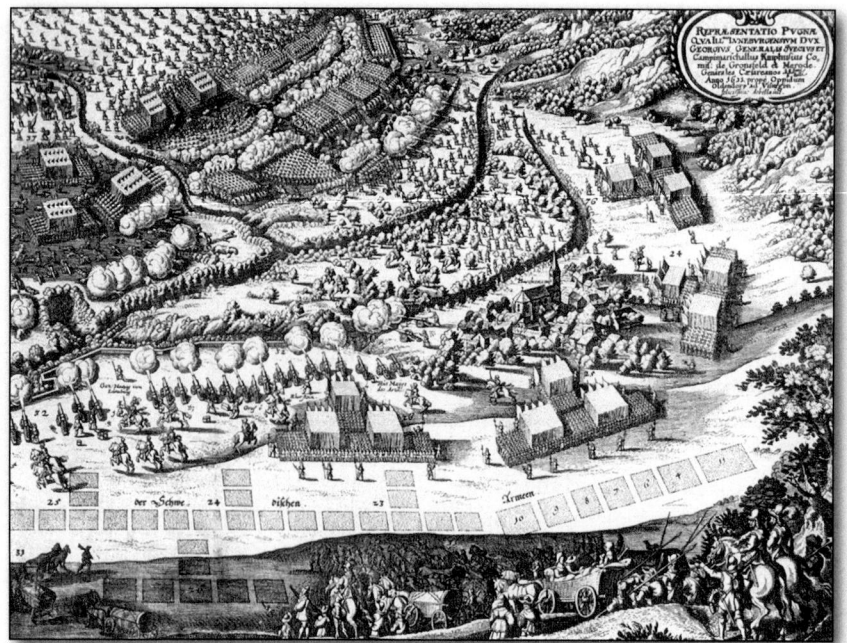

The 'Battle of Oldendorf on 8 July 1633', engraving of Merian (1644). In this decisive combat, the Swedish army commanded by George, Duke of Brunswick-Lüneburg and Marshal Dodo zu Innhausen und Knyphausen defeated an Imperial army commanded by Field Marshal Jobst Maximilian von Gronsfeld, Count Johann of Merode and Lothar Dietrich Freiherr von Bönninghausen. We can clearly observe the formation of the 'Swedish brigade' of three battalions, made up of four companies each, forming a T. The Catholic troops continue to maintain the formation of the mixed type, similar to the Spanish tercio, but with a very large coverage of firearms. (Author's collection)

why he put so much effort into improving its use in the Swedish army. It is often said that Gustavus ordered the infantry to do without pikemen, but this is not true. Swedish units of that time continued to have pikes, but the King reduced the number of soldiers carrying pikes, and also shortened the pike length from 16 feet (5.8 metres) to 11 feet (5.4 metres). This also happened in the Spanish Army.[10]

When it came to the Swedish army's firearms, Gustavus increased their presence. The Swedish infantry was initially armed with light calivers (called *rör* or *bösser*). The first muskets arrived in Sweden around 1592, from a Dutch ship,[11] and by the early as the seventeenth century, the use of muskets was widespread. Years later, as had the Dutch, the Swedes lightened their muskets, reducing the weight of their bullets[12] and shortening their weapons. They used lighter materials and removed the musket rest. They replaced the matchlock by the snaphance flintlock; the paper cartridge was introduced, and bandoleers to carry them. Because the Swedish musket was shorter, the loading of the weapon was faster, increasing the rate of fire. The heaviest old musket was in service for several decades and was known as the 'full musket'; the shortened weapon was called 'ordinary musket' or 'half musket'. Due to these improvements, Gustavus eliminated calivers from the Swedish army from around 1620.[13]

The Swedish King wanted firepower to be the defining element of a battle, and that is why he experimented with it. On one hand, he established

---

10 Brzezinski, *Gustavus Adolphus Infantry*, p.20.
11 Brzezinski, *Gustavus Adolphus Infantry*, pp.16–18.
12 The Swedish musket shot balls of about 36 grams, less heavy than the standard of the Spanish musket – of about 55 grams – but heavier than that of the arquebus, of between 10 and 15 grams.
13 Brzezinski, *Gustavus Adolphus Cavalry*, p.25.

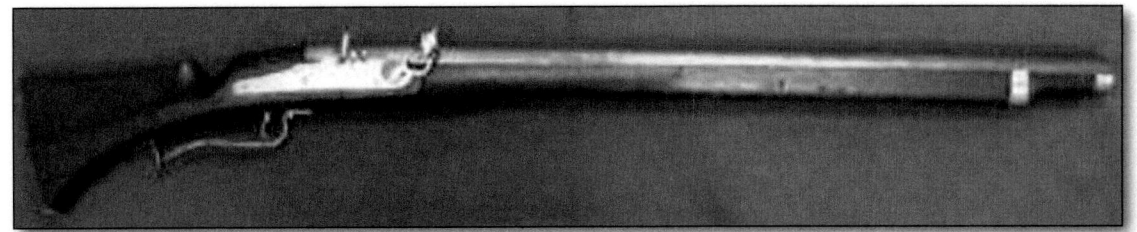

Swedish musket, dated 1626, with the effigy of Gustavus Adolphus. It has the following measurements: length 143.5cm; calibre 3.4cm; weight 5.05kg. (Armémuseum, AM.030305)

that his fire units to extend his frontage; on the other, he modernised the firing drills. So, the Swedish Army put this into practice in its wars with the Poles: first, reducing the size of companies; secondly, units formed into two ranks fired their muskets at the same time, beginning the introduction of 'volley fire' or 'salvo' techniques. But as early as 1631 the Swedes used several firing systems, firing two, three, and even more ranks at the same time. This improved the firepower of its units, but also managed to increase the deadly and psychological impact of Swedish fire on its enemies.

Turning to the Swedish cavalry, it was initially divided between cuirassiers and primitive mounted arquebusiers. The former was partially protected with armour, equipped with pistols and swords while the latter were armed with an arquebus, maybe a pistol, and a sword. However, Gustavus eliminated the use of the arquebuses and emphasised the use of pistols, and in doing so created a new type of Scandinavian cavalry, called *lätta ryttare*, or light cavalry, with very versatile functions, intended for both shock combat and scouting.[14]

The third type of cavalry in service in the Swedish army were dragoons. Closer to infantry than cavalry, this type of soldier appeared in France in the last years of the sixteenth century, in the Protestant forces of Henry Bourbon, King of Navarre. The first evidence of this type of cavalry in Sweden is from the year 1610.[15]

The first units of 'Swedish' dragoons were mostly French and Italian mercenaries, commanded by officers of these nationalities (De la Barre, De la Chapelle and Carnissini). Their use on campaign began in operations against Poland in 1626, with half a dozen companies. At the landing in Pomerania (1630), the Swedish Army had only one company of dragoons, under the command of Frenchman, Captain Daniel de Saint Andre. The first regiment of dragoons was created in 1631, under the command of German Georg Christof von Taupadel: this unit reached a strength of 1,200 men in 12 companies. In the following months, more dragoon regiments were created, but the number of companies in these were fewer, ranging from four to eight.[16]

Some chronicles describe that initially the Swedish dragoons were armed with short 'pikes', about three metres long, while others carried light muskets. In fact, it could be that the Swedish dragoons, just as those in the Catholic armies, initially retained closer organisational ties to their infantry origin,

---

14 Brzezinski, *Gustavus Adolphus Cavalry*, p.4.
15 Brzezinski, *Gustavus Adolphus Cavalry*, p.15.
16 Brzezinski, *Gustavus Adolphus Cavalry*, p.15.

Illustration from the book 'Military art on horseback. Instruction of the principles and foundations of cavalry' ('Art militaire à cheval. Instruction des principes et fondements de la cavallerie') written by the officer Johann Jacobi Wallhausen, in 1616. He was born around 1580 in Wallhausen, near Bad Kreuznach, but little is known about his life. He probably became a soldier in the Netherlands, then entered the service of the city of Gdańsk, where he became colonel-sergeant. In a contract signed in February 1617 with John VII of Nassau-Siegen, he became the head of the Siegen war school, the first in Europe. Like many authors of the early seventeenth century, he considered the 'gendarme' (gens d'armes, heavy cavalry) to be the elite of the cavalry and the lance as the most effective of the offensive weapons. He was very reluctant to use portable firearms which he deemed unworthy of a true gentleman. In this illustration we see the four types of horsemen proposed by Wallhausen: the gendarme – with a heavy medieval lance, the cuirassiers, armed with pistols, the arquebusiers with arquebuses, and the dragoons, armed with both arquebuses and pikes, to fight on horseback or on foot. (Author's collection)

carrying pikes and firearms in the same proportion as an infantry company. However, from 1631 or 1632, the dragoon's only weapon would be the shortened musket.[17]

Dragoon units were used to deploy to the front or flanks quickly in support of an infantry unit, thanks to their mobility on horseback, but they were also used in reconnaissance and ambush operations.

Unlike Swedish infantry, conscripted from the male population on a territorial basis, Swedish cavalrymen were mainly volunteers. Since cavalry was also recruited at the territorial level, the basic formation was the company. But as of 1627, the companies were grouped into five regional regiments, each of four companies, but in 1631 the strength was increased to eight companies per regiment, of 125 troops each: 23 officers and staff, and 102 men. These eight companies formed a regiment of 1,000 soldiers. There were 13 cavalry companies permanently in service: six Swedish native, four Finnish and three companies raised and paid by the Swedish high nobility.[18] During the German campaigns, the mercenary cavalry regiments in the service in Swedish Army had 26 staff and 99 men per company.[19]

Gustavus placed his cavalry in the classical manner, on the wings, although he did occasionally place them behind the infantry, or located it between the intervals of the various brigades and infantry regiments.

---

17 Brzezinski, *Gustavus Adolphus Cavalry*, p.16.
18 Brzezinski, *Gustavus Adolphus Cavalry*, pp.5–6.
19 Brzezinski, *Gustavus Adolphus Cavalry*, pp.7–10.

THE ARMIES

The attacking tactics of Swedish cavalry was to deploy to sweep the enemy riders or infantry from the vanguard, then to retreat to the flanks, and wait for the Swedish infantry attack, supported by artillery fire. Then, depending on the development of the battle, the cavalry would charge the enemy flanks or the centre to support their infantry. Swedish cavalry was to be used as a means to deplete enemy reserves or to create confusion so that Swedish infantry could dominate the heart of the battle.

For that reason, the first line of horsemen used pistols as their initial weapon, to disrupt the enemy ranks and free the way for the following ranks to close with the disordered enemy using cold steel. The cavalry squadrons were initially deployed in four ranks, then only three, instead of the 10 ranks of other armies.[20]

This method of cavalry combat was different from that used in the rest of Europe, where the 'caracole' was norm. Here, riders armed with pistols or carbines trotted towards the enemy in successive waves, firing their weapons and retreating, so that the next line of riders could fire their shots, and so on. Only a few units maintained the use of the sword or lance in combat, and close combat with cold steel were not widespread, or were developed by 'irregular' units, such as Albanian *stradioti*, Croats, or Hungarians.

On the contrary, Gustavus insisted on the use of shock as the predominant combat tactic of the cavalry, returning to the use of cavalry as a shock weapon, using speed in place of firepower.

During the various wars with the Poles, the Swedish cavalry[21] faced the prestigious Winged Hussars but the Swedes had smaller horses and their men were not as well trained as their Polish counterparts. The Poles had warhorses, larger and heavier than those of the Swedes, and were armed with medieval-style lances, some 5 metres long.[22] They were also armed with several pistols.

Most of the Swedish riders didn't have pistols at this time, or only one, and they did not have the firepower or the experience to develop the tactic of

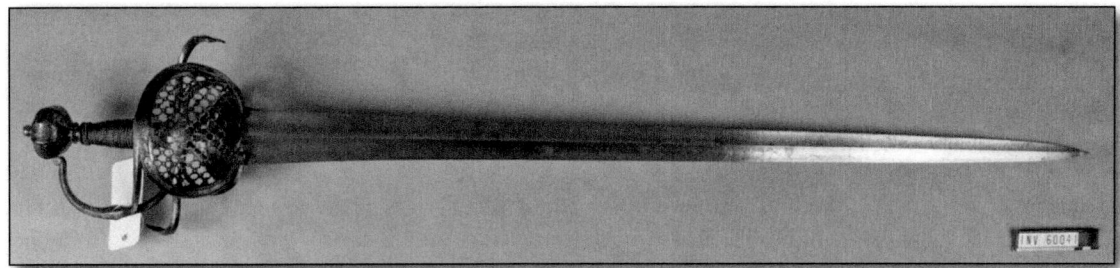

Cavalry sword, with a total length of 112.0cm, length of the blade of 91.0cm, with a width of 5.3cm, and a weight of 12.50kg. The blade is double edged, at the top it is quite wide, but it tapers quite a bit towards the tip. On both sides it is adorned on the top with engraved ornaments and on the outside with an image of Bernard of Saxe-Weimar in a medallion frame. Inside, in addition to the ornaments, there is a portrait of Gustavus Adolphus within the same type of frame as the portrait outside. However, on the sheet it bears the inscription 'ME FECIT SOLINGEN 1652' (I was manufactured in Solingen in 1652). All this suggests that the handle and bowl of the sword were manufactured around 1630 and belonged to an officer of the regiments of Bernard of Saxe-Weimar, when he was in the service of Sweden. The blade was later repaired in 1652. (Armémuseum, AM.060041)

---

20 Brzezinski, *Gustavus Adolphus Cavalry*, pp.7–10.
21 Brzezinski, *Gustavus Adolphus Cavalry*, p.4.
22 Brzezinski, *Gustavus Adolphus Cavalry*, p.23.

the 'caracole' as in other countries. Since the size of the Swedish horses could not be changed, Gustavus devised a method to improve the effectiveness of his cavalry by ordering a reduction in the amount of armour worn by the riders in order to win more freedom of movement, as less weight meant that Swedish horses would gallop faster and leave less time for the enemy to fire.

The King did not forget firepower, so he also introduced the use of musketeers to accompany the cavalry, as Henri IV of Navarre had done similarly. To increase the effectiveness of the cavalry charge, he placed groups of musketeers in detachments of between 50 to 200 men among the horsemen, to repel or disrupt attackers by their fire, and as in the Polish campaigns, breaking the charges of the winged hussars. These musketeers, when the Swedish cavalry charged, could follow them at the run and re-enter action quickly, but at times the cavalry lost some of the effect of the charge, because of the slow speed of the musketeers trying to keep up with them.[23]

Since the experience of Breitenfeld showed that if the cavalry fled, it left the musketeers terribly vulnerable, so Gustavus equipped these mixed groupings of riders and musketeers with two regimental guns for each detachment.[24]

Regarding artillery, Gustavus unified and reduced the calibre of artillery pieces, adopting three types of artillery: siege, field and regimental. In addition, in order that the guns had better mobility, he shortened them and lightened their carriages.

With the heavy artillery, Gustavus had four types of cannons: 48 pounder, 24 pounder, 12 pounder and six pounder guns. However, the effectiveness of the 24 pounder gun for siege warfare resulted in a decision to cease making more 48 pounder cannon, as they were more expensive and laborious to use. Ultimately then, the siege artillery was equipped with 24 pounder guns, weighing 60, 30 and 15 quintals (6,000, 3,000 and 1,500kg).

The field artillery used 24, 12 and six pounder guns, weighing of 27, 18, and 12 quintals respectively (2,700, 1,800 and 1,200kg). But he abandoned the use of 6 pounder cannon and adopted the 3 pounder cannon as regimental artillery. With these changes the Swedish Army simplified its artillery base into just three types, 24, 12 and three pounders, greatly simplifying the supply of ammunition. The pieces were commanded by officers (*styckjunckare*), and served by gunners (*konstapel*) and assistants (*hantlangare*).[25]

As for the use of the heavy artillery on the battlefield, the King used the 24 and 12 pounders in the traditional way. At Breitenfeld he placed three cannon in front of the central squadron of each regiment of the first Swedish line. His main tactical innovation was to reorganise the heavy pieces into batteries to concentrate fire at selected targets.[26]

Gustavus assigned guns to infantry units organically, to increase their firepower. This was the regimental artillery. Gustavus considered the importance of firepower in the frontline and sought to maximize it by

---

23 Brzezinski, *Gustavus Adolphus Cavalry*, p.26.
24 Brzezinski, *Gustavus Adolphus Cavalry*, p.27.
25 Brzezinski, *Gustavus Adolphus Cavalry*, p.27.
26 Brzezinski, *Gustavus Adolphus Cavalry*, p.19.

THE ARMIES

4 pounder regimental (regementsstycke) model. The piece is from 1632 and has a decoration in relief, with images of musketeers, drums and pipers. It also had a decoration formed by a dolphin on each handle, but only one remains. (Armémuseum, AM.061448)

hauling genuine field artillery to support his infantry while it manoeuvred, and in firefights. Other armies of this time emphasised the use of heavy large calibre artillery, positioned in the rear or at other times in the vanguard, their main mission being counter battery fire and the weakening of the enemy defence. But Gustavus changed the focus. He wanted his infantry brigades to have light cannons, capable of following their advance, and able to deploy in the front line to support their musketeers' fire.[27]

But the path to success was not easy. This concept of 'field artillery' was a matter addressed in all armies, with a greater or lesser degree of success, to provide their infantry with effective, mobile artillery support.

In 1622–1623, mathematician and engineer Philip Eberhard designed and tested a leather cannon. It was later demonstrated in Stockholm in 1625. Over the next three years several inventors tried to improve the prototype, but it did not succeed in removing the propensity of the barrel to overheat and burst, which is why this type of cannon was replaced in 1629 with a weapon that would be known as the 'regimental cannon' (*regementsstycke*), a 3 pounder, in order to replace the ordinary cannon type in the Swedish army, the *Murbräcker* type.[28] These new guns were less likely to overheat than ordinary guns and had a rate of fire about 50 percent greater than the older guns.[29]

As a result of a fusion of engineering development with copper production in Sweden, the barrel of this new artillery piece was made of a bronze and

---

27 Brzezinski, *Gustavus Adolphus Cavalry*, pp.15–16.
28 It is unknown who was the inventor of this type of artillery, although the engineer Schildknecht claimed that it had been a German named Siegroth. The presence in Sweden of Hans Heinrich Siegroth and his son David Friedrich, who worked for Gustavus Adolphus in the 1620s, from Hessen-Kassel is confirmed (Brzezinski, *Gustavus Adolphus Cavalry*, p.18).
29 Negredo, *Guerra*, p.152.

copper alloy with tin, reinforced by iron hoops, held in place with boiled leather binding. The barrel was shortened, and a small powder charge was used, which helped the reduction in the weight of the barrel considerably, to 50kg. The first regimental pieces of this pattern were introduced into units in 1629, and the Swedes produced them on a massive scale in German territory from 1632. Being much lighter guns, they were easily deployable next to infantrymen. In addition, their reloading system with wooden cartridges made them very fast and their firing rate was eight shots for every six of a musketeer. The main task of the regimental artillery was to fire cannister at enemy infantry before contact, either in attack or in defence.[30]

These guns were hauled by two horses with a small limber and needed only two crewmen, one designated as a gunner (*konstapel*), to load and fire, and another was his assistant (*hantlangare*), who was also the driver of the limber with which the piece was pulled. For each pair of cannon there was an officer (*styckjunckare*) who oversaw fire discipline.[31]

Initially two guns were assigned to each regiment. Later five heavier pieces, with a greater range, would be introduced. At Breitenfeld, Gustavus had 42 regimental guns, distribute six per brigade (three per battalion), facing only Imperial 25 cannon. With the innovations in the size, weight and standardisation of ammunition, Gustavus had genuine field artillery, which allowed him to dominate the battlefield during his German campaign.[32]

In 1630 the Swedish artillery was organised into a single regiment of six companies. Three of these contained the heavy pieces, one company contained all the regimental guns, while another company was designated as fireworkers and included grenadiers and explosives experts. The sixth company were sappers entrusted with offensive and defensive duties around the artillery. In 1632, the regiment had a strength of 1,200 men, most of them of Swedish origin, although some officers were foreigners.[33]

Gustavus also refined and standardised gunpowder charges for each calibre of gun. Bagged powder in pre-measured cartridges improved rates of fire and increased accuracy. The logistics train was essential for effective artillery. Horses, limbers and carts and their drivers were not drawn from civilian contractors, such as in the Spanish Army, but were instead affiliated with the artillery regiment. The heavy cannon travelled with the siege train, each piece hauled by large teams of draught animals. The light pieces always travelled ahead, along with the infantry and cavalry for quick deployment.[34] In Nördlingen, the Swedish-German army had 20 of their 12 and 24 pounders, 42 regimental three pounder guns, and six siege guns and mortars.[35]

Looking at the nationalities serving in the Swedish army during the war in Germany, when Sweden landed in Pomerania in 1630, the main component of its army were native Swedish troops, as well as Finnish units and Livonians

---

30 Brzezinski, *Gustavus Adolphus Cavalry*, p.22.
31 Brzezinski, *Gustavus Adolphus Cavalry*, p.18.
32 Brzezinski, *Gustavus Adolphus Cavalry*, p.19.
33 Brzezinski, *Gustavus Adolphus' Cavalry*, p.19.
34 Brzezinski, *Gustavus Adolphus' Cavalry*, p.19.
35 Guthrie, *Battles*, p.400.

from the Swedish Baltic Empire (*Stormaktstiden*).[36] However, as the months passed, casualties, desertion and disease reduced their ranks, and the King had to resort to the support of his German allies (Saxony), volunteers (Scottish, English, French) and mercenaries,[37] which made up a large percentage of his armies. Some of these German units were newly raised, but others consisted of veterans who had been fighting for several years. This compensated for the low quality of replacements for casualties among the veteran Swedish units. In 1621 native Swedish and Finnish troops made up 85 percent of the Swedish army, whilst in 1630/1631 they comprised just over 50 percent.

The German Army of Bernard of Saxe-Weimar

At Nördlingen, Swedish native units were in a minority, as most were located in the garrisons of northern Germany and in Johan Banér's field army. Guthrie states that 'of all the major battles Nördlingen was the one with the smallest proportion of Swedes in the ranks of its own army'.[38] The chief of the army was Swedish, Gustav Horn, as were other senior officers, such as Young Oxenstierna, together with the Yellow and Horn Infantry Regiments and the Kurland and Livonia cavalry units.[39]

The core of the 'Swedish' Army in Nördlingen were Germans: from Heilbronn League troops (Bernard and Hohenlohe) and minor allies (Württemberg, Rheingrave), and volunteers and mercenaries from all parts of Germany. Also noteworthy is the involvement of several 'Scottish' regiments (Monro, King, Forbes, Ramsay).[40]

These units from Sweden's German allies had adopted Swedish formations and organisation, as well as their fire discipline. They even assimilated the practice of using the colour patterns for their uniforms, flags and titles, such as the Yellow and Black regiments.

On campaign, as was also the case in the other armies, the reality was very different from the theoretical organisation. The brigades comprising the Swedish-German army in the battle of Nördlingen presented a high degree diversity in terms of unit strengths. The Yellow Brigade had about 1,400 troops, formed from the Yellow and Zerotin regiments. The brigades of Thurn and Bernard each had three regiments, with a total of about 1,250 soldiers. Pfuhl's brigade had four regiments totalling 1,700 men while Horn's had five infantry regiments but only 1,200 soldiers in total. The Scottish brigade, of seven regiments had a mere 1,700 men, while Rantzau's brigade, with eight regiments totalling 2,000 men.[41]

---

36 Andersson, Ingvar: *A History of Sweden*. Praeger, Nueva York, 1956; Frost, Robert I.: *The Northern Wars. War, State and Society in North-eastern Europe 1558–1721*. Routledge, New York, 2000; Roberts, Michael: *The Swedish imperial experience 1560–1718*, Cambridge UP, Cambridge, 1984.
37 Brzezinski, *Gustavus Adolphus' Infantry*, pp.11–16.
38 Guthrie, *Battles,* p.397.
39 Guthrie, *Battles,* p.397.
40 Guthrie, *Battles,* p.397.
41 Guthrie, *Battles,* p.398.

THE BATTLE OF NÖRDLINGEN 1634

24 pound cannon model, also called ½ kartaun. It has the inscription 'M.W. Mei F. Gedan Anno 1666', from which it can be concluded that it was probably manufactured by the foundry Michael Weinholdt, in Danzig, 1666. It is 97.0cm long and weighs 15.7kg (Armémuseum, AM.061505)

INV 61505

The Imperial Army

At the beginning of the seventeenth century, the Holy Roman Empire did not have a permanent army in the modern sense of the term, as did Spain, Holland or Sweden. The conglomeration of states that made up the Empire was reluctant for the Emperor to have a permanent armed force, since they feared that it would be used to limit their privileges.[42]

The Empire was divided into 10 military regions,[43] called Imperial Circles (*Reichskreis*) that had to supply troops to serve the Emperor in the case of a threat.

These troops were largely local militias raised by the privileged estates (feudal nobility, the clergy and rich merchants). However, as the number of recruits varied depending on the population, a province's resources and the type of threat, the Imperial representatives and those of the states and cities were engaged in long and arduous negotiations. In theory, one man out of every 30 enlisted in the infantry could be recruited, and one in every 100 for the cavalry.

The states and the cities also provided the clothing, the equipment, the arms, pay and supplies for these troops, many of whom deserted. In practice, these Circles provided regiments of mercenaries, paid for by member states, be they Electorates, Duchies or small city states.[44]

Since the Emperor, despite his position and the large population in Germany, could not have a reliable and permanent basis for national Imperial recruitment, the Habsburgs' mode of recruiting troops was sustained by two

---

42 Brnardic, *Imperial Armies. Infantry*, p.3.
43 Bavaria, Swabia, Upper Rhineland, Lower Rhineland-Westphalia, Franconia, Lower Saxony, Austria, Burgundy, Rhine and Upper Saxony (Dotzauer, Winfried: *Die deutschen Reichskreise in der Verfassung alten Reiches und ihr Eigenleben. 1500–1806*. Wissenschaftliche Buchgesellschaft, Darmstadt, 1989).
44 Brnardic, *Imperial Armies. Infantry*, p.12.

THE ARMIES

'The enrolment of troops' (1633), by Jacques Callot. This is the second sheet of the total of 18 that make up the series called 'The Great Miseries of War' (Les Grandes Misères de la Guerre, in French); these realistic and heart breaking drawings represent the destruction unleashed against civilians during the Thirty Years' War; although no specific campaign is represented, but the set seems to be inspired by the actions of the army that Cardinal Richelieu sent in 1633 to occupy the Duchy of Lorraine, Callot's homeland. Each engraving has a title in verse of six lines below the image, written by the famous collector of prints Michel de Marolles. They all show wide panoramic views, with many tiny figures. In this sheet we look at the start of any campaign: the enlistment of soldiers, the payment of their first wage and their training. (Palais des Ducs de Lorraine)

sources: hiring entire units of mercenaries or mandatory recruitment within the Habsburg hereditary territories.

It was faster and more feasible to recruit entire mercenary units. The Emperor dealt only with the unit's chief, a genuine warlord, who was contracted to recruit, arm and supply a certain number of soldiers, in exchange for a number of privileges; perhaps a noble title, money, a right to levy war taxes and contributions and so forth.[45] So, to raise a regiment, a warrant was usually issued to an officer, which was called *Werbepatent* (levy patent) or *Werbekontrackt* (levy contract), stating what locale in which he was to recruit his company, the number of men required, and whether they were to be infantry, horse or dragoons.

In the first half of the sixteenth century, these mercenary units were well-known as the *Landsknechts*, and their fighting methods were similar to Swiss pikemen, with whom they always maintained absolute enmity, both for their mercenary rivalry and for their different nationality.

The *Landsknechts* were organised into regiments (*regiment*), led by their Colonel (*Obrist*), who was the contractor for all the soldiers. These German regiments theoretically had 10 companies, called *Fahne* (it means 'flag') of 400 men, which were subdivided into 40 sections of six to 10 men.[46]

But from the second half of the sixteenth century and especially in the beginning of the seventeenth century, German infantry was organised into regiments of 10 companies of 300 men each, divided into squads

---

45 Brnardic, *Imperial Armies. Infantry*, p.13.
46 Brnardic, *Imperial Armies. Infantry*, p.16.

(*Korporalschaften*) of 25 men, with a total of 3,000 soldiers armed with the usual range of weaponry.

However, in practice regimental contract patents indicate that most units were contracted to contain 2,000 soldiers, and after several months of campaigning, this force would be reduced to in the region of 1,500. In some extreme cases, a veteran regiment might only have 500 men remaining.[47]

The *prima plana* (company's staff) of the company had 40 members: three officers – a captain (*Hauptmann*), lieutenant (*Lieutenant*) and second lieutenants (*Fahnrich*); the non-commissioned officers (NCO) were a sergeant major (*Wachtmeister/Deldwebel*), the accountant (*Fourier*) and the sergeant (*Führer*), subaltern (*Unterschreiber*), medical staff (*Feldscher*), up to 12 corporals (*Korporal*) and 20 squad chiefs (*Gephreite*), two drums or pipers. Each regiment had a regimental staff of over 40 members, with the colonel (*Obrist*), who was generally the 'owner' (*Inhaber*) of the regiment, and his second in command, the lieutenant colonel (*Obristleutnant*).[48]

Although in the sixteenth century the proportion of firearms was lower than the pikes and other weapons (swords and halberds), prior to the outbreak of the Thirteen Years' War[49] (1593–1606), a German regiment theoretically had 3,000 troops, with 1,600 were musketeers, 1,200 pikemen and 200 halberds. However, throughout the conflict it was proved futile having halberdiers or skirmishers armed with sword and shields, and therefore units increased their firepower, increasing the number of musketeers and arquebusiers to double that of the pikemen.[50] That is why before the outbreak of the Thirty Years' War, in theory, an infantry regiment had 1,500 musketeers, 300 arquebusiers and 1,200 pikemen, but at the end of the conflict the proportions changed significantly and only one in five men carried pikes.[51]

At the outbreak of the Thirty Years' War, the Empire had only 5,000 troops, recruited during the Uskoks War (1615–1617), so a new army had to be recruited very quickly. In less than a year, Ferdinand of Styria had raised 30,000 troops to start the campaign against Frederick V of the Palatinate in Bohemia.[52]

From 1625 onwards, with the entry of Denmark into the war, Emperor Ferdinand II saw how his military machinery depended largely on the will and resources of the Catholic League, led by Duke Maximilian of Bavaria, and whose goals were not entirely in line with those of the Habsburg monarchy.

Because of this, the Emperor accepted General Albrecht Wallenstein's (1583–1634) proposal to raise an Imperial Army of 24,000 men, free of any

---

47 Brnardic, *Imperial Armies. Infantry*, p.15.
48 Brnardic, *Imperial Armies. Infantry*, p.16.
49 To know some more about this conflict: Bagi, Zoltán Péter: 'The Life of Soldiers during the Long Turkish War (1593–1606)' in *The Hungarian Historical Review*, Vol. 4, 2, Cultures of Christian-Islamic Wars in Europe (1450–1800), 2015, pp.384–417; Finkel, Caroline: *The Administration of Warfare: The Ottoman Military Campaigns in Hungary, 1593–1606*. Vwgö, Vienna, 1988; Mugnai, Bruno y Flaherty, Christopher: *Der Lange Türkenkrieg (1593–1606): The long Turkish War*. Soldier shop, Bergamo, 2014–2015.
50 Spring, *The Bavarian Army*, p.50.
51 Brnardic, *Imperial Armies. Infantry*, p.11.
52 Brnardic, *Imperial Armies. Infantry*, p.4.

THE ARMIES

Albrecht Václav Eusebius z Valdštejna, by Anthony Van Dyck (1629). Better known as Wallenstein or Waldstein. He was born into a Protestant family of the lesser Bohemian nobility, but in 1604 he converted to Catholicism. At the age of 20 he enlisted in the Imperial army, serving on the Hungarian border and later in the Friuli War. When the Bohemian revolt broke out, he saved the royal treasure from Protestant hands. From that point his rise was unstoppable. A paradigm of the 'Impresario' of war, he enlisted and maintained at his expense more than 50,000 soldiers in the service of Emperor Ferdinand II. The dependence that the Emperor had on Wallenstein was precisely what led to his downfall. As a general, Wallenstein was prudent. He preferred to fight defensively most of the time, and he did not like siege warfare, because of the high losses likely. In terms of his character, it was said of him that he was choleric, superstitious, distrustful of both friends and cruel towards his enemies. (Rijksmuseum RP-P–1908-4118)

cost to the Imperial treasury. Wallenstein's financial agent, Hans de Witte, advanced the money required to recruit troops, with an Imperial commitment to be reimbursed for war taxes and contributions that would be levied in the conquered territories. In just a few weeks, Wallenstein recruited 14,800 infantrymen, and 7,600 cavalry.[53]

As for the deployment of Imperial units on the battlefield, at the beginning of the Thirty Years' War, the Imperial regiments formed in battle following the model of the Spanish tercio, both because it was a proven success on the battlefield, but also because the senior commanders of the Imperial army (for example, Bucquoy, Tilly) had served in the Spanish Army of Flanders.[54]

The Imperial army adapted the tercio's mode of a 2,000 to 3,000 infantry block, divided into 60 to 100 ranks, each of 30 to 50 men. As in the Spanish army, the Imperial detachment of pikemen (*Pikenierhaufen*) was the tactical unit, which was protected by musketeers (*Musketierabteilungen*). On the battlefield, like the Spaniards, the Imperial soldiers deployed their units arranged as on a chessboard (in *echequier*), in two or three lines, with the artillery at the front while on the flanks were the heavy cavalry, supported by the light cavalry.[55]

But that changed after the Imperial defeats in the battles of Breitenfeld and Lech, and with the death of General Tilly. The new Imperial Commander-in-Chief, Albrecht von Wallenstein ceased using the old tercio deployment model and reorganised German imperial infantry according to the Dutch model. 'Brigades' were created as operational units, from 900 to 1,000 men each,[56] with regiments of 500 men. He also incorporated light cannons at the

---

53 Brnardic, *Imperial Armies. Infantry*, p.5.
54 Brnardic, *Imperial Armies. Cavalry*, p.21.
55 Brnardic, *Imperial Armies. Cavalry*, p.21.
56 Spring, *Wallenstein's Army*, pp.29–42.

regimental level, and even trained musketeers to accompany cavalry units, following the Swede's example.[57]

Thus, the typical Imperial battle formation changed from the 'tercio' model to the 'linear' model. In battle now the companies and regiments would be grouped together into units of 1,000 infantrymen, but because the units were often so lacking in strength, several regiments came together to make up the required one thousand men, and for that reason, the aggregation of these diverse regiments was known, in Dutch-Swedish style, as a 'brigade', or 'battle'.[58] At the deployment level, they had twice as large a frontage as the depth of the formation.[59] The depth of the pike block was 10 ranks, and between 6 and 10 ranks of musketeers were positioned on the front and on the flanks. This type of deployment was used at both Lutzen and Nördlingen by both the Imperialists and Bavarians.[60]

Turning to the Imperial cavalry, during the sixteenth century it had been recruited specifically for a campaign and at the end of hostilities the units were disbanded. The main component was mercenary units, or semi-professional feudal contingents. The basic unit was the *Fahnlein* (detachment), with a variable number of troops (50 to 100 men).[61]

With the Ottomans threatening the eastern border, some of these units were recruited on a permanent basis by the Empire, so that in the early seventeenth century, Emperor Rudolf II organised this cavalry into permanent companies, but with variable strengths of between 100 to 250 men. Four or five companies formed a regiment, which in theory had about 1,000 troops, but in practice was around the 600–800 mark. On campaign, the cavalry companies often had only 40 or 50 men.[62] German cavalry was mainly divided into two classes of troops, the Cuirassiers (*Kürassiere*) and the Harquebusiers (*Arkebusier*).[63]

In the sixteenth century the cuirassiers were initially armed with a lance and sword, but later were given pistols, but kept the sword and full armour, which was almost impenetrable to bullets. In the Graz Armoury there are two sets of heavy armour weighing 42kg, although the usual weight was around 25kg.[64] The armoured cuirassier was one of the most formidable opponents on the battlefield of the Thirty Years' War. Mounted on big horses, deployed in lines 6 to 12 ranks deep, they were totally threatening.[65]

Harquebusiers were armed with a form of carbine, called a 'harquebus' – initially wheellock, and later snaphaunce or dog lock flintlock, sword, and pistols, protected by a breastplate and a buff coat. Initially, the harquebusiers

---

57 Brnardic, *Imperial Armies. Infantry*, p.22.
58 Brnardic, *Imperial Armies. Infantry*, p.15.
59 In the Spanish manuals, this type of formation was known as a picture of double front or doublet, in which there were the double the of number pikemen in the front, in relation to their depth. The *sargento mayor* (sergeant major) distributed the musketeers to support the formation.
60 Guthrie, *Battles*, p.377.
61 Brnardic, *Imperial Armies. Cavalry*, p.6.
62 Brnardic, *Imperial Armies. Cavalry*, p.6.
63 Brzezinski, *Gustavus Adolphus Cavalry*, p.3.
64 Brnardic, *Imperial Armies. Cavalry*, p.17.
65 Brzezinski, *Gustavus Adolphus Cavalry*, p.24.

THE ARMIES

Lobster-Tail Burgonet (Zischägge), probably second quarter seventeenth century, from Northern Europe. The term 'Zischägge' refers to a distinctive type of seventeenth-century helmet consisting of a hemispherical bowl, a brim with sliding nosepiece (nasal), cheekpieces, and a long-laminated tail over the back of the neck. The single nasal-bar type was characteristic of Continental Europe, whilst the three-barred type with a pivoting peak was more widely used in the British Isles. The German word 'Zischägge' is a corruption of the Turkish 'chichak', which refers to a similar helmet used throughout much of the Ottoman world. It became popular in Europe, especially for cavalry and officers, from 1600 to the end of the seventeenth century, and it was widely used during the Thirty Years War and English Civil Wars. (Metropolitan Museum of Art, 14.25.499)

German Three-Quarter Armour (early seventeenth century). Dimensions: weight 25.75kg; weight of helmet approx. 2.25kg. This armour comes from the private collection of Count Zierotin, of Castle Blauda in Bohemia. This type of armour generally served as equipment for cuirassiers. Because they were mass produced, they are also called 'Munition armour', to be stored in large armouries, to equip both foot soldiers and cuirassiers. Munition armour was of a standard pattern with interchangeable pieces. It was often made of iron or sometimes an alloy of iron containing a small amount of phosphorus, which gave a marginal increase in toughness. (Metropolitan Museum of Art, 29.152.4a–m)

were intended to provide fire support, to the cuirassiers, when they were still charged with lances, but later, the harquebusiers had their specific role in combat, to either operate independently against the enemy, or provide infantry with support, or for scouting purposes.[66]

As the conflict progressed, a new type of mounted soldier appeared in the Catholic army, the dragoons. As in the Swedish army, or in the Spanish, initially they were not considered cavalry, but mounted infantry they were organised as infantry companies with the ranks of soldiers and officers the same as an infantry company, but in the long term they became a specific type of cavalry, gradually replacing the harquebusiers, who disappeared as such at the end of the Thirty Years' War.

---

66 Brnardic, *Imperial Armies. Cavalry*, p.3.

23

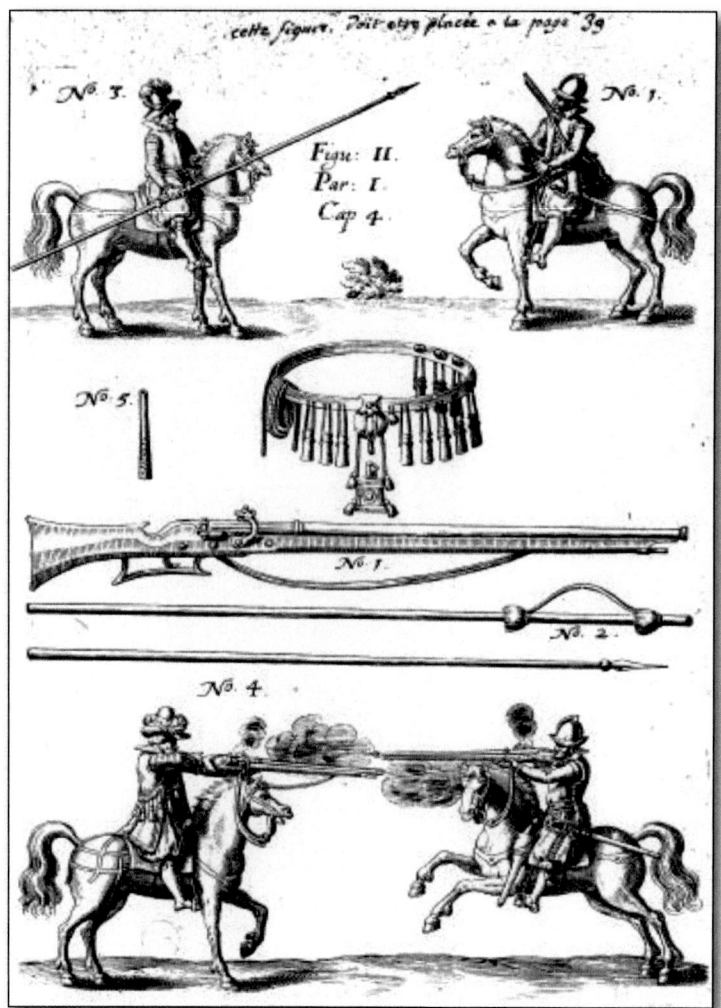

Illustration from the book 'Military art on horseback. Instruction of the principles and foundations of cavalry', by Johann Jacobi Wallhausen. We can see the equipment of a dragoon, made up of a light spear about 3 m long, and a matchlock – wheellock arquebuses appear in other treatises. (Author's collection)

Most dragoons were armed with shortened muskets, about 1.38 metres, and with a smaller calibre, usually about 15 mm. Dragoons wore no armour.[67] Catholic dragons, being deemed infantry units, initially had pikes and a dragoon company was supposed to have 200 troops, half with pikes and half with muskets. In theory, the pikemen were in 10 ranks, while the musketeers in two, divided into two 50-man detachments on each flank of the pikemen. This formation, then, was similar to that of the infantry. In fact, some units were temporarily transferred from being pikemen to dragoons simply because of the need to have a mounted troop.[68]

The Empire was also served by national contingents for its cavalry,[69] in the shape of men of Hungarian, Croatian or Albanian ethnicity, operating as light cavalry. Their tasks were scouting and exploration and the 'small wars' of raiding, pillaging and causing mayhem among the civilian population. These riders were armed with pistols, carbines, heavy maces and eastern-style swords.

At the beginning of the Thirty Years' War, the Empire had only two cavalry regiments. One was the cuirassier regiment of the Spanish Baltasar de Marradas, and the other the harquebusier regiment of Henri du Val, Count of Dampierre. Within a matter of a few months, four regiments of cuirassiers and four of harquebusiers were recruited to crush the Bohemian revolt.[70]

Imperial cavalry was organised into companies of 99 soldiers, with staff of 12 men. The cavalry regiments consisted of a varied number of companies, from between four to 16. As the conflict progressed and when the needs of war demanded, when individual companies were too understrength, they were grouped together into squadrons, often of two or three companies. The squadron thus became the basic combat unit of the cavalry, forming up

---

67 Brnardic, *Imperial Armies. Cavalry*, pp.34–35.
68 Spring, *Bavarian Army*, p.115.
69 Brnardic, *Imperial Armies. Cavalry*, pp.37–43.
70 Brnardic, *Imperial Armies. Cavalry*, p.12.

THE ARMIES

The Landeszeughaus (Graz) is considered the largest preserved historical armoury in the world, containing 32,000 objects: including armour, firearms and polearms, swords, and cannons from the fifteenth to the eighteenth century. Here we have a panoramic view of the room dedicated to armour: in the foreground, various examples of cavalry armour, of the kind used by cuirassiers and we can see the total protection they offered. On the shelves on both sides there are hundreds of infantry helmets (morion, cabasset, burgonet) and breastplates and armour for pikemen and horsemen. (Author's photos)

between five and ten rows deep. At the beginning of the conflict, however, the terms company and squadron were often used as synonymous terms.[71] At the time of Lutzen and Nördlingen, the Imperial cavalry contained squadrons of about 300 riders, with a depth of five or six ranks.[72]

With the entry of Denmark into the conflict, Emperor Ferdinand II became more aware of his enormous military reliance on the Catholic League, and especially Bavaria, so he accepted General Wallenstein's proposal to create a fully independent Imperial army. In 1625, this army had 7,600 mounted troops organised into 17 regiments (nine of cuirassiers, five of harquebusiers, two of dragoons and one of Croats). And after the battle of Lützen, the Imperial army theoretically had more than 40,000 cavalry in 28 cuirassiers regiments, 21 harquebusier regiments, 11 of dragoons and 10 irregular Croat and Hungarian regiments.[73]

---

71 Brnardic, *Imperial Armies. Cavalry*, p.6.
72 Guthrie, *Battles*, p.377.
73 Brnardic, *Imperial Armies. Cavalry*, p.13.

At the outbreak of the war the Imperial artillery was still organised as had been in the middle of the sixteenth century, with a great variety of calibres of cannon. The basic measure of the pieces was called *Kartaune*, which was equivalent to a piece of 50 pounds. Thus, there was the fourth *kartaune* (12 pounds) and the middle *kartaune* (24 pounds). Light pieces continued to be called falconettes (One pounder, four, six, eight, 12 and 25 pounders), together with other types of pieces with specific names (*schlangem, werfer*) and of various calibres. Such diversity was a real problem for master gunners, in order to obtain the right cannonballs which is why in the early 1630s the calibres began to be simplified and the guns were built only in the eighth-barrel (6 pounds), quarter-barrel (12 pounds) and half-barrel (24 pounds) calibres, although many older pieces remained in service.[74] Heavy pieces generally deployed in large batteries of up to 12 pieces, located in half-fortified locations, with almost no mobility. Once located, it was very laborious and slow to move them, so they remained in the second line. The rate of fire was also very slow, and they were generally active during the first phases of a battle, to prepare an attack and for counter-battery fire.

In imitation of the Swedish army, from 1633 the Imperial and Bavarian armies included two light pieces in their infantry regiments, although their profusion and use were not as successful as in the Protestants armies. These guns were moved by their gunners who would manhandle them forward as the infantry unit advanced. When the musketeers reloaded, the regimental cannons fired.[75]

At the battle of Nördlingen, the imperial army was able to deploy 34 heavy guns, 116 light ones and four mortars.[76]

The Army of the Catholic League

Bavaria entered the Thirty Years' War on 8 October 1619, when Duke Maximilian of Bavaria, as head of the Catholic League, ordered the recruitment of an army of 30,000 soldiers for the spring of 1620.[77]

Like in the other armies raised in Germany, the regiments of the League were theoretically 3,000 strong, divided in 10 companies of 300 soldiers, but contracts stored in the archives indicate that they were usually of 2,000 soldiers, and in some cases just 1,000.[78] On campaign, there was no standard theme, as some regiments had less than 10 companies, while other units had more. Rarely did any have the on-paper establishment of anywhere near 300 soldiers per company, because of desertion, sickness and losses in battle.

The organisation, chain of command, recruiting and training of the Catholic League army were similar to those of the Imperialists. However, at the beginning of the conflict these aspects were not managed effectively,

---

74 Brnardic, *Imperial Armies. Infantry*, p.41.
75 Brnardic, *Imperial Armies. Infantry*, p.42.
76 Brnardic, *Imperial Armies. Infantry*, p.41.
77 Spring, *Bavarian Army*, p.1.
78 Spring, *Bavarian Army*, p.49.

THE ARMIES

Maximilian I, Duke of Bavaria, by Joachim von Sandrart (1643). He was Duke of Bavaria from 1597 and an Elector of the Holy Roman Empire from 1623. Through various reforms, he strengthened by economising his duchy, with which he managed to have fully autonomous military and political power. He did not always have the same interests as the Emperor Ferdinand. Maximilian was a very religious man, uncompromising and hard on the Protestant faithful, and he promoted the Catholic Reformation. (Kunsthistorisches Museum, GG 8035)

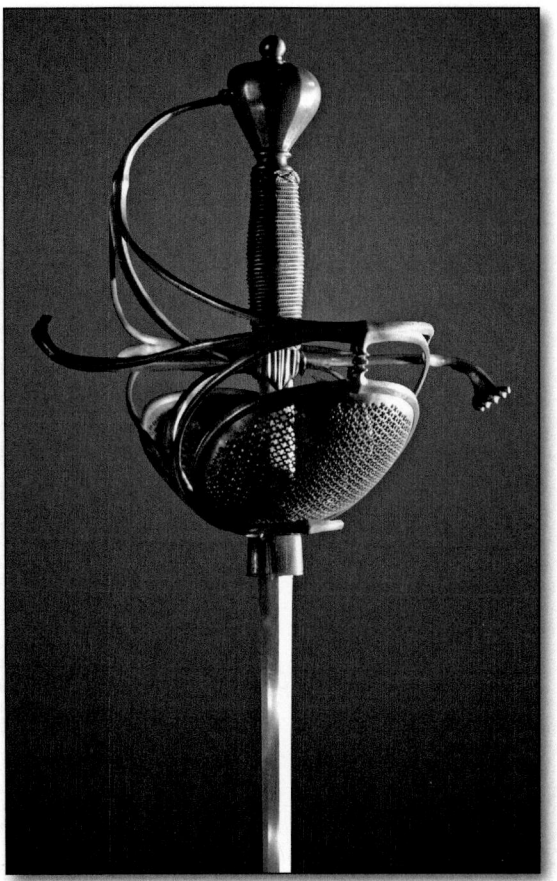

Pappenheim-hilt rapier. Originating in Germany in 1630 it was popularised by the Imperial general Count Pappenheim. Pappenheimer swords feature an elegant set of shells and loops, offering excellent finger protection. It was a weapon that served both for thrusting, and had a sharp blade to cut both on foot and on horseback. (Open source)

while those responsible for them in the Imperial Army had prior experience having served in Flanders and Italy in the service of Spain, and others in Hungary against the Turks (Thirteen Years' War, 1593–1606).

The Bavarian regiment had a regimental staff consisting of the colonel (*obrist*), lieutenant colonel (*obristleutnant*), major (*obristwachtmeister*), chaplain (*kaplan*), quartermaster (*quartiermeister*), wagon-master (*wagenmeister*), provost (*profos*) and provost assistant (*profoshilfs*). Each infantry company had its own *prima plana*, consisting of captain (*hauptman*), lieutenant (*leutnant*), flagman (*fahnrich*), two sergeants (*feldwebel*), three corporals (*korporal*), 25 squad leaders (*gephreite*), one surgeon (*feldscherer*), three drums (*trommel*) and one piper (*spülen*).[79]

In terms of recruiting a voluntary system was in place between 1618 and 1632, but when the Swedes invaded Bavaria, Duke Maximilian decreed the forced enlistment of recruits to defend the country. Thus, on 30 June 1632

---

79 Spring, *Bavarian Army*, p.50.

he ordered a general muster of all men between 18 and 40 years of age, to ascertain the potential number of men available for war.[80] Unlike the Dutch, Spanish and Imperial armies, which formed ethnically national units, that is, units, be they companies, battalions or entire regiments, with soldiers from the same nation, in the case of Bavaria and the League, soldiers from as far away as Bohemia, Greece, France, Spain or Italy served side-by-side in the same unit.[81]

Furthermore, unlike in the Imperial or Spanish Army, which disbanded regiments when their strength fell to an operationally unviable level, in the Bavarian army new companies were raised to strengthen the regiments. This had financial benefits as the cost was lower because new patents or contracts were not granted to new colonels, and the time and effort taken to recruit individual companies was less than that needed to raise an entirely new regiment from scratch.[82] In fact, Bavaria raised 21 infantry regiments during the entire conflict, of which only five were dissolved.[83]

At the beginning of the war the Bavarians were using the classic Spanish deployment of the tercios. However, after the defeat of Breitenfeld, the Bavarians abandoned the tercio system and adopted the Dutch linear system.[84]

Bavarian cavalry banner. It presents the typical symbols seen on Bavarian banners: the monogram 'M' of Maximilian, Duke of Bavaria, in gold, surrounded by a laurel wreath, a symbol of reward for poets, athletes and warriors in ancient Greece and Rome. The background of the flag is blue, associated with the colour of the Virgin Mary's mantle. The banner is dated between 1600–1625, and it is not known to which unit it belonged or when it was captured. Its measurements are as follows: width 55cm; height 64cm; length 252cm. (Armémuseum, AM.081230)

Bavarian cavalry regiments also had a wide disparity in strengths, from 100 to 500 for each cavalry regiment. The cavalry had similar organisation to the infantry. Each cavalry regiment had a staff or *prima plana*, and each cavalry company had its own, consisting of a captain (*rittmeister*), a lieutenant (*leutnant*), a sergeant (*wachtmeister*), a quartermaster (*fourier*), two corporals (*korporal*), a scribe (*musterschreiber*), a surgeon (*feldscherer*), three trumpets (*trumpeter*) and one saddler (*sattler*).[85]

Like other contemporary armies, in 1634 the Bavarian cavalry was divided into four types: cuirassiers, harquebusiers, dragoons, and light cavalry (Croatians), following the same pattern as Imperial units. Dragoons, considered infantry, had their own organisation at the company level, having a captain, lieutenant, ensign, sergeant major, sergeant, two scribes, a farrier, one surgeon and three corporals.[86]

Bavarian artillery was divided into six basic types: cannon, culverin, bastard culverin,

---

80 Spring, *Bavarian Army*, p.35.
81 Spring, *Bavarian Army*, p.33.
82 Spring, *Bavarian Army*, p.41.
83 Spring, *Bavarian Army*, p.50.
84 Spring, *Bavarian Army*, p.105.
85 Spring, *Bavarian Army*, p.1 and 49.
86 Spring, *Bavarian Army*, p.52.

minion, falcon and falconet. Siege mortars were also available. A muster from 1622 indicates that more than 550 horses and 129 limbers were needed to move the artillery (sorted by type, for example, shot, gunpowder, grapeshot). The firing rate of the largest Bavarian cannon was 10 shots per hour. The falconets, the smaller pieces, could fire 20 times per hour.[87] The prestigious guns guarded in the Munich arsenal, called the '12 Apostles', were pieces of extraordinary size and beauty, and when King Gustavus Adolphus sacked the Bavarian capital, five of those behemoths were taken away.[88]

The Spanish Army

For the British reader, the Spanish Army of the Thirty Years' War is a great unknown.[89] On the other hand, the other warring armies in the Thirty Years' War, such as Swedish,[90] Dutch,[91] Imperial,[92] Bavarian[93] and French[94] are much better understood to the European reader.

British historians have barely mentioned Spanish military involvement or have described the Spanish Army as if it were still organised as it was in the sixteenth century. Thus, in his vast book *The Thirty Years' War*,[95] Geoffrey Parker describes Spanish participation in the conflict almost exclusively from a political point of view, and when he mentions the military aspect, he does not go into detail in describing the Spanish Army, but rather presents some merely descriptive military action. In his work, the military weight of the war was essentially only developed by the Empire, Bavaria, Sweden, Denmark and Saxony.

In the same vein, Victoria Wedgwood, in her book *The Thirty Years' War*,[96] also considers Spanish participation only from a political point of

---

87 Spring, *Bavarian Army*, p.53.
88 Spring, *Bavarian Army*, p.53.
89 Notario López, Ignacio&Iván: The Spanish Tercios, 1536–1704. Men-at-Arms 481. Osprey, Oxford, 2012; Picoult, Pierre: *The armies of Philip IV of Spain (1621–1665). The fight for European supremacy.* Helion, Warwick, 2019.
90 Fredholm Von Essen, Michael: *The Lion from the North. Volume 1. The Swedish army of Gustavus Adolphus, 1618–1632.* Helion, Warwick, 2020; Roberts, Michael: *Essays in Swedish History.* Weidenfeld & Nicolson, London, 1967; Brzezinski, Richard: *The Army of Gustavus Adolphus (1). Infantry.* Osprey, London 1991, Brzezinski, Richard: *The Army of Gustavus Adolphus (2). Cavalry.* Osprey, London, 1993.
91 Van Nimwegen, Olaf: *The Dutch Army and the Military Revolutions, 1588–1688.* Boydell Press, Rochester, 2010; Van Der Hoeven, Marco (ed.): *Exercise of Arms. Warfare in the Netherlands (1568–1648).* Brill, Leiden, 1997.
92 Brnardic, Vladimir: *Imperial Armies of the Thirty Years' War (1). Infantry and Artillery.* Men-at-Arms 457. Osprey, Oxford, 2009; Brnardic, Vladimir: *Imperial Armies of the Thirty Years' War (2). Cavalry.* Men-at-Arms 462. Osprey, Oxford, 2010; Spring, Laurence: *In the emperor's service. Wallenstein's army, 1625–1634.* Helion. Warwick, 2019.
93 Spring, Laurence: *The Bavarian Army During the Thirty Years War, 1618–1648: The Backbone of the Catholic League.* Helion, Warwick, 2017.
94 Parrott, David: *Richelieu's Army: War, Government and Society in France, 1624–1642.* Cambridge University Press. Cambridge, 2001.
95 Parker, Geoffrey: *La Guerra de los Treinta Años.* Editorial Antonio Machado, Madrid, 2004.
96 Wedgwood, Cicely Veronica: *The Thirty Years War*, Nova York Review of Books, New York, 2005.

view, and attributes them with a Machiavellian role with the sole purpose of maintaining Catholic religion in Germany.

And in his book on the Bavarian army during the Thirty Years' War,[97] Laurence Spring refers to Nördlingen in its chronology as a battle in which the Bavarian-Imperialists defeated the Swedes, without mentioning the decisive Hispanic participation.

When describing the Spanish Army, historiography is based on the notion of the tercio, which was the organisational unit of Spanish infantry, officially instituted based on three rules: the decree from Emperor Charles V to Pedro Álvarez de Toledo y Zúñiga, Viceroy of Naples (23 October 1534), the Genoa Ordinance of 15 November 1536 and the Instruction of Alfonso de Ávalos Aquino y Sanseverino, Marquis of Vast, to the Tercio de Lombardía (August 1538).[98] In 1587 the Governor-General of Flanders Alessandro Farnese (1545–1592), Duke of Parma, completed the Tercios legal corpus with the promulgation of two Ordinances concerning the ranks of Auditor General and Provost, as being responsible for justice and military accounting.[99]

The exact origin of the word 'tercio' is not known. The first time it was used in an official document is in the Genoa Ordinance of 1536. Spanish sources indicate that it may have come from the name of a Roman legion that had garrisoned Hispania (*Legio Tertia*, which in fact never was in Spain); other scholars explain that its name comes from what in the Ordinances of 1497 there were three different groups of weapons – pikemen, crossbowmen and arquebusiers[100] while a third explanation states that it also comes from Latin *tertia*, but refers to the third part of the personnel of a Roman legion. Indeed, the theoretical number of troops in a Tercio was 3,000 – divided into 10 companies of 300 troops, while a complete Roman legion, according to Titus Livius, had 6,000 Roman infantrymen and 3,000 auxiliary soldiers, totalling 9,000 troops, of which a third part would be 3,000.

In fact, in his book 'Discourse on how to reduce military discipline to better and former state', the veteran *maestre de campo* (the general-in-chief of a tercio) Sancho de Londoño wrote that:

> The Tercios, although instituted in imitation of such legions, can be compared in a small way with them, that the number is half less, and though formerly there were three thousand soldiers, by whom they were called Tercio, and not Legions, as ancients say, even if they do not have more than a thousand men; formerly in every tercio there were twelve companies, though often there are more in some, and in others less than 12.[101]

---

97 Spring, *Bavarian Army*, p. X.
98 Navarro Méndez, Joaquín: 'La instrucción de 1536 u Ordenanza de Génova (la génesis de los Tercios)' in Revista Ejército, 827, March 2010, p.108.
99 Moreno, *Las Ordenanzas de Alejandro Farnesio*, pp.431–458.
100 Notario, *Spanish Tercios*, p.12.
101 Londoño, *Discourse*, pp.11–12. Traditionally it is accepted that Maurice of Nassau was inspired by History, reading of texts of the Greeks and Romans, to carry out his military reforms in the Dutch infantry, but the Spaniards also introduced reforms.

THE ARMIES

Monument to Isabella of Castile at Paseo de la Castellana (avenue) in Madrid (Spain), by Spanish sculptor Manuel Oms (1842). Depicted person: Gonzalo Fernández de Córdoba, 'The Great Captain'. The general always maintained a friendly relationship with Queen Isabella; on the contrary, with King Ferdinand the relationship was one of military and service collaboration, but it was not so cordial. The King demanded explanations of the expenses incurred by his military expeditions and Gonzalo presented the following detailed account: One hundred million ducats in picks, shovels and hoes to bury the dead of the enemy. One hundred and fifty thousand ducats in friars, nuns and donations to the poor, to pray to God for the souls of the King's soldiers who fell in combat. One hundred thousand ducats in perfumed gloves, to preserve the troops from the stench of the enemy's corpses. One hundred and sixty thousand ducats to replace and fix the bells destroyed from so much ringing of victory. Finally, for my patience in having listened to these trifles from the King, who demands an account from the one who has given Him a Kingdom, one hundred million ducats. (photo courtesy Luis García)

But the origin of the tercios goes back to the establishment of a permanent professional army in Spain, conceived during the War against Granada (1482–1492). Ferdinand II of Aragon and Isabella I of Castile, known as the Catholic Kings, reorganised their royal hosts and noble warriors, both of them with medieval roots, to provide themselves with a permanent and well-organised force. Units called *batallas* (battles), consisting of 500 men, with an amalgamation of soldiers with various weapons: hand gunner (primitive arquebuses), crossbowmen, pikemen, halberds, and shield bearers (*rodeleros*, infantrymen armed with swords and shield). Each battle was divided into 10 platoons of 50 men, commanded by a platoon chief. The union of several battles formed a division.

In 1493 an Ordinance standardised all troops in a basic unit called *capitanía* (captaincy) similar to a company, with 500 troops, commanded by a captain. His second was a lieutenant, who was also responsible for defending the unit's flag. Each captaincy was divided into groups, led by a sergeant.[102] But over time, it was found that apart from a permanent tactical structure (the *capitanías*), a larger organisational unit was needed, and so emerged the *coronelía* (colonelship) commanded by a colonel, which in 1502 were instituted by King Ferdinand II, following the recommendations of the chronicler and soldier Gonzalo de Ayora (1466–1538), to provide a permanent superior structure to the *capitanías*.[103]

---

102 Notario, *Spanish Tercios*, p.4.
103 Notario, *Spanish Tercios*, p.5.

These reforms were applied, especially by Gonzalo Fernández de Córdoba (1453–1515), known as the 'Great Captain,'[104] in the Italian Wars campaigns.[105] Indeed, for the first Spanish expeditionary force in Naples (1495–1497), the army was divided in *capitanías* of 500 men (200 pikemen, 200 shield bearers and 100 arquebusiers). But in 1504, Gonzalo Fernández de Córdoba organised his force based on the new Ordinances: the *coronelías* were theoretically composed of 6,000 men, grouped into 12 *capitanías*, but in practice, they ranged from 12 to 16 *capitanías*; and in the expedition to Oran (1509), the *coronelías* were formed by between eight to 16 *capitanías*.[106]

After the conquest of Naples by 'the Great Captain', Spanish military doctrine changed thanks to his practical contributions on the battlefield. Key were the consolidation of an operational army, mobilised throughout the year, and the ability to act at great distances from the Iberian Peninsula. Infantry had pre-eminence over heavy cavalry (infantry would now be the backbone of the army, with cavalry being left to perform secondary tasks, and be required to coordinate with infantry) and the recruitment into Spanish service of foreigners to fill the numerical weaknesses of the Hispanic contingent.[107] However, current Anglo-Saxon historiography, in its study of the so-called Military Revolution, has ignored or downplayed the innovations and warlike actions of Gonzalo Fernández de Córdoba.[108]

The conflict in Italy was resumed by Emperor Charles V and I of Spain (1500–1558) and it was through the 'laboratory' of the Italian Wars that the Spanish learned a number of key lessons in mobilising their armed forces. Traditional models of military mobilisation used in the war against the Moors (the so-called *Reconquista*) were not valid for offensive actions in distant locations.[109] In addition, they became more aware of the need for a large, highly trained and motivated permanent armed force with the ability to work through any warlike scenario, and for extended periods of time, not just for a single campaign or for only one year, but for many years or as long as required.

In Italy the best units were allocated to fight French expansionism, and when there were no battles, the soldiers remained within the Italian fortresses to protect them. These Spanish garrisons in Italy, known as the *Presidios*,

---

104 About the contributions of the Great Captain in the Hispanic armies: Rodríguez y Mesa, *Del Gran Capitán a los Tercios*, pp.147–152.
105 About the several Wars of Italy that led to confrontation between France and Spain, with their respective allied Italian states: Barbasán Lagueruela, Casto: *Las primeras campañas del Renacimiento*. Imprenta J. Peláez, Toledo, 1890; Mallett, Michael Shaw, Christine: *The Italian Wars, 1494–1559. War, State and Society in Early Modern Europe*. Longman, Harlow, 2012; Oman, Charles: *A History of the Art of War in the Sixteenth Century*. Methuen, London, 1937; Taylor, Francis L.: *The Art of War in Italy, 1494–1529*. Cambridge University Press, Cambridge, 1921.
106 Notario, *Spanish Tercios*, p.5.
107 Rodríguez y Mesa, *Del Gran Capitán a los Tercios*, p.150.
108 Rodríguez y Mesa, *Del Gran Capitán a los Tercios*, p.149: Geoffrey Parker does not summon even a single time the Great Captain (Parker, Geoffrey: *The revolution…*), and Black minimised his innovations, attributing his successes to the errors of the French (BLACK, *European Warfare*, pp. 72–73).
109 Rodríguez y Mesa, *Del Gran Capitán a los Tercios*, p.152.

'The conquest of Oran', painting by John of Burgundy (1514), when an army led by Pedro Navarro on behalf of the Cardinal Cisneros, seized the North African city (1509), which was controlled by the Kingdom of Tlemcen. The fleet had 80 naos and 10 galleys, plus additional small boats. They carried around 8,000 to 12,000 infantrymen and 3,000 to 4,000 cavalrymen. In this image we see the Cardinal, with his purple-red habit, and General Pedro Navarro, surrounded by knights still armed in the medieval manner, and by infantry (called 'peones', Spanish medieval term) with armed with spears also in the medieval manner. The flag that can be seen is the Cardinal's personal banner, with the symbols of his rank as Cardinal of Toledo. (Capilla Mozárabe de la Catedral de Toledo)

constituted the strategic reserve of soldiers of the Hispanic Monarchy. They were all highly trained soldiers who had gained experience in fighting against the French, against the Turks or against the Barbary pirates, and thanks to their experience, were well disposed to perform in any operational theatre, given their training, professionalism and experience.[110]

To organise these units in the Presidios, in 1534 and 1536 the new Ordinances were drafted. It was in this context that the first Tercios – known as *Tercios Viejos* (Old Tercios) – were created, in 1534, with units quartered at the Italian fortresses: one in the Kingdom of Sicily, another in the Duchy of Milan (or the Kingdom of Lombardy) and another in the Kingdom of Naples.[111] In 1536 the Tercio of Sardinia and the Tercio de Galeras (the first

---

110 Rodríguez y Mesa, *Del Gran Capitán a los Tercios*, p.153.
111 Navarro Méndez, Joaquín: 'La instrucción de 1536 u Ordenanza de Génova (la génesis de los Tercios)' en *Revista Ejército*, 827, March 2010, p.108.

Marine Corps in modern history) were created. The other units that were created later were known as *Tercios Nuevos* (New Tercios), or simply Tercios.

The Tercio was an administrative unit that, at the same time, could be constituted as a combat unit. Each had a certain number of companies,[112] which could either be in the same territory, garrisoned in several cities, or could fight in theatres of very far from each other.[113]

In 1534, the Tercios had 10 companies with 300 members each, eight of the companies being 'pikemen' and two were 'arquebusiers'. The Tercio had its own *prima plana* or staff, carrying out the military and command functions of the unit, as well as the administration and payment of wages. This staff consisted of 29 members, the head being the chief of the Tercio called *maestre de campo* (as a general of the Tercio) and his second was the *sargento mayor* (sergeant major).[114]

Both types of companies had the same number of men and the same *prima plana*, that was made up of 11 members: one *capitán* (captain) and his page, one *alférez* (second lieutenant, as second in command of the company and in charge of protecting the flag), one sergeant, one flagman, two drummers, one flautist, one chaplain, one quartermaster and one barber (acting as a surgeon).

The pike companies consisted of the 11 members detailed above, 135 *coseletes* (pikemen wearing back and breast plates who were heavy pikemen), 44 *picas secas* (unarmoured pikemen), 90 arquebusiers and 20 musketeers. The arquebusier companies also had 11 members of the *prima plana*, 35 *picas secas*, 239 arquebusiers and 15 musketeers.

The Spanish companies were also divided into platoons of 25 men at the command of an NCO, known as a *cabo de escuadra* (squad corporal). In addition, informally, the soldiers were grouped in *camaradas* (comrades), groups of six to 12 soldiers, who shared food, lodging, and so forth, this being a social structure very important for morality and 'esprit de corps'.

The organisational model of the Tercios rooted in Italy was spreading throughout Spanish domains. Thirty years later, in 1567, to quell the rebellion in the Netherlands, the Third Duke of Alba, Fernando Álvarez de Toledo y Pimentel (1507–1580), known as the *Duque de Hierro* (Iron Duke), left Milan for Flanders at the head of the four Spanish Tercios based in Italy (Sardinia, Sicily, Naples and Lombardy); but these units' composition varied (3,500 being the largest, then 2,000, 1,800 and 1,500) and the number of companies also varied (10 was the norm, but there were 15 and even 19).[115]

That is why once in Flanders, the Duke of Alba instituted the custom that in the Netherlands the Spanish Tercios would have 12 companies of 250 men, while maintaining the practice that in Spain and Italy the Tercios would continue to be of 10 companies of 300 men. The pike companies of 250 men had 11 members of *prima plana*, 111 *coseletes*, 108 *picas secas* and 20

---

112 For more detail on the main ranks in the Hispanic Army: Piccouet, *Armies*, pp.122–125; Notario, *Spanish Tercios*, pp.14–17.
113 Mesa, *La pacificación de Flandes*, p.195.
114 For a more detailed description: Notario, *Spanish Tercios*, pp.14–17.
115 Mesa, *Innovaciones militares*, p.541.

musketeers, whilst the arquebusier companies had 11 officers and assistants, 224 arquebusiers and 15 musketeers.[116] As for the proportion of shot to pike, not counting the members of the *prima plana*, in the Tercio of 10 companies, the proportion was 48.79 percent, while in the Tercio of 12 companies it was 23.64 percent.[117]

This theoretical model remained in place for several decades, but the reality was very different as companies generally had more firearms than the rules dictated, but on campaign, if the enemy were strong in cavalry, companies increased the number of pikes in order to better defend themselves.

Nonetheless, military literature and military instruction, theoretically, continued to emphasise the prevalence of pikes over firearms, but this was due to creative accounting. The arquebusiers were paid more than the pikemen, and at this time, infantry could only defend against cavalry attacks by forming a large square of pikemen, at least until the invention of the bayonet, so each Tercio had to have enough pikemen in order to defend the unit in these situations.

During the reign of Philip II, the proportion of pikes to firearms would continue to grow in favour of the latter and in 1594 it was ordered that the new companies recruiting in Castile to serve in Italy should have 125 pikemen, 100 arquebuses and 25 muskets. In 1598 it was ordered that a company of 250 soldiers should have 130 pikemen, 100 arquebuses and 20 musketeers, and then in 1603 the order was issued requiring that half of the companies in the Tercios would be made up of pikes, and the other half with firearms.[118] But in reality, the muster records of these troops show us that the proportion of firearms was higher than that prescribed in the Ordinances. For example, the musters of Spanish companies in Sicily in 1572 and 1574 show that between 70 and 80 percent of the infantry had arquebuses and muskets, and in 1601 the Flanders Army musters record that 62 percent of Spanish infantry used muskets and arquebuses.[119]

The Ordinances of 1632 reorganised the infantry companies of the Spanish and Italian Tercios. Like any reform, its measures were not immediately implemented, although there were also units that were ahead and already applying these measures.[120] With the new Ordinances, only one

---

116 Throughout these decades of continuous combat, several Ordinances were issued that adapted the organisation of Tercios to the circumstances they found themselves in. (Piccouet, *Armies*, p.139).
117 By the end of the sixteenth century the Spaniards already understood definitively that firearms were the main weapon of the battlefield and that the pike would end up becoming obsolete. In 1586, the Spanish veteran official Martín de Eguiluz wrote 'in this Era, the Arquebusiers and Musketeers are very useful', and he thought that in a company of 100 men, 35 pikemen was enough(Eguiluz, *Discurso*, p.167).
118 Rodríguez y Mesa, *Del Gran Capitán a los Tercios*, p.170.
119 Rodríguez y Mesa, *Del Gran Capitán a los Tercios*, p.171.
120 One of the most controversial aspects of the 1632 Ordinances was the exception of seniority in service for members of the nobility. Historically, the Spanish tercios had served as a means of social advancement and in the sixteenth century many *maestres de campo* had ascended on merit from the humblest layers of society (Julián Romero, Sancho de Avila, etc). The Ordinances of 1632 maintained a strict system of promotions, based on seniority in lower employment to be able to ascend to higher employment. However, the Ordinance also considered belonging to the nobility as an element of merit for promotion, and a distorting element at that for the whole

THE BATTLE OF NÖRDLINGEN 1634

Battle of Heiligerlee, as depicted by Frans Hogenberg (circa 1570). The Battle of Heiligerlee (Heiligerlee, Groningen, 23 May 1568) was fought between Dutch rebels and the Spanish army of Friesland. It was the first Dutch victory during the Eighty Years' War. We can see how the Dutch arquebusiers in the foreground advance against the Spanish, and behind them a charge of reiters armed with pistols attack the Spanish guns. In the distance, fighting between units of pikemen can be seen. (Open source)

type of company was created, containing all weapons (pikes, arquebuses and muskets). However, in the Iberian Peninsula the Tercios would have 12 companies of 250 men, while in Italy and Flanders, Tercios would have 15 companies of 200 men, so in each case, the theoretical number of an establishment of 3,000 men was maintained.

In Spain then, the Tercios had 12 companies, with 11 members of *prima plana*, 90 pikemen, 60 musketeers and 89 arquebusiers. In Italy, the Tercios consisted of 15 companies, each with 11 senior staff, 70 pikemen, 40 musketeers and arquebusiers. Theoretically, infantry stationed in Italy and

---

officers and non-commissioned officers corps, who generally belonged to the social class of the 'hidalgos', the low nobility, with hardly any great wealth or influence, or from the popular classes, who were clearly not 'noble'. For example, to be a *maestre de campo* it was necessary to have served eight years as captain, but being noble, having served eight years in total in any capacity in their military career was enough. And to be considered for promotion to be a captain, 10 years of experience were necessary as a soldier or *alférez* (second-lieutenant or ensign), but for a person deemed to be noble this requirement was reduced by almost half.

Flanders had 37 percent pikemen, 42 percent of arquebusiers and 21 percent musketeers, that is, a 2 to 1 ratio in favour of firearms. Despite the obvious decrease in the number of pikes, during the rest of the seventeenth century the number of pikes remained stable as a consequence of the greater pre-eminence of cavalry, especially from the 1640s onwards. Pikes as a defensive weapon would remain until the beyond introduction of the bayonet.[121]

But as soon as he arrived in Flanders from the German expedition in 1636, the Cardinal-Infante Fernando ordered that his army reintroduce the two types of companies, arquebusiers and pikemen, both with 200 men. So, the Tercios of Flanders thus had 15 companies, two of arquebusiers (with 11 commanders and staff, 159 arquebusiers and 30 musketeers) and 13 companies of pikemen (with 11 members of company's staff, 69 pikemen and 120 musketeers). This put the percentage of weapons at 31 percent pikes, 11 percent arquebuses and 56 percent muskets.[122]

The Hispanic Monarchy, with territories in the Iberian Peninsula, America, Africa, Flanders and Italy, was also the first global monarchy, with the difficult problem of defending such extensive and unconnected territories. The enormous complexity of this led to the development of a military system different from the other European nations that were still largely based on traditional feudal or private methods, but in Spain, recruitment was based on a royal monopoly, and without the King's permission (*patente*) one could not recruit volunteers. These soldiers, once enlisted, were held accountable only to the King, and were exempt from ordinary civil jurisdiction (the military had their own laws, known as *fuero militar* (military law).[123]

During the sixteenth and first half of the seventeenth century all units of the armies of the Hispanic Monarchy whether in Spain, Flanders or Italy, were made up of volunteers, and the way to access the army was to enlist

Showcase of weapons from the seventeenth century, in the Castel Sant'Angelo (Rome). First, an Italian cup sword; Swiss cuirass half armour, a brandistock, a morrion, the raised crest indicating that it is Italian, because Spanish morrions were straight – and a bulletproof breastplate. All the pieces are Italian except the armour and the breastplate. (Author's photos)

---

121 Rodríguez y Mesa, *Del Gran Capitán a los Tercios*, p.171.
122 Hrncirik, *Spanier auf dem Albuch*, p.43.
123 Rodríguez Y Mesa, *Del Gran Capitán a los Tercios*, pp.154–156.

in one of the many levies and recruitment activities that were being made throughout Spain and Italy.

The recruiting process began when a captain or second lieutenant (with aspirations to be promoted to captain) applied for a license from the King to recruit a company. The administrative documents (patent letter and letter of conduct) established the number of soldiers, recruiting area and meeting point for the company to be presented to the King's representatives, and in return the officer was confirmed as captain of the company, and was able to choose who would fill the rest of the unit's command positions. The officer travelled to the assigned enlistment area, moving through the villages, and with the beating of a large drum that captured the people's attention, proclaimed the adventures and high fortune that could be expected from the life of soldier. Once he had assembled the number of people required to form the company, he went to the agreed mustering point of the company, after which the unit was garrisoned in some Spanish fortress or was transferred by sea to the Italian *presidios*.[124] The company was recruited, paid and uniformed at the expense of the kingdom, but the captain had to advance his own money to pay for the enlistment bounty and the maintenance of his men until they met with the King's representatives.

Once the new unit personnel were assembled, the rookies (*bisoños*) were trained and strengthened through a hard routine of physical (marches, swimming) and military training, using the pike, swords and firearms drill, until they were considered ready for combat. The training process took months, conducted by experienced veterans. It was then that due to the constant wars involving Spain around the world, the unit was sent an active service. On most occasions these new companies consisted of veteran sergeants, the recruits, now well-trained, and by former soldiers enlisting in search of fortune. They were very well-trained units, hence the reputation of the Spanish units was so prestigious.

The 'esprit de corps' of the Spanish soldiers of the Tercios was very high;[125] for them, honour (*honra*) and prestige (*reputación*) were fundamental, and an oath was binding, even if it cost their life. This feeling came no doubt from the deeply rooted Catholic tradition of these times, which manifested itself in such deep respect for religion, but also exposed it to the evil effects of intolerance.

According to legend, at the end of the battle of Rocroi (19 May 1643), where the Duke of Enghien, Louis II of Bourbon-Conde, defeated the Spanish army of Francisco de Melo, a French officer asked a Spanish soldier how well the troops that the Spanish had fought that day, to which the Spanish soldier simply replied: 'Just count the dead'.[126]

---

124 Notario, *Spanish Tercios*, p.18. About the recruitment of the tercios in Spain. Thompson, *War and decadence*, pp.129–180; Parker, *The Ejército*, pp.71-73; Quatrefages, *Los Tercios*, p.423; Andújar, *Ejércitos*, pp.141–146; Martínez Ruiz, *Los Soldados del Rey*, pp.901–904; Rodríguez Hernández, *Los Tambores*, p.87.

125 About the motivation of the military life: Thompson, *Milicia*, pp.115–133; Carrasco, *Guerra y virtud*, pp.135–162; Puddu, *El soldado gentilhombre*, pp.148–175.

126 At the Battle of Rocroi, the French had about 6,000 dead and 2,500 wounded, while the Spanish lost 2,000 killed, 3,000 wounded and 3,826 prisoners, of whom 2,000 were repatriated to Spain.

This engraving, made by Nicolas Cochin, is entitled 'Les Cornettes, Guidons et Drapeaux pris sur les ennemis en la bataille de Rocroy portés en cérémonie à nostre Dame par les cent Suisses' and represents the triumphal entry into the cathedral of Paris of the flags and banners taken from the Spanish at the Battle of Rocroi, which took place on 19 May 1643 between the French army under the command of the young Louis II of Bourbon-Condé, at that time Duke of Enghien and 21 years of age, later Prince of Condé, and the Spanish army under the command of the Portuguese Francisco de Melo, captain general of the Tercios of Flanders. Various research works have made it possible to match some of the flags to the Hispanic Tercios that fought in the battle: Spanish Albuquerque's tercio, Italian Tercios of Strozzi, Visconti and Jorge de Castellví, and the German Frangipani's regiment. Some flags and trophies from the battle were deposited in the Château de Chantilly, in the Galerie des Batailles, commonly called 'Les Trophées de Rocroy'. (BNF)

A characteristic element of the Spanish military system was the *reformado* (reformed) officers and non-commissioned officers:[127] These were men that, due to lack of money or for disciplinary reasons, the units to which they belonged had been dissolved or absorbed into other companies. These reformed officers and unofficial officers lacked a position in the new unit and became part of it as ordinary soldiers, but their experience was considered by the officers and in combat their service was highly appreciated as they commanded and maintained order in the front ranks during combat.

Besides the *reformados*, another type of combatant common in the Spanish Tercios was the figure of the 'particular' (*particular*), 'adventurer' (*aventurero*) or 'entertaining' (*entretenido*): often these were noble people (*hidalgos*), even of the higher nobility, who wished to gain prestige in the sight of King and for that reason they asked for permission to accompany a general, to be part of his entourage, hence the name 'entertaining' as the general paid some of their maintenance, and in combat, the 'adventurer' could fight in the front ranks and thus gain prestige. Frequently these individuals were former soldiers, but were not now on active service, unlike the *reformados* who were technically still enlisted, but were taking up arms again for the chance of being noticed. Their goals were to be awarded a position in the administration or supply of the army, thus being in a position to make a fortune on the acquisition of war booty and by 'irregular' bookkeeping.

In terms of armament, the pikes used by the Spaniards during the Italian Wars (late fifteenth and early sixteenth centuries) were slightly shorter than the French, Swiss or German ones. A Spanish pike measured five to five and a

---

(Quesada Sanz, Fernando: 'Los mitos de Rocroi' in *La aventura de la Historia*, 97 (November 2006), Arlanza Ediciones, Madrid).

127 Notario, *Spanish Tercios*, p.14.

THE BATTLE OF NÖRDLINGEN 1634

The 'Salón de Reinos' (Hall of Realms) or so-called 'Salón grande' ('great hall') was the best illustrative example of the military power of the Hispanic Monarchy, in the old Buen Retiro Palace in Madrid, built between 1630 and 1635. This room housed the best paintings, almost all now preserved in the Prado Museum. The room owes its name to the fact that the coats of arms of the twenty-four kingdoms that formed the Hispanic Monarchy in the time of Philip IV were painted on it. Both artists belonging to the old generation worked on the battle canvases, in the case of Carducho or Cajés, who had already worked in the service of Philip III, as well as the younger ones, trained in naturalism, in the case of Maíno, Zurbarán, Pereda and Velázquez himself, favourite of Philip IV. We have here 'The Battle of Fleurus', painted by Carducho (circa 1635). We can see in the background a combat between two infantry 'escuadrones': the first line is firing, the second is pointing and the next 3 lines are ready with the loaded weapon, while the last is reloading. Higher up is a cavalry attack, to the caracole, which is repulsed by the fire of arquebuses, while the pikemen lower their weapons to repel the charge. We can distinguish very well various Spanish flags, all of them with the Burgundy Cross in the centre. (Museo del Prado)

half metres and weighed 3.5kg, dimensions maintained during the sixteenth and seventeenth centuries.[128]

The Spaniards always preferred the arquebus to the musket, as it was lighter and had a higher rate of fire. The Spanish arquebus measured one metre in length, weighed seven kilogrammes, and fired a lead bullet weighing 22–24 grams. It had a rate of fire of two or three shots per minute, with a maximum range of 100 metres, but was only effective at 30 metres, but it was simple to handle and could be mastered quickly.[129]

---

128 Piccouet, *Armies*, pp.169–171.
129 Piccouet, *Armies*, pp.171–174.

Spanish muskets, known as the 'Biscayan type', were heavier and more accurate than other European muskets. They measured between 1.3 to 1.6 metres, weighed more than 10kg and it was necessary to use a forked rest to aim and shoot. Its firing rate was one shot per minute, and it required 44 actions to reload. Its main advantage was the weight of the ball (24 to 42.5 grams) and the greater effective range of 50 to 75 metres and maximum range of 300 metres that allowed the Spanish musketeers to be lethal to a distance superior to the other European armies.[130] In 1632 Captain Miguel Pérez de Ejea reported that 800 feet (222 metres) was the longest range at which the Spanish muskets were taking effect.

In the Swedish or Dutch armies, the arquebus and the musket were intended to be rationalised, so that the troops could use the same type of weapon and to avoid logistical problems. On the contrary, it is considered that the Spaniards were old fashioned in maintaining arquebuses and muskets. But the Spaniards were always clear that the arquebuses were used on the battlefield in a continuous and very fast fire, and that the muskets were used to engage at long distances and to be very effective with their heavier bullets.

As for the use of the Tercios in combat, scholars generally consider they fought in a single monolithic block of 3,000 pikemen, with small units of arquebusiers and musketeers at their corners, as the paintings of battles depict the Tercios in combat. The reality was very different.

The combat unit that we can see in the pictorial representations of the sixteenth and seventeenth centuries is not a Tercio as such, but an *escuadrón* (squadron), a tactical infantry unit formed with the soldiers of a Tercio, or several, who were formed by a combination of ranks and files of pikemen.[131] The *escuadrón* was formed by a specific number of troops, not the number of companies or their parent unit. The *cuerpos volantes* (mobile units) were also created, which were 'ad hoc' units formed to respond to a specific threat or to achieve a specific goal, with a philosophy very similar to the German *Kampfgruppe* in World War II.[132] The need to operate in theatres of operations so diverse and so distant from one another, with such difficult transport and communications, shaped the versatility and adaptability of the Spanish troops.[133]

The Spaniards wrote a myriad of manuals for the *Arte de Escuadronear* (The Art of the Squadron), and it was the responsibility of the *sargento mayor* of every Tercio to know the exact number of troops under his command so that they could be grouped into one *escuadrón*. There were countless formations, based generally on square root mathematical formulas, but generally reduced to four types: *escuadrón cuadrado* (square squadron), *escuadrón prolongado* (extended squadron), *escuadrón de terreno* (terrain

---

130 Notario, *Spanish Tercios*, p.35.
131 The Spanish pikemen, arquebusiers and musketeers were armed with swords, called *ropera*. The Spanish infantrymen were trained in the handling of the sword (called *Destreza*, skill), and stood out in individual combat skills compared to the other armies (Piccouet, *Armies*, p.168).
132 Mesa, *Military Innovations*, p.544.
133 Piccouet, *Armies*, pp.125–144.

squadron) and *escuadrón de gran frente* (large front squadron), chosen based on whether depth or a wider front was sought.

Indeed, when the commanders wanted to have greater firepower on the front line, a 'large front squadron' was formed, in which the front was twice as large as the depth. If the general wanted to have the same number of files as the front, the 'square squadron' was used. The most commonly used deployment in battle was the 'extended squadron', which was rectangular in shape, with longer sides facing the enemy. With more men at the front, it allowed more shooters to fire continuously until they were ordered to retreat inside the squadron.[134]

For example, if you wanted to form a large front squadron and had 450 pikemen, the depth to front ratio was one to two, and would consist of 30 files wide, and 15 ranks in depth (30 x15). In addition, the firepower would be provided by two detachments on each wing, with 5 files wide and 15 ranks deep, the four bodies forming an independent unit of 600 men.[135] To this formation could be added more pikemen and shot, usually adding to the right of the formation, increasing the depth and/or the frontage.[136]

In fact, the flexibility of the infantry squadron allowed that in the Battle of Fleurus (29 August 1622), the Spanish Tercio Viejo de Naples was reinforced with Burgundian troops, which merged into it, as they had learned to do in instruction drills. And at the Battle of Nördlingen, the Tercio de Idiáquez was repeatedly strengthened with arquebusiers from other units.[137]

To form up in these formations, it was considered that a soldier occupied one square foot of space and that one square foot had to be set free on each side and three more in front and behind, which were distances separating them from the four companions around them. Therefore, the squadrons did not form up with the soldiers drawn up close to each other, but rather took into account that each of them must have remained with the appropriate intervals between ranks and files during the combat.

When deploying the army in battle, the *maestre de campo* decided, depending on the number of available troops, the number and type of enemy, and the terrain, the tactical form he wanted to deploy. The *sargento mayor*, knowing the number of pikes and other weapons the unit had, with its experience and use of mathematical rules, calculated how many ranks and files the squadron would have, and advised the captains of the companies that would be part of it. The squadron was silent so that the orders could be executed effectively. All the Spanish soldiers knew perfectly well how they should enter and exit the squadron, and what position they should occupy once they were inside.

In essence, the basic squadron could be described, from the inside out, as a formation where the flags and senior officers were protected in the centre, then came the *picas secas* (unarmoured pikemen) and in the outer ranks the *coseletes*, with their breastplates. The flags were always left in the centre, in the

---

134 Mesa, *Military Innovations*, p.545.
135 Hrncirik, *Spanier auf dem Albuch*, p.45.
136 Piccouet, *Armies*, pp.176–178.
137 Notario, *Spanish Tercios*, p.39.

THE ARMIES

Illustration from the book 'Military Compendium and Squadron Treaty'(Compendio Militar y Tratado de Escuadrones) (1643) by Sargento Mayor Miguel Lorente Bravo. Throughout the seventeenth century, countless books written by former officers were written in Spain, in which the battle tactics, organisation of units and the logistics of armies were explained. All of them also taught how to 'escuadronear', to form ad hoc units based on the available troops, the terrain and the enemy. Using complex mathematical formulas, it was the task of the sergeant major of the tercio to be able to locate the companies in this type of unit. In this illustration, as complex as it is implausible, a total of 1,566 pikemen are available and a 360º self-defence is required: 4 rectangular squadrons are formed, with a 24 man frontage and 11 soldiers deep, as well as 4 triangular squadrons that they are inserted in the formation, of 21 soldiers frontage and 11 deep. (Author's collection)

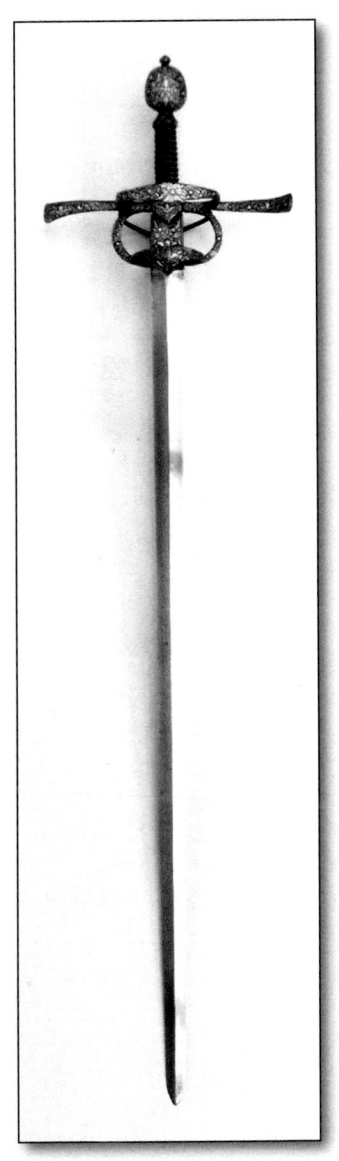

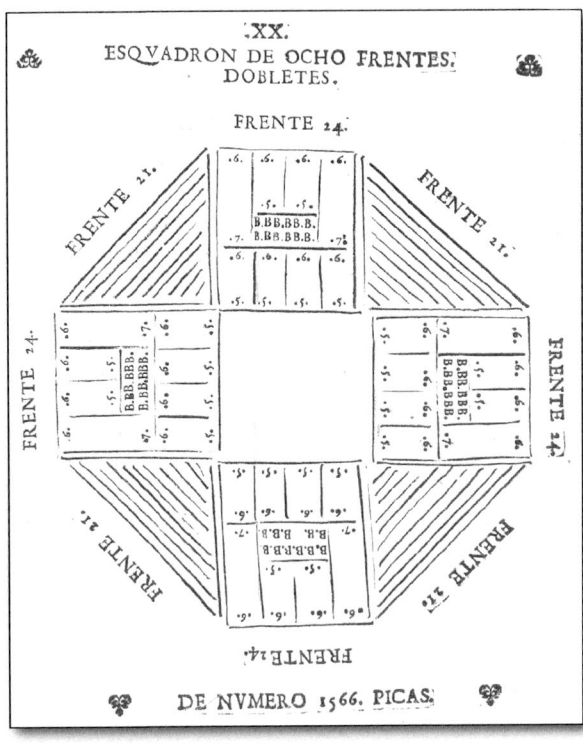

Rapier, early seventeenth century, probably German. Made of steel, silver and iron. Its dimensions are: overall length 117.6cm; blade length 101.3cm; width 28.9cm; weight 1.616kg. As for its decoration, on the obverse it has a portrait of the head of a monk within a shield; on the reverse, the Bavarian coat-of-arms. The term 'rapier' sword designates a certain kind of sword with a long straight blade, wielded with one hand. The origin of the term could be French, Italian or in Spanish: in this language, it means 'sword that goes with the clothes' (ropera), because it was worn as an accessory. Unlike the longer and wider war swords, the rapier was carried because it was fashionable to do so and as a weapon of personal defence and was the traditional weapon for duels of honour. In each country a specific fencing style was developed for this weapon: in Spain, fencing with the rapier sword had the name 'Verdadera destreza de las armas' (true skill of arms); in Germany, the Deutsche Fechtschule; or the French and Italian schools of fencing. (Metropolitan Museum of Art, 42.50.12)

most protected place. The mathematical tables of military drills in squadrons made it possible to calculate, even allowing for leaving a kind of inner square to protect flags, ammunition and even carriages.

In the front rank of the squadron, the most dangerous, were the officers and sergeants, and the stronger and more experienced soldiers with better armour. It was a place of honour, which is why the *particulares* soldiers were often found there too, so that, if they survived, they could reap the reward of their valour. Soldiers worked hard to keep their equipment in good condition so that they could be privileged to be part of the front line.

At each corner of the squadron were the *mangas* (detachment), consisting exclusively of arquebusiers, which provided the firepower that the squadron needed to weaken the enemy before the pikes of both units collided. The *mangas* operated independently of the squadron and could be chosen for specific actions, such as defending an enclave or individually attacking a position. Indeed, detachments of arquebusiers and musketeers could be deployed as a skirmish screen in front of the formation to weaken the enemy with their fire, or to line a parapet in a trench, and, if necessary, could be pulled back to the *escuadrón* for safety. The Spanish arquebusiers were multipurpose soldiers, very useful for the class of combat that the Spaniards practiced, and the arquebusiers became the prototype soldier of the Tercios of the sixteenth century.[138]

Musketeers and some arquebusiers formed the *guarniciones* (garrisons), permanently located on the front and sides of the squadron, which moved at their own pace and, in case of defence, entered the formation.

In the event of a cavalry attack, the musketeers could volley fire at a distance, and the arquebusiers would advance a few metres, take one or two shots, and return into the formation.[139]

The shot in the Hispanic Monarchy's armies were trained to fire in a number of ways. On one hand, the ranks of shooters fired, then knelt on the ground to reload; another system was to use the cavalry's 'caracole' technique, adapted to infantry. This was firing by ranks, where a rank advanced a few steps, fired and marched to the rear of the formation to reload. Shooters could also operate in open order, which consisted of firing at independently in a skirmish line.[140]

This is why the Tercios did not fight in the way they are represented in contemporary engravings, which only conveyed a stylised image to simplify their placement on the battlefield. Indeed, this monolithic image of the Tercios would contrast so much with the deployments created by Maurice of Nassau, forming their troops in companies of 120 men, which by joining four of them obtained battalions of 480 troops, and two of these a regiment of 960 men; in fact, these 1,000 men is very similar to the number of soldiers who formed the Spanish squadrons.[141]

---

138 Rodríguez y Mesa, *Del Gran Capitán a los Tercios*, p.170.
139 Rodríguez y Mesa, *Del Gran Capitán a los Tercios*, p.169.
140 Piccouet, *Armies*, pp.178–179.
141 Mesa, *Military Innovations*, p.544.

Spanish cavalry has generally been considered to be the weakest weapon in the Spanish army and was not modernised like that of other armies, but Spanish cavalry since the end of the fifteenth century adopted the use of firearms, but also units in the medieval manner (known as *Compañías de lanzas* or lance companies), as well as other European armies (*Gendarmes* in France or *Bandes d'Ordonnaces* in Flanders), were also in use. Therefore, from 1494 the Spanish regular cavalry was grouped under the title of *Guardas de Castilla* (Guards of Castile), and divided in two types, heavy and light cavalry. The first were grouped under the heading of *Hombres de Armas* (Men-at-Arms), and those of the light cavalry were called *Jinetes* (riders).

However, the Guards of Castile rarely fought outside of the Iberian Peninsula as they were part of the Royal Guard, but their organisational model applied to the cavalry units that were recruited in Spain, Flanders and Italy who took part in all European and African scenarios. A heavy cavalry company consisted of 37 men-at-arms, a captain, one trumpet, one armourer and one blacksmith, while the light cavalry was divided into companies of 100 men, further divided into *Caballos-celadas* (horsemen with helmets), armed with lances and sword, and of *Arcabuceros a caballo* (Harquebusiers), armed with a wheel-lock arquebus or carbine, pistols and a sword. Both types had a captain, one lieutenant, one sergeant, one trumpet, one armourer, one blacksmith and 94 men.

But in the armies of Emperor Charles V fighting in Europe, most of the heavy cavalry came from the Burgundian and Flanders Ordinance Companies (similar to the French *Gendarmes* companies) and cavalry recruited from all over Germany (cuirassier and lancer cavalry, especially those called *Reiter* or *Schwarze Reiter*. Their main weapons were two or more pistols and a sword and most reiters were well armoured with helmets and cuirasses).

In the days of King Philip II, the cavalry of the Spanish army was divided into companies of *Gente de Armas, Caballos Celadas, Arcabuceros a caballo* y Spanish *Herreruelos* (riders armed with firearms, such as reiters).[142]

The riders of the *Gente de Armas* units were covered in armour from head to knee, armed with a heavy lance and sword and their horses were also protected. The maintenance of such units can be explained for a number of reasons. The social order of the post-medieval society, in which the nobility and its entourage maintained a significant social, economic and military role, and on the other, the high degree of training required by these units which would have a detrimental effect on the overall effectiveness of the army if not maintained, losing the use of units that had been trained heavily and with expensive equipment.

The *Caballos Celadas* were light cavalry, also armed with lances but with lighter body armour than the *Gente de Armas*, and their horses were smaller and unprotected. They accompanied the *Gente de Armas* and exploited their success when the former broke through the enemy formation.

Beside these riders, the Spanish cavalry maintained units armed with pistols and light arquebuses. in the days of Philip II, these were the German

---

142 Rodriguez Y Mesa, *Del Gran Capitán a los Tercios*, pp.177–179.

THE BATTLE OF NÖRDLINGEN 1634

'The Skirmish Between Cuirassiers', painting by Sebastiaen Vrancx (circa 1635). The Battle of Lekkerbeetje or Lekkerbeetken (5 February 1600) was a cavalry duel previously fought at Vughterheide, near 's-Hertogenbosch, between 22 Brabant knights in the service of Spain, and 22 French knights serving in the army of the Dutch Republic. In the winter of 1599–1600, during the winter inactivity, the garrison of 's-Hertogenbosch, commanded by Anthonie II Schetz, Baron de Grobbendonk, captured a French lieutenant of cavalry in the service of the Dutch Republic. The prisoner wrote to his captain, Pierre de Bréauté – a 19-year-old Norman nobleman – asking for money to be sent to ransom him. Bréauté replied that he should be ashamed of having been captured, as any of his men would have to be worth two enemies. Gerard Abrahams, a lieutenant of cuirassiers in the Spanish army in Flanders, listened to the contents of the letter and challenged Bréauté to a duel. The two officers obtained the permission of their commanders, and the battle took place on 5 February 1600. The battle began with a trumpet signal from the heralds. Abrahams was the first to die, when he was shot in the neck in the first charge and his brother also died next. Bréauté fought with great courage but was wounded and taken prisoner. The Flemings won and executed Bréauté in revenge for the death of his officer Abrahams. The fight was commemorated in songs, poems, stories, paintings and engravings. There are paintings of the battle made by Joost Cornelisz Droochsloot, Sebastian Vrancx, Simon Johannes van Douw, Gerrit van Santen and Esaias van de Velde. (Rijksmuseum, SK-A–1409)

mercenary 'reiters', as found in other European armies, and the Spanish *Herreruelos* and *Arcabuceros a caballo*. From the second half of the sixteenth century onwards, all of these units were simply referred to as *Arcabuceros a caballo*, suggesting that their main weapon was an arquebus, but also armed with a pair of pistols.

By the time of King Philip IV, the Ordinances of 1632 officially eliminated the lance units and established the consolidation of cavalry armed with firearms: the *Caballo Coraza* units (armoured horse), armed with guns and a sword, and who were protected by armour. The evolution of the Art of War in the Hispanic world – mainly France and Italy – had shown that armoured cavalry armed with lances no longer served in a useful military context where sieges predominated, especially in Flanders, and battles were rare, with skirmishes and firepower predominating. In short, heavy cavalry units were expensive to train and maintain, making it much more effective to equip them with firearms and to provide them with more mobility by reducing their armour.

When in contact with the other European armies, around the 1630s, the figure of the dragoon also appeared within the ranks of the Spanish cavalry. They evolved the same as in other armies, first as infantry soldiers who were mounted on horseback because of particular circumstances. Later, they evolved into multi-purpose cavalry units.

On the battlefield, the cavalry was organised in squadrons formed by a variable number of companies (from two to four), who in practice were not at the full paper establishment of 100 troops. For example, in a muster of 1573, the cavalry of the Duke of Alba had one squadron of 136 riders per company, whereas in the first battle of the Dunes (2 July 1600), the Spanish cavalry had an average of 68 horsemen per company.

In combat, Hispanic cavalry military tactics consisted of first attacking with the Harquebusiers, who, by using fire in successive waves (the *caracole* technique), weakened the enemy's front ranks and morale, then followed by the charge with the lance, to break the enemy line. Paradoxically, the use of the sword by the Swedish cavalry was considered a distinguishing element of the military revolution initiated by Sweden, giving the cavalry more 'aggressiveness', while at the same time, the use of the lances for the Spaniards as a distinguishing element of their 'aggressive charge', is considered an anachronism.[143]

The use of the lance was not limited to the Spanish cavalry. In the middle of the seventeenth century General Raimondo Montecuccoli of the Imperial Army described the ideal tactics of a cavalry charge. The lancers had to attack first, in such a way that their shock power would weaken the enemy ranks, and they would then be relieved by the cuirassiers, who would fire their guns to break the enemy unit.[144]

Spanish artillery was officially born in the reign of the Catholic Monarchs, who in 1495 maintained a permanent detachment of 72 gunners to serve their field artillery, although in the castles and fortresses there were many other pieces with their respective gunners.

The manufacture of artillery pieces was initially a specialist task, and at the outset there was a wide variety of calibres and designations to refer to, such as cannon, medium cannon, sakers, minions, falconets, culverins. As in other countries there was an enormous diversity of types and sizes, which posed a real problem for the supply of munitions. The first initiative to rationalise the calibres came in the reign of the Emperor Charles V, who reduced the 23 recognised calibres to only seven. In 1609, a reform conducted by the Spanish master gunner Diego Ufano (1550–1613), reduced the number of guns to six types, and later to only four (48, 24, 12 and six pound cannon), although in practice other small types such as three and four pounders continued to be used.[145]

---

143 Mesa, *Military Innovations*, p.548.
144 Spring, *Bavarian Army*, p.115.
145 Brzezinski, *Gustavus Adolphus Cavalry*, p.18.

Illustration from the military treatise "The Perfect Gunner: Theory and Practice" ("El perfecto artillero: theorica y pratica"), by Julio César Firrufino (1648). Firrufino was professor of Mathematics and Fortification at the Casa de Contratación de Indias ("House of Trade of the Indies") in Sevilla. He wrote various works on artillery, both for armies and navies. His best known work was the "Perfect Gunner", which is an encyclopedic treatise, based in Niccolò Fontana Tartaglia's ideas. In this illustration we see a 48-pound cannon, that would have been used in sieges and to beat large infantry formations. The legend in Spanish reads "On fire, I forgive nobody" ("Encendido, a nadie perdono"). (Author's collection)

The terminology was also unified, based on the 48 pound barrel reference, which was also called the 'full cannon'. From there, the various calibres became known as a fraction of this type, the 24 pounder became the 'demi-cannon', the 12 pounder, the 'quarter cannon', and the 6 pounder the 'eighth of cannon'. The Spanish style of categorisation spread throughout Europe, adopted first of all by those who had more contact with the Spanish armies such as their French and Dutch enemies.[146]

In Flanders (1570) a standard Spanish battery had 24 pieces of artillery: six heavy guns, two culverins, four medium culverins and 12 falconets. Each battery was directed by one captain general, eight lieutenants, one artillery commander, seven auxiliaries, 96 artillerymen or soldiers (three for the falconets and five for each of the other pieces), 10 gunners, 24 conductors, a chaplain, a doctor, a farrier and 75 assistants, totalling 226 men and around 180 to 200 horses. In practice, however, field or siege batteries consisted of varying numbers of pieces, of different calibres, depending on actual availability.

The Spanish Tercios were a part of the armies of the Hispanic Monarchy, which had territories in Italy and Flanders. It was in these regions that troops were recruited, either serving as their garrison, or being assigned to other operating theatres. In addition, like other European armies, the Kings of Spain were well-supplied with German mercenaries, with their own regimental structure.

Units that were not Spanish were known as *Tropas de Naciones* (Troops of the Nations).[147] Several historical studies give different, but approximate

---

146 Brzezinski, *Gustavus Adolphus Cavalry*, p.19.
147 Piccouet, *Armies*, pp.151–154.

figures, of the composition of the armies of the Hispanic Monarchy. Depending on the theatre of war and the year, native Spaniards made up between 15 to 25 percent of the army, the rest being Italians (25 percent), Walloons and Burgundians (25 to 40 percent) and Germans (25 percent). There were also contingents of Irish and British, but in smaller numbers (10 percent as a maximum).

The Italians and the Irish were privileged to be organised in Tercios the same as the Spaniards. The Walloons were first organised as the Germans, in regiments of 3,000 men, but in 1602 they were authorised to reorganise into Tercios, in the Spanish way.

In Nördlingen, the Spanish army consisted of the typical amalgamation of nationalities that formed the backbone of its European empire. The Tercios of Spanish infantry were the nucleus, but frequently they were not the largest contingent, but were the elite force of the army. Generally, the largest contingents were Italian, from Milan (Lombardy) or Naples and Sicily. The third ethnic component was from the Spanish Netherlands (Walloon soldiers from Catholic Flanders and Burgundians from Franche-Comté).

Cavalry banner, captured by the Swedes in the early 1630s. Damask silk canvas, with green floral print and painted decoration. On one side is the Virgin; on the other side, a coat of arms in gold against black with a crowned lion and seven red roses. The text that was under the image of the Madonna is hardly distinguishable anymore, but according to tradition, they are considered Walloons, so the unit of origin could be from the Spanish Army on the Rhine or the army of the Duke of Feria. (Armemuseum, AM.081410)

2

The Leaders

The Catholic Army

Ferdinand of Habsburg (1608–1657), was the son of Emperor Ferdinand II (1578–1637) and his first wife Maria Ana of Bavaria (1574–1616). On 8 December 1625 he was crowned King of Hungary and 27 November 1627, King of Bohemia. As Imperial heir, he unsuccessfully sought command of an army and campaigned alongside General Wallenstein, who he repeatedly opposed. This led to resentment by the young prince, who in the Imperial court in Vienna joined the opposition faction aimed at Wallenstein and manufactured the conspiracy that led to his deposition in early 1634.

In 1631, after years of negotiations with the Spanish branch of the Habsburgs, he married the Spanish infanta, his cousin Maria Ana of Spain (1606–1646), with whom six children were born, including his successors, as Emperor, Ferdinand IV and Leopold I.

After the assassination of the mercenary general Wallenstein, and despite his limited military experience, his position as heir to the Empire and his regal figure meant great deal to the veteran officers of the Imperial Army and the League. His collaboration with Matthias Gallas at a political and military level was successful.

After Nördlingen, his position in the Imperial court was powerful, following the overthrow of influential Minister Hans Ulrich von Eggenberg. He then engaged in political affairs, while his brother the Archduke Leopold William (1614–1662) assumed a military role. In 1635, Ferdinand participated as Imperial Commissioner in the peace talks in Prague. On the death of his father, he was crowned Emperor of the Holy Roman Empire as Ferdinand III on 15 February 1637.[1]

Matthias Gallas (1584–1647) was born Matteo Galasso in the Italian city of Trento. He began his military career in Flanders as a soldier in the service of Spain. Later he was destined to take part in Saboya's campaign (1616–1617). At the beginning of the Thirty Years' War, he was serving as a captain in the Italian fortress of Riva, where he met a young captain named Johann

---

1 Guthrie, *Batallas*, p.370; Hengerer, Mark: *Kaiser Ferdinand III (1608–1657): Eine Biographie*. Böhlau Verlag, Vienna, 2012.

THE LEADERS

Emperor Ferdinand III, by Frans Luycx (c1637–1638). He was the eldest son of Emperor Ferdinand II and Maria Anna of Bavaria. He received his religious and scientific training through Jesuits at his father's Court. He always had great respect for his father and the rest of the family and tried to reach an agreement in case of differences of opinion. According to sources, he spoke seven languages (he was fluent in German, Latin, Italian and Spanish, and to a lesser extent, French, Czech and Hungarian). He tried to hold a military office, but Wallenstein did not want him to. Finally, from 1634, he commanded the Imperial army. Politically, he had to compromise between the demands of France and Sweden to achieve the Peace of Westphalia, in exchange for increasing his power as sovereign of the Austrian hereditary lands and as King in Hungary and Bohemia. Ferdinand was a patron of the arts and sciences, very musical and himself a composer. He married three times and had 11 children. (Kunsthistorisches Museum, GG_8024)

von Aldringen, with whom he had a long friendship. He sought permission to enlist in the Catholic League Army, where thanks to his previous experience he was granted the position of colonel, under the command of General Tilly, distinguishing himself during the battle of Stadtlohn (6 August 1623) and in the conquest of Krempe (November 1628).

In early 1629 he sought permission to join the Wallenstein army at the request of his friend Aldringen. When Emperor Ferdinand II sent an army to defend the dynastic rights of his second wife Leonor of Mantua, against Carlo I Gonzaga, Duke of Nevers, who was endorsed by France, Gallas and Aldringen were promoted to *General-Feldwachtmeister (major-general,* or major general of field guards), under the command of Ramboldo XIII, Count of Collalto, *Feldmarschall* (Field Marshal) of the Empire. The two friends married Isabella and Livia, of the Arc's noble family, near Lake Garda. After capturing Mantua, Gallas was rewarded with the title of Count of Campo, where his family came from.

After Gustavus Adolphus's arrival in Pomerania, Imperial troops destined for Italy were called up to fight in Germany but did not arrive in time to take part in the Battle of Breitenfeld (17 September 1631). Wallenstein appointed him as a subordinate general in Bohemia, fighting the Swedes in 1631–1632. For his service in the Battle of Alte Veste (9 September 1632) he was promoted to the rank of *Feldmarschalleutnant* (Lieutenant Field Marshal).

He came to the attention of Emperor Ferdinand II, who convinced him to join the conspiracy to assassinate Wallenstein. Gallas, Piccolomini and Aldringen kept the Imperial court informed of Wallenstein's actions and plans. They were the instigators of Wallenstein's murder in Cheb, in the hands of Imperial officers Leslie, Butler and Gordon. All the conspirators were rewarded by the Emperor, but it was Gallas who received the greatest reward, the lands formerly granted to Wallenstein in Friedland and Reichenberg, and 500,000 guilders. In addition, he was rewarded with the operational command of the main Imperial field army, serving as second to the command of Ferdinand, King of Hungary, with Piccolomini as his subordinate. Gallas was jovial and affable, friendly and popular with officers, and he had energy and organisational talent.

After the successful Battle of Nördlingen, he was named Duke of Lucera (a territory in Puglia) and *Grande de España* ('grandee') by King Philip IV, thus belonging to the Spanish higher nobility. However, his military career began to decline. He failed several times against the Swedes under General Johan Banér in 1637 and 1638, after which he was removed from command. Due to his tendency toward alcoholism and his unfortunate campaigns in Lorraine and Alsace (1635), Pomerania (1638) and Denmark (1644), he was called *Heerderverber* (the army destroyer).[2]

He had a prominent role in the Imperial retirement from Magdeburg (1644), besieged by the troops of Swedish General Torstenson and was later relieved of his command. He again served as a commander in the field following the Swedish victory of Khankov (6 March 1645) but due to his age and exhaustion, he asked to be allowed to step down.[3]

Ottavio Piccolomini (1589–1656) was born in Florence, and he showed a keen interest in the profession of arms when he was a child. At the age of 16 he enlisted as a pikeman in a company serving Spain, and in 1617 was sent to Bohemia by the Grand Duke of Tuscany, in a cavalry regiment to assist the Emperor in his fight against the Bohemian rebels. Piccolomini fought in the Battle of the White Mountain (1620) under General Bucquoy's command, and later in the Bohemia and Hungary. In 1624 he participated in the war that had broken out in Lombardy, in the service of Spain, in the Imperial regiment of Gottfried von Pappenheim. In 1627 he returned to Imperial service as commanding officer of Wallenstein's army. He fell into a bout of depression on charges of extortion but was later exonerated and promoted to colonel.

He later left for Italy, embedded in Italian politics due to his family obligations. He returned to Germany when he learnt of the news of the landing of the Swedish King Gustavus II Adolphus. For his service in the Battle of Lutzen he was promoted to *General-Feldwachtmeister* (major-general). The attitude and actions taken by Wallenstein from 1633 were not favoured by Piccolomini, who distanced himself from his general. Joining the plot that ended with Wallenstein's assassination, he was rewarded with the rank of *Feldmarschall*, 100,000 guilders and the ownership of Náchod (Orlické). However, the imperial court preferred Gallas to replace Wallenstein.

Famed for being brave and responsible, and with his brilliant service record, in 1638 he was honoured with the German title *Reichsgraf* (Count of the Empire). In 1639, for his services against France (Compiègne, Thionville, Diedenhofen) he was rewarded by King Philip IV of Spain with the Duchy

---

2   Guthrie, *Batallas*, p.370.
3   Hallwich, Hermann: 'Gallas, Matthias Graf von', in *Allgemeine Deutsche Biographie*: (ADB). 8, Duncker & Humblot, Leipzig 1878, pp.320-331; Rebitsch, Robert: *Matthias Gallas (1588–1647). Generalleutnant des Kaisers zur Zeit from Dreißigjährigen Krieges. Eine militärische Biographie.* Aschendorff Verlag, Münster, 2006; Spring, *Wallenstein's Army*, p.22.

General Ottavio Piccolomini, by Anselm van Hulle (c1650). Enlisted at the age of 16 as a pikeman, he fought in Italy in the service of Spain, and then went to Bohemia, in the army of General Bucquoy. He took part in many of the battles of the first stage of the Thirty Years' War. He joined Wallentein's service, becoming a colonel. After the battle of Lützen, the Emperor promoted him to general-feldwachtmeister. During the 1630s he served successively under Wallenstein, the Empire and Spain. From 1645 he returned to the Imperial army and was rewarded with the rank of Generalissimo towards the end of the war. He had three children, and all died in battle After the war he retired to his possessions and died in an accident when he fell from his horse. (Deutsches Historisches Museum, Gm 95/65)

of Amalfi, he received the title of grandee and was inducted into the Order of the Golden Fleece.

During the following years he was repeatedly in the service of Spain and the Empire, until in 1648 he was promoted to *Reich Feldmarschall* (Field Marshal of the Empire), and *generalissimo* of all the Imperial armies until the end of the conflict.[4]

Fernando de Austria (1609–1641), Prince ('Infante') of Spain, Cardinal-Archbishop of Toledo was the younger brother of King Philip IV of Spain and cousin of King Ferdinand of Hungary. Planning for a religious life, political and military circumstances in the Spanish Netherlands led to his appointment as governor. But in order to gain experience in the affairs of state and tasks of government he was appointed Viceroy of Catalonia (1632) and afterwards of Italy (1633).

He had no prior military experience at Nördlingen. After the battle, he remained in Germany with his army for a few more weeks to assist his cousin King Ferdinand of Hungary, but eventually had to continue on his way to the Spanish Netherlands. There, as governor-general, he campaigned victoriously against the Dutch rebels and against the French. However, the economic problems and joint superiority of their enemies led to limited success on his part. While on campaign, he became ill with a stomach ulcer, aggravated by a permanent state of exhaustion due to the pressure of the exercise of his command, and he passed away in Brussels on 9 November 1641.[5]

---

4   Bierther, Kathrin: 'Piccolomini, Ottavio', *Neue Deutsche Biographie* (NDB). Band 20, Duncker & Humblot, Berlin, 2001, pp.408–410; Spring, *Wallenstein's Army*, pp.19–20; Weyhe-Eimke, Arnold von: *Octavio Piccolomini in the Herzog von Amalfi*. Steinhauser & Korb, Pilsen, 1871.
5   Houben, Birgit: 'La casa del Cardenal Infante don Fernando de Austria (1620-1641), in Martínez Millán, José y Hortal Muñoz, José Eloy (coord.): *La corte de Felipe IV (1621-1665): reconfiguración de la Monarquía católica*. Polifemo, Madrid, 2015, pp.1679-170; Palencia, C.: *El Cardenal Infante Don Fernando de Austria*. Speech pronounced in the opening of course of Real Academia de Bellas Artes y Ciencias Históricas de Toledo. Toledo, 1946; Puig, Rogelio: 'El cardenal-infante don Fernando de Austria, evocación militar de una gran figura histórica', in *Saitabi*, 8, 35–38, 1950–1951, pp.66–71.

THE BATTLE OF NÖRDLINGEN 1634

The Cardinal-Infante, by Gaspar de Crayer (1639). This painter was a pupil and successor of Rubens and was also influenced by Van Dyck. He was the accredited painter for the churches of Brabant and Ghent. King Philip III, very religious, wanted his son Fernando to join the Catholic clergy, so with only 10 years' experience he was appointed Archbishop of Toledo and shortly afterwards he was appointed Cardinal. Fernando was not ordained a priest, something not uncommon at that time when a member of the royalty or aristocracy held an ecclesiastical office. Fernando, like the entire Spanish reigning Habsburg family, was characterised by pale skin, blond hair and blue eyes, inherited from his predecessor Philip the Handsome of Flanders. The Archbishopric of Toledo was the richest Catholic diocese, after that of Rome. The Archbishop of Toledo in Spain claimed Primacy in Spain, as the primate above all other episcopal sees in Spain. (Museo del Prado, P001472)

Diego Mexía de Guzmán y Dávila (1585–1655), Duke of Sanlúcar and Marquis of Leganés is a fine example of the Spanish military aristocracy. As the third Duke of Alba, Fernando Álvarez de Toledo and Pimentel. He was cousin of the *Valido* (prime minister) Gaspar de Guzmán y Pimentel, Count-Duke of Olivares, and son-in-law of famous General Ambroggio Spínola.

From 1600 he had been fighting in the Netherlands, where he served for more than twenty years as a chamberlain official and *gentilhombre* (gentleman) of Archduke Albert of Austria. He was very competent, an expert in siege operations, but cautious. During the campaigns of 1620–1622 he had the rank of *maestre de campo* in the army of his father-in-law Spinola. In 1625 he was in Castile and Andalusia to organise a defence against the English landing in Cádiz. In 1628 he accompanied Spinola to visit the siege of La Rochelle, where they met with Louis XIII and Cardinal Richelieu, informing King Philip IV that France would sooner or later declare war on Spain, once the Huguenot rebellion was over.

He returned to Flanders, where he was appointed *maestre de campo general* (General Field Master) in 1630 by Archduke Isabel Clara Eugenia. After the death of the Duke of Feria (1633), he was appointed *Gobernador de las Armas* (governor of arms, second-in-command of the whole army) of the Alsace army, mustering the surviving units to join the Cardinal-Infante's army, where he served as his chief of staff. Leganés was the true Spanish strategist at the battle of Nördlingen.

On 24 September 1635 he was named governor and commander-in-chief of Army of the State of Milan. During the following years (1635–1641) he had to face the threat of a coalition of France and the Dukes of Parma, Mantua and Savoy who sought to destroy Spanish supremacy in Italy. Later he was assigned to the Army of Catalonia, where he won both victories and

Diego Mexía de Guzmán y Dávila, 1st Marquis of Leganés, by Anthony van Dyck (ca. 1634). He began his military life serving in the Flemish army, while still a teenager, at the end of the sixteenth century, like many other nobles of his time. He rose through the military ranks, as a cavalry captain and 'maestre de campo'. He married the daughter of Ambrosio Spínola and was a cousin of the Count-Duke of Olivares. In 1622 he participated in the Palatinate campaign against Frederick V of the Palatinate. In 1626 he was appointed captain-general of the Flanders cavalry, and in 1630 he was appointed 'maestre de campo general' of the Flanders' Army in the field. In 1633 he was appointed Governor of the Arms in the army of the Duke of Feria in Alsace, and later second-in-command of the army of the Cardinal-Infante. He fought in Catalonia against the Catalan rebels and their French allies. The Marquis was also known as an art collector and although his collection included works by such Spanish painters as Velázquez and Ribera and Italian artists such as Titian, he particularly focussed on the large number of works by Flemish artists such as Rubens and Van Dyck. (National Museum of Western Art, P.1987-0002)

suffered defeats against the French armies and the Catalan rebels. From 1648 retired from military life.[6]

Charles IV of Lorraine (1604–1675) belonging to the ducal family of Lorraine, and came to power through dubious means, marrying close his cousin Nicole of Lorena, who he later sought to separate from power by accusing her of witchcraft and thus attempting to achieve an official church-sanctioned separation. The strategically placed Duchy of Lorraine was subject to the political and military pressures of France, eager to reach the natural border of the Rhine, which forced Duke Charles to cede government to his younger brother Nicholas Francis in 1634. This did not stop the French invasion, and both brothers had to go into exile, being welcomed into the service of their two uncles, Emperor Ferdinand II and Duke Maximilian of Bavaria. Duke Charles entered the Empire's service to fight the Protestant armies and French expansionism.

Charles IV won several victories from 1638–1640, especially in the Franch-Comté, in the service of the King Phillip IV of Spain. Charles participated in the relief of the siege of Dole and defeated the army of Bernard of Saxe-Weimar. From this position of force, he negotiated with France the treaty of Saint-Germain-en-Laye (2 April 1641), so he regained his status as Duke, but accepted the duchy becoming a French protectorate and pledged to conclude no alliances with the Habsburgs. But after a few months, he participated in

---

6   Arroyo, *El marqués de Leganés*, pp.145–185; Guthrie, *Batallas*, p.371; Hrncirik, *Spanier auf dem Albuch*, p.112.

the plot of Louis of Bourbon, Count of Soissons, provoking another French invasion. He would not return from exile until 1659. Throughout the years of service with the Empire and Spain he commanded several armies, with several successes but also defeats, at the hands of generals Horn, Bernard of Saxe-Weimar and Turenne.[7]

Giovanni Maria Serbelloni (1590–1638), Count of Castiglione d'Adda and Lord of Romagnano was a native of the Duchy of Milan and closely linked to military service with the Spanish Monarchy; his older brother died in 1617 in the siege of Vercelli. He was promoted to *maestre de campo* in 1617 and in the following years participated in the conflict over the strategic passage of La Valtellina (in the Lombardy region of northern Italy, bordering Switzerland), being rewarded for his services with the rank of *Comisario general* (commissioner general) of Hispanic troops in Lombardy. In 1633 he was promoted by the Spanish governor of Lombardy, the Duke of Feria, to the rank of artillery general upon completing the formation of the Alsace army. When Feria fell ill, Serbelloni succeeded him as interim commander-in-chief. During the winter of 1633–1634 he was responsible for the defence of Munich. After the arrival of the Cardinal-Infante, he was given the command of the survivors of the Alsace army and was confirmed in the rank of *Gobernador de la Artillería* (Commander-in-Chief of the artillery).

With the outbreak of the war against France (1635) he returned to northern Italy, where he held the supreme command of Spanish troops who fought the French against the Duke of Rohan at La Valtellina, and he participated in the decisive Battle of Morbegno, where he was wounded. In 1637 he was part of the main Spanish army which besieged the border fort of Leucata (France), where he was again wounded. He died in 1638 in Perpignan.[8]

The three Catholic armies present at Nördlingen had their own military structures and traditions. In addition, the leadership had three princes and great military personalities, with their egos and personal motivations. But such a disparate combination worked at a military level, generally demonstrating remarkable harmony and ability.

It is noteworthy that the two Ferdinands became great friends, and their rising rule was enough to smooth any tension between the generals. This atmosphere of collaboration contrasted with the rivalry between Bernard and Horn.[9] While the two Ferdinand cousins were exercising the role of political and institutional figures, with their significant presence with the troops. Both Gallas and Leganés served as chiefs of staff, providing the necessary experience, so that both princes could make wise decisions. At a secondary level, tactical and operational, general officers like Piccolomini, Serbelloni and Werth executed the orders accurately and effectively, thanks to their many years of experience.

---

7   Fulaine, Jean-Charles: *Le duc Charles IV de Lorraine et son armée: 1624–1675*. Editions Serpenoise, Woippy, 1997.
8   Hrncirik, *Spanier auf dem Albuch*, pp.111–112.
9   Guthrie, *Batallas*, p.371.

THE LEADERS

The Protestant Army

Bernard of Saxe-Weimar (1604–1639) was the eleventh son of Duke Johann de Sachsen-Weimar. The young Bernard was distinguished in the Battle of Wimpfen (1622). He left for the United Provinces (1623) where he studied military organisation, tactics and siege warfare. In 1626 he enlisted in the Danish Army, with which he fought for several years, during which he pondered the importance of creating a German-led, Protestant army instead of foreign powers. In 1631 he fought under the flag of Hesse.

For his valour he was distinguished by King Gustavus Adolphus with the rank of colonel in the German cavalry regiment from his personal guard (1631). Later he was in the entourage of Chancellor Oxenstierna as a military adviser and was later promoted to *Generalmajor* of the Protestant army operating in Swabia.[10] In addition, Bernard was granted the territories of the former Bishops of Wurzburg and Bamberg, and he received the title of Duke of Franconia. The armies of Bernard and Gustaf Horn invaded Bavaria in 1633, defended by Johann von Aldringen, but the operation was not completely successful.

After the defeat of Nördlingen and the Swedish debacle, in 1635, Bernard went into the service of France. He was both Commander-in-Chief of the Heilbronn League and general in the service of France, so this double position led to difficulties in subsequent campaigns. Depending upon what was most convenient he sometimes acted as chief of the Protestant cause, but in others acted according to French interests.

In 1638 Bernard emerged victorious in the battles of Rheinfelden, Wittenweiher and Teugen-Hausen, capturing Rheinfelden, Freiburg and

Bernard of Saxe-Weimar, by Michiel van Mierevelt (1630). Bernard was the eleventh son of Duke John II of Saxony-Weimar and Dorothy Mary of Anhalt. He received a good education and was a very religious man, professing a fervent Protestant faith that led him to enlist in the army at the age of 18, participating in the battles of Wiesloch (1622), Wimpfen (1622) and Stadtlohn (1623). He later took part in the campaigns of Christian IV of Denmark, and after the landing of Gustavus Adolphus in Pomerania, he put himself at his service. As a reward for his courage, he rose to command an independent army and was named Duke of Franconia. He later became the military leader of the League of Heilbronn, serving in France. Richelieu promised to provide Duke Bernard with £4 million a year in grants during the war to support an army of 12,000 foot and 6,000 horsemen with the necessary artillery, and in a secret article he was granted Alsace, on condition that he did not expel the Catholic religion. Between 1635–1638 Bernard fought for the Protestant cause, but also to consolidate his own personal power in Alsace. Bernard died on 18 July 1639 in Neuenburg am Rhein, while preparing for a new campaign against the Imperialists. The suspicion that he died of poison that could have been administered to him at the request of Richelieu is not proven. Sweden, France and Holy Empire fought for Bernhard's legacy. (Deutsches Historisches Museum)

---

10 Guthrie, *Batallas*, p.371.

THE BATTLE OF NÖRDLINGEN 1634

Breisach, respectively. France confirmed to him that Alsace and Haguenau would be given as reward for his service. But his health began to deteriorate, and he died on 18 July 1639 in front of the walls Neuenburg of the Rhine, at the beginning of its siege.

His true ambition was to constitute a reigning dynasty in an extensive territory, which he believed was his right by his years of service and conviction in fighting for a rightful Protestant victory. Of undoubted military valour and ability, experience had led him to think that battles could be won not only by strategy, but also by valour and determination in belief of victory, that is, by refusing to acknowledge the possibility of defeat. But if this reasoning served at Lutzen and Rehinfelden, it could have contributed to the Nördlingen disaster.[11]

Gustav Karlsson Horn (1592–1657), Marshal of Sweden was born into an illustrious noble family with a long military tradition. He studied at several European universities and learned the military profession under the supervision of Maurice of Nassau in the Netherlands. He participated in the wars against Russia and Poland, and at the age of 35 was promoted to Field Marshal by King Gustavus Adolphus, and he became his most trusted officer.

His involvement at Breitenfeld was significant and he was then sent by the Swedish King to Upper Franconia, conquering Mergentheim, the capital of the Teutonic Order, and the Bishopric of Bamberg, and then went to the Rhineland, where he occupied Koblenz and Trier, before continuing to Swabia.

Gustaf Horn af Björneborg, attributed to David Beck. Horn belonged to a military family. He studied at various German universities and served in the army of Maurice of Nassau. He fought against Poland and in 1628 he was appointed field marshal. He was second in command, after Gustavus Adolphus himself, in the German campaign (1630–1632). After his capture at Nordlingen, he spent eight years in captivity until his release in a prisoner exchange, in exchange for three imperial generals, with the promise not to fight against the Holy Empire again. He then held administrative positions. Later he led Swedish troops against Denmark and Poland in the 1650s. From the chronicles it is deduced that Gustaf Horn was one of the best Swedish generals in the Thirty Years' War, along with Johan Banér and Lennart Torstensson. Horn was an expert tactician in defensive warfare and sieges, but he was risk averse. He was stubborn, meticulous, and finicky, intelligent but little given to vigorous actions. (Nationalmuseum, NMGrh 654)

---

11 Schubert, Friedrich Hermann: *Bernhard, Herzog von Sachsen-Weimar*, Neue Deutsche Biographie (NDB). Band 2, Duncker & Humblot, Berlin 1955, pp.113–115.

THE LEADERS

Clash of Cavalry (1649), by Pieter Meulener, who specialised in battle painting, and was a disciple of Sebastian Vrancx. In this work we can see the harshness of close-range combat: exhausted ammunition, the Spanish horseman, recognisable by the red ribbon, in this case tied around the neck, but frequently tied around the waist, uses his pistol as if it were a mace. His enemy, a Dutch horseman, defends himself with the sword. In the background we see other close-range gun fights, and musketeers can be seen in the distance. (Museo del Prado, P001883)

After the death of the Swedish King, both Horn and Johan Banér were responsible for leading the Swedish army in Germany, while his brother-in-law Chancellor Axel Oxenstierna took control of the civilian government. However, Horn's strategic leadership was overshadowed by the directives of Chancellor Oxenstierna and the imposing military figure of Bernard of Saxe-Weimar.

Horn had no reputation for audacity but did for tactics and he had shown this in the battles of Breitenfeld and Pfaffenhofen. Cautious and pessimistic in nature, he disliked sharing command with a person like Bernard,[12] who disapproved of his character, his insubordination (the two argued over their seniority over each other) and the divergence of their political motivations. While the former continued to stumble into Swedish hegemony, the latter already showed their ambitions of a purely German-led policy.

After his capture at Nördlingen, he remained a prisoner until 1642. He returned to operational command during the Swedish war against Denmark in 1644, directing the attack on Scania, conquering the while province except for the cities of Malmö and Kristianstad.

---

12 Guthrie, *Batallas*, p.372.

In 1651 he was named Earl of Pori, and the castle of Marienborg was handed over to him. In these later years, Horn also served as governor-general of Livonia. At the outbreak of the war against Poland in 1655, he was responsible for defending Sweden from Polish attacks.

Johann Philipp Cratz von Schaffenstein (1585–1635) came from a Catholic family with a long military tradition. Like his brothers, he served for years in the Imperial Army. He was known as a valiant and capable officer. However, a personal ambition, which would end his life, also began to stand out in him. Thus, in spite of General Tilly's recognition, Cratz went to Wallenstein's army, accepting his promise of a better position, but after a quarrel with his new general, he left and marched under the command of the Duke of Lorraine (1627) and later in the Army of Bavaria (1631).

He regained the esteem of Tilly, who proposed him as his successor, but Duke Maximilian of Bavaria preferred General Aldringen. This caused a great deal of resentment in Cratz, who was appointed commander of the fortress of Ingolstadt. When Wallenstein regained his pre-eminence in the Catholic armies, Cratz decided that he had suffered too much humiliation and entered negotiations to surrender Ingolstadt and to receive a field command in the Protestant army. The plot was discovered and Cratz fled to meet the Swedish-German coalition.

In Nördlingen, Cratz was the second in command after Bernard and his value was unquestionable, leading the cavalry that fought in the plain of Nördlingen. But after his capture he was tried and beheaded for high treason, for the attempt to surrender the fortress of Ingolstadt. [13]

---

13   Guthrie, *Batallas*, p.372; Spring, *Wallenstein's Army*, pp.25–26.

3

The War in Germany

The Defenestration of Prague and the First Years of the War

One of the reasons for the outbreak of the Thirty Years' War was the poisonous religious hatred that existed between the various religious persuasions in the Holy Roman Empire and the Kingdom of Bohemia. To understand why it is necessary to go back to the Schmalkaldic War (1546–1547) that put the Emperor Charles V against a coalition of Protestant princes, led by John Frederick I, Elector of Saxony and Landgrave Philip I of Hesse. The defeat of the Protestant Schmalkaldic League at the Battle of Mühlberg (24 April 1547) only paused the conflict, which flared up again in 1552 with the so-called Princes' Revolt, which eventually led to the Peace of Augsburg (1555), by which Emperor Charles V recognised the power of German princes to have their subjects forced to profess the religion that their sovereign would select (a principle of the *cuius regi, eius religio*) but recognised their right to emigrate to another state if they did not agree with the religion chosen for them.[1]

Despite this small attempt at coexistance among the different religious dogmas within the states of the Empire, controversy and animosity were not resolved. In addition, the Calvinists did not sign the Peace. In 1608 several Protestant states created the *Protestantische Union* (Protestant Union), with the purpose of protecting their interests. But the response from the other religious side was not unexpected and Catholics created the *Katholische Liga* (Catholic League) in 1609. On both sides they pressed Emperor Rudolf II, who yielded power to each league, leaving an Imperial government that was weak and almost powerless.[2]

In 1608, in view of Rudolf's delicate physical and mental health, the Imperial family held a number of meetings where it was decided that the Emperor transfer to his brother Matthias the Kingdoms of Hungary, Austria

---
1   Parker, *Guerra*, p.25.
2   Parker, *Guerra*, pp.33–45.

and Moravia, and with an official heir, the Imperial Habsburg family ensured control of these kingdoms. Rudolf agreed, but later, in an outburst of frantic activity, recanted and sought to regain power. That is why he sought the support of the Czech nobility and granted them, by the *Majestätsbrief* (Letter of Majesty), religious freedom to the nobles and cities of Bohemia. The document for Bohemia was signed on 9 July 1609, and that of Silesia on 20 August. In exchange for freedom of worship, the Emperor urged them to recruit a military force to defend his position.[3]

But Rudolf found himself out on a limb and was eventually cut off from power and died in January 1612. He was succeeded by his brother Matthias I (1557–1619), who was advised by his friend the Bishop of Vienna, Melchior Klesl, to practice a conciliatory policy with between the Catholics and Protestants, with a view to regaining the Imperial authority and prestige lost by Rudolf. However, the various Catholic and Protestant factions were too enraged to allow for a peaceful conclusion to the complicated politico-religious climate in the Empire.[4]

In 1616 the health of Emperor Matthias I was very delicate. However, what worried his Imperial family most was his mental state and the absence of a natural heir. In the face of Turkish pressure (as an external enemy) and religious tensions in the Empire, in the form of internal dissent, the Imperial court decided to confirm his successor by naming his cousin Archduke Ferdinand of Styria as heir.

Traditionally, this honour was granted to the 'King of Bohemia', elected by the Bohemian Crown Lands Diet (formed by the states of Bohemia, Moravia, Silesia and Lusatia). It was an elective monarchy, that is to say that the representatives of the Bohemian States elected their future king and from the mid–sixteenth century onwards, this honour had been given to the Imperial heir to the Habsburg House.[5]

But in 1617, under pressure from the Austrian Imperial court to elect Ferdinand of Styria, who was considered ultra-Catholic and, therefore, an enemy of Bohemian religious freedoms (basically made up of the Bohemian Brothers, Calvinists and Lutherans), an anti-Habsburg movement grew. However, Ferdinand's candidacy succeeded as King of Bohemia, and by the Treaty of Graz (1617) the new King of Bohemia was guaranteed support for the Imperial throne by his Spanish cousin, King Philip III, in exchange for control of Alsace, the recognition of Spanish rights to the possession of the Imperial fiefs in Italy, especially the Duchy of Milan, and recognition of the pre-eminence of the Spanish branch over the House of Habsburg, in all Europe.[6]

Ferdinand was an uncompromising Catholic devotee, and in Bohemia he tried to apply his own Catholic Counter-Reformation, by limiting the influence of Protestants and promoting Catholic worship. At the political level, he was in favour of centralising power and reaffirming the Habsburgs'

---

3   Parker, *Guerra,* p.13.
4   Parker, *Guerra,* p.45.
5   Parker, *Guerra,* pp.49–51.
6   Bordeau, *Men and money,* p.29.

authority over their possessions. In addition, he reintroduced servitude and sought to limit the power of the Bohemian nobility.

Those measures made Ferdinand even more unpopular. He was inflexible in his desire to prevent the expansion of Protestantism in Bohemia. Although Matthias and Klesl wanted a relaxation in the religious conflict, Ferdinand did not. In 1618 he forced the Emperor to order the halting of construction of some Protestant chapels on royal land. When the Bohemian estates protested against this order, Ferdinand had the Assembly of Nobles dissolved. But some of them, enraged by the monarch's authoritarianism and bureaucratic proclamations, presented themselves at the Hradcany Palace on 23 May 1618, and threw out of the window the Imperial representatives Jaroslav Martinitz and Wilhelm Slavata, along with their secretary Philip Fabricius. All three survived the assassination attempt, but the Defenestration of Prague was the trigger for Bohemia's rebellion against King Ferdinand.[7]

However, with the death of Matthias and the ascension to the Imperial throne of the Archduke and King of Bohemia, now Emperor Ferdinand II (1578-1637), the conflict entered another dimension.[8] The Bohemian nobility, arguing the established concept of the elective monarchy, on 22 August 1619 removed the crown of King of Bohemia from Ferdinand and granted it to Elector Frederick V of the Palatinate, from the House of Wittelsbach, who accepted on 26 August. Frederick had also been a rival to Ferdinand in the fight for the imperial crown.[9]

Frederick V of the Palatinate was the head of the Protestant Union. He had important international ties as he was the son-in-law of the King of England James I (1566-1625) and nephew of Maurice of Nassau (1567-1625), Stadtholder of the Netherlands. He was therefore an influential member of the Imperial nobility, a paladin of the Protestant cause and had important international support. He was crowned king in Prague on 4 November 1619. However, Frederick's expectations were not met as the Protestant Union did not break off hostilities in support of Frederick, and by the Treaty of Ulm, Protestants and Catholics pledged not to go to war.

Frederick was left alone defending his throne in the winter of 1619-1620 and was therefore known as the 'Winter King' (*Winterkönig* in German). Emperor Ferdinand sent troops, as did the Catholic League, headed by Duke Maximilian I of Bavaria. During the summer and autumn of 1620 Catholics recaptured much Bohemian territory, and on 8 November at the White Mountain, outside Prague, the Bohemian and Imperial armies fought. Within hours, the Protestants were defeated, and Frederick and his court had to flee to their German possessions. It was then that the war shifted to the West. The Palatinate was invaded by the Imperialists, Bavarians and the Spaniards, who joined the conflict, although from the outset they had funded Ferdinand II with money and supplied military advisers. On 6 August 1623 the Protestant forces of Christian of Brunswick were annihilated by the Catholic troops of Tilly at the battle of Stadtlohn. Frederick V of the Palatinate was forced to

---

7 Parker, *Guerra*, pp.63-65.
8 Parker, *Guerra*, pp.64-80.
9 Borreguero, *Guerra*, p.186.

THE BATTLE OF NÖRDLINGEN 1634

The Battle on the White Mountain, by Peter Snayers (1620). It was fought on 8 November 1620. An army of 27,000 men of the combined armies of Ferdinand II, Holy Roman Emperor led by Charles Bonaventure de Longueval, Count of Bucquoy and the German Catholic League under Johann Tserclaes, Count of Tilly, defeated 15,000 Bohemians and German mercenaries under Christian of Anhal at Bílá Hora ('White Mountain') near Prague. It can be seen how the two armies deployed in the Spanish way, that is, in units similar to the Tercios, with the pikes in the center and the muskets on the outside. (Bavarian Army Museum)

sign an armistice with Emperor Ferdinand II, ending the 'Palatinate Phase' (1618–1624) of the Thirty Years' War.[10]

However, in 1624 a large coalition of Protestant states was formed to contest the power of the Habsburgs, that is, Spain and the Holy Roman Empire. England, the United Provinces of the Netherlands, Sweden, Denmark, the Duchy of Brandenburg, and Catholic France, the Duchy of Savoy and the Republic of Venice joined in an anti-Hapsburg alliance.

This new stage of the Thirty Years' War is known as the 'Danish Phase' (1625–1629), for King Christian IV of Denmark became the de facto leader of the Protestant cause in Germany. The Danes wanted to help the cause of their co-religionists and to satisfy the political aspirations of Frederick of the Palatinate, but they also aspired to be compensated for their efforts by being given control of the Imperial Circle in Lower Saxony.[11]

---

10 Borreguero, *Guerra*, pp.186–194.
11 Borreguero, *Guerra*, pp.143–147.

Soldiers plundering a farm during the Thirty Years' War (1620), by Sebastian Vrancx. We observe an unfortunate scene of looting, unfortunately a very common practice. Some soldiers, who could be from either side, loot a house, while some threaten the owner. Others are engaged in drinking, eating and killing animals, and harassing the maiden. Women, teenagers and children feel first hand all the terrors of war. The system of contributions, against the subjugated civilian population, was a very widespread practice. Wallenstein's troops became famous for their rapacity (Deutsches Historisches Museum, 1988/1842)

Although initially successful, the Danes were defeated by Wallenstein on 25 April 1626 at the Battle of Dessau Bridge, and on 27 August by Tilly at the Battle of Lutter am Barenberge, where the Danes had more than 10,000 casualties, loosing much of the Danish officer corps, which caused extreme security issues in the Kingdom of Denmark itself, which had to defend its southern border with scant resources.[12]

At the Eastern Operations theatre, Wallenstein forced the Protestants to retreat to Silesia, evacuating the Habsburg states. That Catholic breakthrough, along with the defeat of the Ottoman Empire in Baghdad, forced Transylvanian Bethlem Gabor to sign an armistice with the Empire, and he withdrew from the conflict.

The forces of the Empire and the Catholic League were also severely depleted, so they did not take military advantage of Denmark's exhaustion and precarious situation. However, the Protestant states of the Lower

---

12 Negredo, *Guerra*, p.110.

Saxon Circle agreed to escalate the conflict. But Catholic demands, such as the installation of Catholic monasteries in the Palatinate and the loss of electoral status in the Imperial Diet, were a humiliation for Frederick V of the Palatinate, and he refused to submit. Emperor Ferdinand II wished for a total victory, militarily and political, and he did not wish to moderate his demands. As a result, there was no peace yet.[13]

Abandoned by Denmark, in the following months the Protestant principalities sought to withstand the new Imperial campaign, as the Catholic League persuaded Ferdinand II to forcefully recapture Lutheran possessions which, in accordance with the Augsburg Peace Accords, they belonged by law to the Catholic Church.[14]

Such was the pressure on the Protestants that the King of Sweden, Gustavus II Adolphus (1594–1632) decided to intervene in their favour;[15] but just as with Denmark, Sweden was confident of being able to use the war to expand its sphere of influence beyond the Baltic, expanding onto German soil, to the detriment of Denmark, Poland and the Hanseatic League. Like Christian IV of Denmark, Gustavus was funded by France, as directed by the Prime Minister, Cardinal Richelieu (1585–1642), as they were opposed to the Madrid-Vienna Habsburg axis.

Swedish involvement

With the landing of the Swedish Army in Pomerania a new period was opened in the Thirty Years' War, which historiography has termed 'the Swedish Phase'. Their military intervention culminated in a plan executed by King Gustavus II Adolphus, both politically and militarily, and it cannot be forgotten that Frederick V of the Palatinate always trusted that the Swedish King would establish himself as a strong defender of German Protestants.[16]

Both the Swedish Parliament and the Council of State had given the King full power to intervene in the Holy Roman Empire, and in passing to eliminate the Habsburgs on the Baltic and on defeating the traditional enemy of Sweden, Poland. In fact, the Swedish expeditionary army, of about 14,000 men, was suitable for this and not for a far-ranging campaign in Germany, so during the following months Gustavus Adolphus was engaged in recruiting more troops and in obtaining the support of the Electors of Saxony and Brandenburg, who joined the Swedes as Tilly's army advanced to attack Leipzig and began implementing the Restitution Edict in Saxony.

Thus, the plan devised to transform the Swedish intervention, which could be considered a foreign invasion, was completed in an operation in support of German Protestants, with the alliance with Duke John George I of Saxony, Duke George William of Brandenburg, Landgrave William V of Hesse-Kassel and Bernard of Saxe-Weimar. In addition, thanks to an

---

13 Negredo, *Guerra*, pp.112–114.
14 Negredo, *Guerra*, p.123.
15 Parker, *Guerra*, p.90.
16 Negredo, *Guerra*, p.147.

agreement with France, negotiated in 1628 and signed in Barwalde on 23 January 1631, the Swedes would obtain 400,000 thalers annually for five years, to keep under arms 30,000 infantry and 6,000 horse.[17]

The Swedish strategy in Germany was to achieve a series of successive and increasingly ambitious goals, as follows:

- Secure the Oder River line, setting up a natural space for Swedish expansion on the Polish-German shores of the Baltic Sea. This was achieved by landing in Pomerania and advancing south.
- Control the area of the Elbe River. After the Battle of Breintenfeld in 1631, the Swedes advanced their positions, eliminating the Imperial field army.
- Reach the River Meno, directly threatening Bavaria and accesses to the Rhine.
- Move south through Germany. This was the consequence of defeating the Catholics at Breintenfeld. The Swedes defeated the Bavarians and Imperialists on the Lech River and occupied Munich.
- Advancing along the Danube to seize the traditional Habsburg territories.
- Obtain victory and peace including Swedish hegemony in the Baltic Sea and the creation of a protectorate in Germany.

After the overwhelming victory of Breitenfeld's, fortune smiled on Gustavus II, as he gained more support from his German allies, who considered him a rising star who could by his successes increase their own influence and land at the expense of the defeated Catholics. In 1632 the march to the heart of Germany was almost perfect. The Catholics were defeated at the Battle of the Lech on 15 April, and General Tilly died as a result of wounds received there. Munich was occupied on 17 May but was not sacked as it had paid a large ransom to avoid it. But during these successful campaigns, Gustavus had lost half of his native Swedish troops, and was becoming increasingly dependent on the troops of his German allies and on the supplies they could provide him, given the distance from the Swedish base in Pomerania.[18]

The defeat of the main Catholic army forced Emperor Ferdinand II to request the services of Albrecht von Wallenstein. He accepted the challenge of recruiting a paid, well-equipped and well-trained army in only three months, and he succeeded, thanks to his personal financial resources, his contacts, and the promise of loot to all those who enlisted under his flag.[19]

Although the situation was very critical for the Catholics, Wallenstein resisted pressure from the Imperial court and did not go straight into battle with his new army, but continued to train his troops for several weeks, concentrating his army and the remaining troops of the Bavarian army in a large camp near Nuremberg, in the towns of Zirndorf, Oberasbach and Stein, the construction of which about caused about 13,000 trees to be felled. Gustavus decided to attack the position of Alte Veste (2–3 September

---

17 Parker, *Guerra*, pp.148–161.
18 Negredo, *Guerra*, p.158.
19 Negredo, *Guerra*, p.160.

THE BATTLE OF NÖRDLINGEN 1634

1632), but the Swedish-German Army was unable to break the Catholic defences, and the Protestants were defeated not only on the battlefield, but also politically. As the autumn progressed, the Protestants began to suffer increasing issues with their supply and money shortages. The King ordered a retreat north, with his remaining 20,000 men, almost a third of whom had invaded Bavaria a few months earlier.[20]

Wallenstein's army advanced to Saxony in mid-autumn, but he had great difficulty supplying his army and decided to disband his units. His main cavalry force, under the command of Pappenheim, was to occupy Halle, more than fifty miles from Wallenstein's main base, and another part of his army went to Lützen. Perhaps the victory of Alte Veste had led the

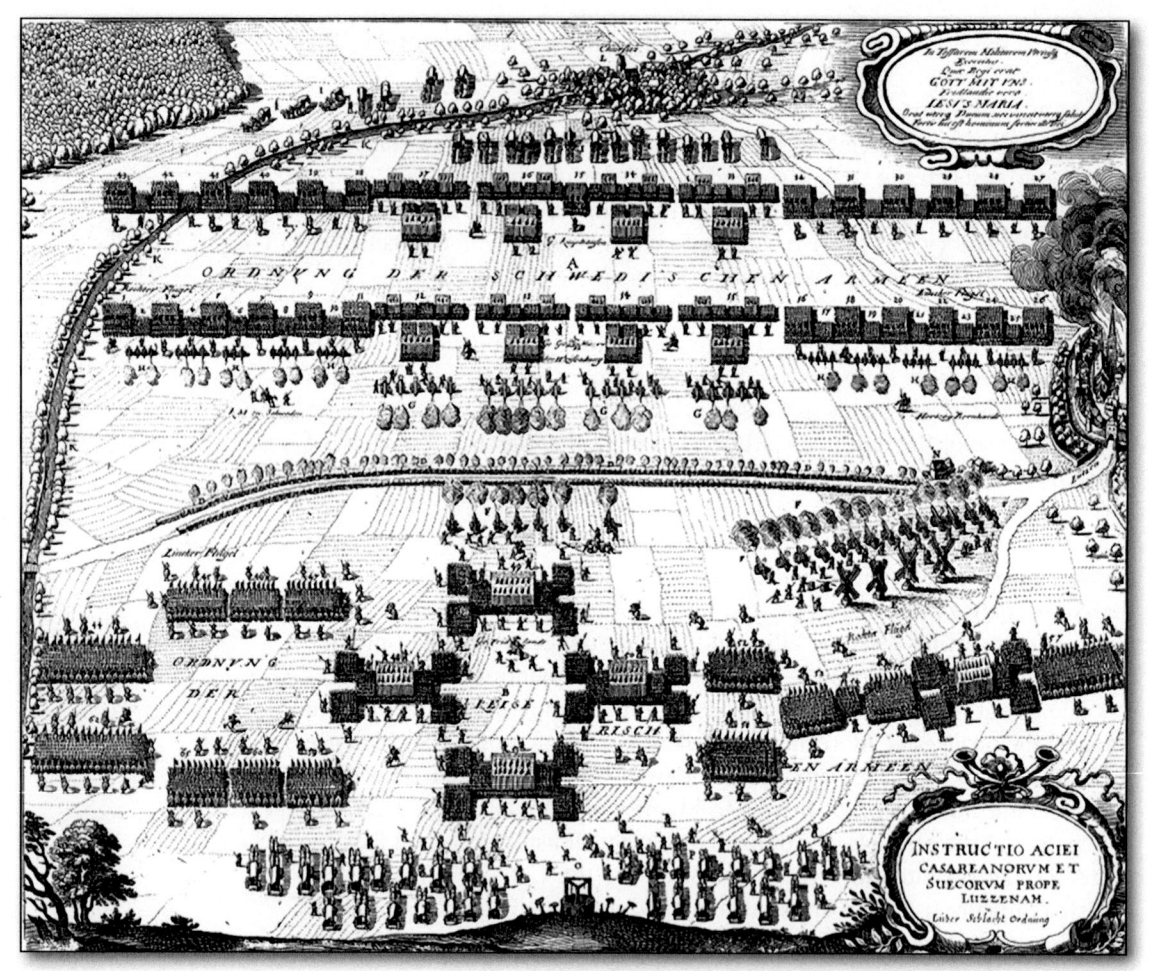

Battle of Lützen (16 November 1632). In this decisive battle between Swedish and Imperial forces, at the cost of numerous losses, Sweden prevailed on the battlefield. Gustavus Adolphus lost his life, but his fame and success remained. In this engraving, the Imperial troops appear deployed in a 'Tercio' type formation, although this was not really the case, but rather they did so in a mixed model, in smaller units. However, we can see what the theoretical model of a 'Tercio' was like; the centre was made up of pikemen and around them, a 'guarnicion' of musketeers, and in the corners, the 'mangas' of arquebusiers. On the contrary, the deployment of the Protestants is more reliable, since they formed in the style of a 'Swedish brigade', although it seems that the usual depth of their ranks was less. (*Theatrum Europaeum*, period 1629–1633, Edition 1646)

---

20 Negredo, *Guerra*, p.161.

THE WAR IN GERMANY

Death of King Gustav II Adolf of Sweden at the Battle of Lützen, by Carl Wahlbom (1855). The brightly illuminated body of the dead King appears to be sliding off his horse. This image recalls the image of Jesus crucified, in the arms of the Virgin Mary; thus, the King is portrayed as a hero and a martyr. The painter abuses explicit romanticism, but recreates the heat of a battle very well, with the various secondary scenes of soldiers fighting to the death, doing anything that would help them survive. Swords, pistols and maces are used to hit the enemy, even if unarmed and on the ground. (Nationalmuseum, NM 1028)

Catholic general to think that his forces were now unbeatable, maybe he underestimated the Swedes, maybe he thought that they were farther away than they really were.

But the reality was that, when Gustavus Adolphus had confirmation that the Catholic army was divided and dispersed he ordered all his troops to march on Lützen. The battle that took place there on 16 November 1632 was one of the bloodiest in the entire Thirty Years' War. Gustavus found his eternal glory, but also his death, as did 3,000 of his men and 6,000 Catholics.[21]

After the Death of Gustavus Adolphus

The death of Gustavus Adolphus[22] and Frederick V of the Palatinate (29 November 1632) could have been another opportunity for peace after almost 15 years of a war that ruthlessly devastated the lands of Germany and Central Europe.

---
21 Negredo, *Guerra*, p.165.
22 In Spain the first news of the death of the Swedish King were known on the 25 December 1632; two days later his demise was confirmed officially. The King Philip IV celebrated mass in gratitude for the death of the 'Lion of the North' (Elliot, *El conde-duque de Olivares*, p.506).

THE BATTLE OF NÖRDLINGEN 1634

Most of the German states involved wished for peace, but that took no account of the personal actions of Albrecht Wallenstein and Axel Oxenstierna, who, on opposite sides, both advocated the continuation of the conflict. They dragged the rest of the country back to the ravages of war. The former, a military veteran, had enriched himself at the expense of the coffers of Emperor Ferdinand II of Habsburg, the latter was the Prime Minister of Sweden who wished to maintain the hegemony of his country in Germany. Yet again it was impossible for a peaceful solution to please all participants in the war.[23]

Gustavus' death led to a crisis in government in Sweden. The heir to the Swedish throne, Christina, was only 6 years old, and the widowed queen, Maria Eleonora of Brandenburg, had fallen into depression following the death of her husband, and was unable to act effectively as regent. The High Chancellor (*Rikskansler*) Oxenstierna took over the government, fulfilling the wishes of the late King, and continued the expansionist policy in Germany. On 12 January 1633 Oxenstierna was confirmed as a Swedish plenipotentiary in Imperial territory, with the power to administer and control all Swedish forces and the lands controlled by them. One of his first actions was to try to regain the confidence of the German princes and to maintain their support for the Swedish war effort as the Germans were demoralised after the King died. As if that was not enough for the Swedes pressure from the Russians and Poles forced Oxenstierna to withdraw native Scandinavian troops and send them to the Baltic to secure control of that area, so longed for by Sweden.[24]

Oxenstierna organised a meeting of his allies in the city of Heilbronn, on 18 March 1633, to strengthen the alliance between them and maintain the leadership of Sweden. The Heilbronn League was formed, with the military circles of Upper and Lower Rhine, Swabia and Franconia. Sweden needed the support of Protestant princes in southwestern Germany to consolidate its presence once Gustavus' aura of invincibility was gone.

To finance the League, the German states would provide 2.5 million *reichstalers* annually. France decided to become more involved in the war and was recognised by the German Protestant princes as the protector of the Protestant cause. In return, France increased its tolerance of Protestants, but it managed to get the money to go directly to the League, and not to Sweden as before. As a result, France stood out strongly in its position as an ally of the German Protestants. Although Sweden had to cede overall control to France, the Swedes retained their position as military commanders.[25]

To lead the Heilbronn League operations in southern Germany, it had been agreed that these would be led by two of Gustavus Adolphus's best generals, namely the ambitious and aggressive German Prince Bernard of Saxe-Weimar, and the cautious Gustav Horn, *Fältmarskalk* (Field marshal) of Sweden.[26]

---

23 Negredo, *Guerra*, pp.167–170.
24 Parker, *Guerra*, p.174.
25 Parker, *Guerra*, pp.174–181.
26 Negredo, *Guerra*, pp.166–167.

Axel Oxenstierna, by David Beck (c1647–1651). He was the son of a family with a long military and governmental tradition in Sweden. He studied at several German universities. In 1609 Oxenstierna was appointed a member of the Royal Council and in 1611 he was appointed a member of the Regency Council. On 6 January 1612 he was appointed Chancellor and his organisation and controls had a positive effect on all parts of the Administration. He advised King Gustavus Adolphus, was appointed governor of several territories and when the king died, Oxenstierna assumed the tutelage of Queen Christina and directed all of Sweden's domestic and foreign policy for over 20 years. The Peace of Westphalia secured Sweden's position as a major power in the Baltic region. (Livrustkammaren, LRK 24339)

One of the first problems the League had to face was the mutiny of Swedish and German troops due to lack of pay. Bernard took advantage of the situation to pressure Oxenstierna who wanted to be granted a hereditary title in Germany as a reward for his services. To remedy the delicate military-political situation, the Heilbronn League raised as much money as it could, paid the troops, provided stipends and property to some officers, and Bernard was appointed Duke of Franconia. Once the mutineers in army had been pacified, operations resumed in southern Germany. Since Bernard and Horn could not agree their strategy, they did agree that they would command their forces independently. So, while Horn's Swedish forces would operate in Baden, Bernard's army, an amalgamation of Swedish and German units, would be based on the Danube, aiming to beat Bavaria.[27]

On the Imperial side, after the relief gained by the death of Gustavus Adolphus, the general situation changed. In a distressed mood Emperor Ferdinand II needed the services of Wallenstein and his army, but the Emperor was increasingly aware that the general was more and more driven by his own ambition and not by service to the Empire. Indeed, Wallenstein was in touch with the court of Vienna, with emissaries from Spain, but also with Bohemian exiles, with personalities from Brandenburg, Sweden and, especially, Saxony. Such contacts were known in Vienna. Opponents of Wallenstein began to murmur in Imperial court about the possibility that he could commit treason. In fact, the truce signed by Wallenstein with the Saxon General Arnim during the summer of 1633 had been consented to, but with much suspicion in Vienna. Paradoxically, this truce had also been tolerated by a disgruntled Oxenstierna.[28]

---

27 Negredo, *Guerra*, p.168.
28 Negredo, *Guerra*, p.170.

But Wallenstein's army was still operational and at Steinau, on 27 September 1633, the Protestants were defeated yet again. This could have been the start of a great offensive, but Wallenstein did not capitalise on the occasion that both his victory and the arrival in Germany of a new Hispanic army under Gómez Suárez de Figueroa, IV Duke of Feria would do to weaken Protestants armies.

Spanish Involvement

From the beginning of the revolt in Bohemia and its extension to the rest of the Holy Roman Empire, Spain had helped the Austrian Habsburgs. On one hand, they were closely related by blood, but on the other, they fought in support of the Catholic religion. Above all, because its military intervention to resolve the conflict served to consolidate the prospect of European hegemony of the Hispanic Monarchy.[29] This aid came in the form of money and volunteers for the Imperial armies, many of whom reached senior military ranks, such as Charles Bonaventure de Longueval (1571–1621), Count of Bucquoy, Johann Tserclaes (1559–1632), Count of Tilly, Guillermo Verdugo (1570–1629), Baltasar de Marradas (1560–1638), Carlo Spinelli (1575–1633).

After resolving the revolt in Bohemia, the Habsburg forces took advantage of the situation to eliminate the power of Frederick V of the Palatinate, and through diplomatic manoeuvring they were able to politically isolate Frederick, and to bring Spain into the military conflict. In August 1620, General Ambroggio Spinola with 20,000 infantrymen and 4,000 cavalrymen from the army in Flanders began their march from Brussels and by early September entered the Lower Palatinate.[30] Spinola pretended to besiege Frankfurt, but later moved to the Rhine, occupying cities on both banks. Another 10,000-strong Hispanic Army, under the command of Gonzalo Fernández de Córdoba (great-grandson of Great Captain) joined the Catholic League army, under Tilly, and invaded the Upper Palatinate, defeating the Protestant armies at the battles of Wimpfen (6 May 1622) and Höchst (20 June 1622).

The Spanish military situation was complicated when in 1621 the Twelve Year truce (1609–1621),[31] agreed with the United Provinces of the Netherlands, was not renewed. Spinola had to retreat from his gains in Germany to secure Flanders, but left Germany with Gonzalo Fernandez de Córdoba to lead an army of 17,000 infantrymen and 2,500 horse. When

---

29 Bordeau, *Men and money*, p.28. In the Battle of White Mountain, the Catholic army included three Walloon Tercios (under the command of the Count of Bucqoy, Count of Henin and the Spanish Colonel Guillermo Verdugo), and the Neapolitan Tercio of Carlos Spinelli, with the regiments of *caballos-corazas* (cuirassiers) of the Walloon Colonel Gauchier and the cuirassiers regiment of Count Baltasar de Marradas (MESA, *Nördlingen*, p.10).
30 Bordeau, *Men and money*, pp.29–30; Mesa, *Nördlingen*, p.10.
31 For more information about this period: Allen, Paul C.: *Felipe III y la Pax hispánica, 1598–1621*. Alianza Editorial, Madrid, 2001; García García, Bernardo José (ed.): *Tiempo de paces: La Pax Hispanica y la Tregua de los Doce Años*. Fundación Carlos de Amberes, Madrid, 2009.

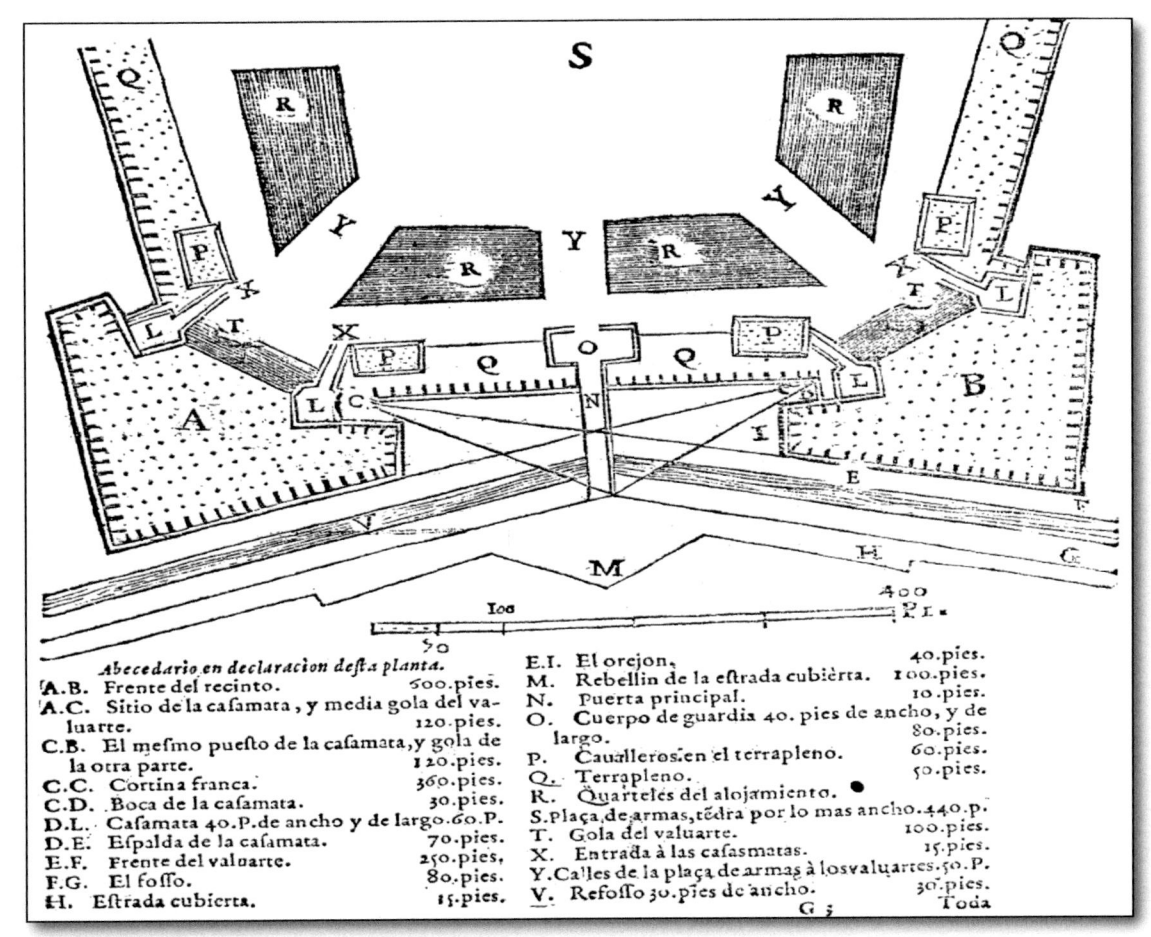

Illustration from the book 'Theory and practice of fortification' ('Teoría y práctica de la fortificación' 1598), by the engineer Cristóbal de Rojas. He was in charge of repairing and improving the defences of the city of Cádiz after the Anglo-Dutch assault of 1596. He worked on the project and design of the San Felipe de La Mamora Fort (Morocco) and was Juan de Herrera's assistant in the construction of the El Escorial Monastery. A century before Sébastien Le Prestre de Vauban became famous, Italian architects created a new fortification system, the 'trace italienne' (bastion fort), based on bastioned construction. In this illustration we see the basic concepts of bastioned fortification, born in Italy and widely applied in the Spanish possessions in Europe, Africa, America and Asia: bastion, casemate, curtain wall, hornwork, lunette, moat, ravelin, tenaille. (Author's collection)

troops of Ernst von Mansfeld (1580–1626) and Christian of Brunswick (1599–1626), dismissed from the Protestant army after successive defeats in the Palatinate, marched north seeking to enlist in the army of the United Provinces, the Spanish under Gonzalo Fernandez de Córdoba defeated them at the Battle of Fleurus (29 August 1622).[32]

With its direct participation in the war, Spain not only strengthened the military power of Catholics in the Empire, but also demonstrated its strength to its traditional Dutch and English enemies, who supported Frederick with money and troops. In addition, Spain obtained several Palatinate cities, ensuring better control of the 'Spanish Road', which ran through Lombardy, Tyrol and Swabia, following the Rhine, through Alsace and Lorraine to

---

32 Esteban Ribas, Alberto Raúl: *La batalla de Fleurus, 1622*. Almena, Madrid, 2013.

the Netherlands (there was also an alternate route of Alsace, Lorraine, Luxembourg and the Bishopric of Liege.

At an international level, at the beginning of the 1630s Spain was entering a delicate period. If the war for the succession of Mantua and Monferrato (1628–1631)[33] was not successful in terms of political aspirations, at least it allowed the forces there to be freed up for service on other fronts. Thus, 10,000 troops divided into eight Tercios and 22 cavalry companies were free to be relocated to the defence of Italy and Flanders. But at the same time, it allowed them to see how French objectives would continue against Spain on all possible fronts, especially in the Netherlands and Germany.[34]

Faced with the rapid Swedish advance, Spain received letters from the Empire in a hurry to form an alliance. The Emperor wished that Austria, Spain and the Emperor's faithful principalities signed a document stating that all efforts should be made to defeat the Protestant enemies. Paradoxically, it was essentially the same proposal made by Spain in 1625 in the Treaty of Aranjuez, but had been forgotten by the Empire for years, as the Austrians only wanted Spanish help in fighting the Danes and their German allies, whereas the Spaniards wanted a reciprocal arrangement and Imperialist help against the Dutch.

The Spaniards did not agree to the Imperial plan, but the catastrophic situation after the glittering landing of Gustavus II Adolphus, almost resulting in the collapse of the Imperial cause, forced Spain to devote a huge amount of resources of all kinds to sustain its Austrian cousins. The Spaniards sent subsidies to the Emperor to finance his army, as well as to the other princes of the Empire to encourage them to support him, and on a military level, an army was sent to the Rhineland Palatinate, both to ensure the loyalty of this province to the Empire, and also to secure passage along the Spanish Road, protecting traffic through the Rhine and the ecclesiastical principalities along the banks of the river. But Cardinal Richelieu acted much faster, and in December 1631 his French troops besieged several locations in the Archbishopric of Metz and forced them to sign a treaty of friendship with Duke Charles of Lorraine. To make matters worse, the Swedish army had also reached the Rhine, and after defeating small Spanish detachments at Stockstadt and Oppenheim[35] appeared to be helping the Dutch isolate Spanish Flanders.[36]

Spain could not afford to have war raging on three fronts simultaneously (Flanders, France and Sweden), so Prime Minister Count-Duke of Olivares sent the veteran general Gonzalo Fernández de Córdoba as ambassador to Paris to try and avoid the open war. Meanwhile, in Madrid, the counsellors of King Philip IV studied the appropriate responses to French aggression. These were an offensive war with a preventative attack through the Pyrenees or a defensive war, keep all their territories fully mobilised and await the French attack. Given the depletion of the economic resources of Spain and especially

---

33   De La Rocha, *El Ejército de Alsacia*, pp.11–13.
34   Elliot, *El conde-duque de Olivares*, p.454.
35   Mesa, *Nördlingen*, p.10.
36   Elliot, *El conde-duque de Olivares*, p.482.

of Castile,[37] the King of Spain preferred to wait for events to unfold, trusting that the resources sent to the Empire and the forces recruited so far would be enough to deter the French from attacking Spain. In any case, he chose to be cautious and prepare for a French attack.[38]

That is why at the beginning of 1632 the Spaniards resumed negotiations with the Holy Roman Empire to sign a military treaty of mutual defence, but in April 1632 the answer came from the Imperial court refusing to enter into any such agreement. There were also reports that the Swedes had devastated Bavaria and that France had again attacked Lorraine, expelling the Spanish garrison from Trier.[39]

With the arrival of the Swedish army in the area of Mainz and the Rhine, together with French advance into Lorraine, this caused Francisco de Moncada (1586–1635), III Marquis of Aitona, extraordinary ambassador and advisor of Princess Isabel Clara Eugenia of Austria (1566–1633), to write alarmedly to the Count-Duke of Olivares, reporting to him that the sum of the powers of Holland, France and Sweden was irresistible and 'would just gobble up the Spanish Netherlands'.[40]

Equestrian portrait of Gaspar de Guzmán y Pimentel, count-duke of Olivares, by Diego Velazquez (1636). Olivares was 34 years old when 16-year-old King Philip IV named him his 'valid' (prime minister). Olivares accumulated great power and was feared by the other nobles, for his talent, great political ability and extraordinary capacity for work. However, after the start of the war with France (1635), the rebellion of Portugal and Catalonia (1640) and hostilities with the Netherlands (80 Years' War), King Philip IV decided to withdraw his position and banish him to one of his estates in 1643. In this portrait Olivares appears in a battle scene, although it is known that he did not fight in any. But the minister wanted to emulate other great nobles who were military, such as the Duke of Feria, the Marquis Spínola or the Marquis of Leganés. Velázquez painted Olivares with an arrogant attitude, an energetic force with which he looks at the viewer. In addition, the figure of the minister and his horse occupies almost the entire painting, thus allegorically showing the real power that Olivares had. (Museo del Prado, P01181)

37 Elliot, *El conde-duque de* Olivares, pp.457–477.
38 Elliot, *El conde-duque de* Olivares, p.485.
39 Elliot, *El conde-duque de* Olivares, p.494.
40 De La Rocha, *El Ejército de Alsacia*, pp.9–17.

To make matters even worse, by the middle of 1633 the health of Princess Isabel Clara Eugenia of Austria had worsened. She was the daughter of King Philip II of Spain, and between 1598 and 1621 had been the sovereign of the Spanish Netherlands, with her husband and cousin, Archduke Alberto of Austria. After Alberto's death, as the marriage had produced no children, the Princess remained at the head of the Flanders government, but only with the rank of governor general. Due to his military experience, it had been Ambroggio Spinola who had led the war in Flanders for several decades, but when the Italian general left for Italy, the various military commanders who remained, such as the Marquis of Santa Cruz, the Marquis of Aitona, Gonzalo Fernández de Córdoba and Carlos Coloma, all with similar rank and experience, had disagreed on who would take over the command, and without collaborating closely with each other, caused bewilderment among officers and men of the army. In addition, the Dutch offensive led by Frederick Henry (1584–1647), Prince of Orange, was about to cause the collapse of the Spanish Netherlands, after Maastricht and Limburg were lost.

In the face of the failure of the Flanders defensive campaign, most generals sought a change of scenery and permission to return to Spain, to avoid being accused of negligence.[41]

To remedy the heartbreaking situation in both Flanders and from Spain, it was good to see that a member of the Spanish royal house was the new governor of the Spanish Netherlands. He followed in the footsteps of Margarita de Parma (1559–1567), Juan de Austria (1576–1578) and Isabel Clara Eugenia, but the death of the latter was expected imminently, and required a member of the family of Philip IV who had the military and political courage and ability to govern the distant lands of Flanders. The young Fernando de Austria, 23 years old and Archbishop of Toledo (which is why he is known in the chronicles as Cardinal-Infante), was ready to assume such high levels of responsibility.[42] In preparation to replace Isabel Clara Eugenia, Philip IV appointed him as Viceroy of Catalonia, where Ferdinand quickly learned the tasks of government and the protocols of the administration.

The main Spanish objective was to regain its power in Flanders. King Philip IV relied on his brother's talent, but he also needed Imperial support to defeat the Dutch. As always, his intention was to help the Empire free itself of all internal and external threats, so that later the Imperialists would help Spain to overcome the Dutch. But the Imperialists always refused to play their part, as they had no strategic interest in the affairs of the United Provinces. For that reason, the veteran ambassador Count of Oñate was sent to Vienna to pressure Emperor Ferdinand II to sign a global peace treaty with Spain, the diplomat Diego Faajardo Saavedra was sent to the court of Maximilian of Bavaria[43] and the diplomat Ottavio Villani was ordered to

---

41 De La Rocha, *El Ejército de Alsacia*, p.19.
42 Elliot, *El conde-duque de Olivares*, p.503.
43 For a major analysis of this period, refer to the writings of the diplomat and politician Saavedra Fajardo: Aldea Vaquero, Quintín: *España en Europa en el siglo XVII. Correspondencia de Saavedra Fajardo. Tomo III: El cardenal Infante en el imposible camino de Flandes, 1633–1634*. CSIC, Madrid, 2008.

meet with General Wallenstein, to gain his support and fidelity to the Spanish military and political aims.[44]

The Spanish King had to decide how his brother would travel to Flanders. Since the Dutch had a powerful fleet, and also because of the risk of storms, the Prince was not advised to travel by sea to Flanders. Instead in 1633 the Cardinal-Infante went to Genoa, and from there to Milan, as the plan was for him to travel from Italy to the Spanish Netherlands along the Spanish Road,[45] the traditional land route followed by the armies of the Hispanic Monarchy to reach Flanders from their Italian domains. It is perhaps worth explaining that this was not a single route, nor a road built for that purpose.

The origin of this military route lies at the beginning of the political and religious uprising in the northern states of the former Netherlands. The unrest throughout the country prompted King Philip II to send a professional army to address the situation and put down all unrest and disorder. As the best troops were stationed in his possessions in Italy, the four Tercios (of Lombardy, Naples, Sicily, and Sardinia), were ordered to march to Flanders. In command was the Duke of Alba, Fernando Alvarez de Toledo y Pimentel, and in 56 days, the 10,000 soldiers of the army marched from Milan to Brussels. It was the first time that this road was used and it was a success.

A solution was thus given to a necessity that would repeat itself on numerous occasions for the next one hundred years. The main theatre of operations for the Spanish in Europe during this period was against the Dutch, hence the necessity of sending troops to Flanders, and the strategic

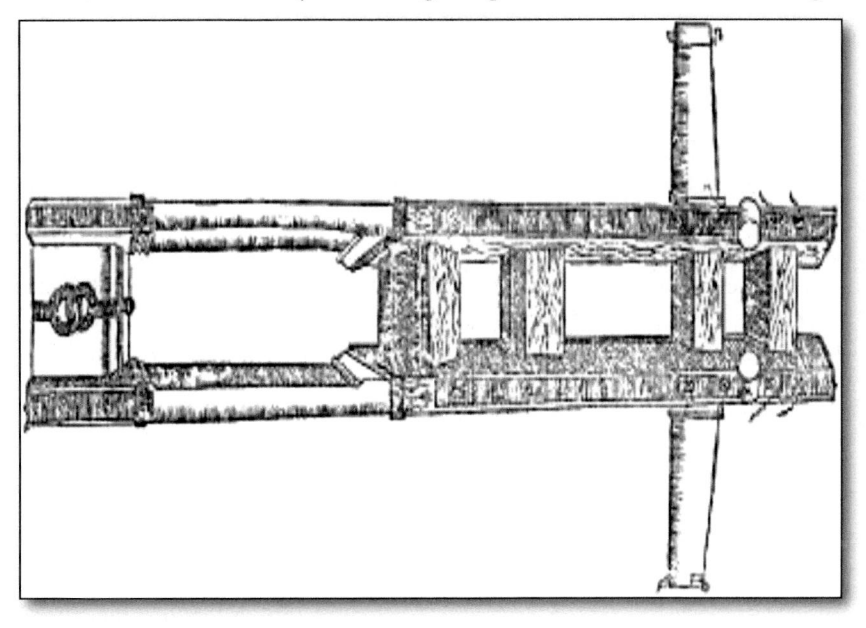

Illustration from the military treatise 'The perfect gunner: theory and practice' by Julio César Firrufino (1648). In this illustration we see the gun carriage of a culverin. The text of the book identifies the various parts and materials with which it has to be manufactured. (Author's collection)

44　Elliot, *El conde-duque de Olivares*, p.509.
45　Martínez Laínez, Fernando: *Una pica en Flandes. La epopeya del Camino Español*. EDAF, Madrid, 2007; Paoletti, Ciro: 'L'Italia e il Cammino di Fiandra', in Congresso internazionale 'Le armi del sovrano. Eserciti e flotte da Lepanto alla Rivoluzione Francese, 1571–1789', Roma, Archivio di Stato, 2001; Parker, Geoffrey: *El ejército de Flandes y el Camino Español, 1567–1659*. Alianza Editorial, Madrid, 2005; Sánchez, Jorge: *El Camino Español. Un viaje por la ruta de los Tercios de Flandes*. Editorial Dilema, Madrid, 2014.

reserve of forces which could be mobilised for the task was in Italy. This is the reason why, whenever troops were needed in Flanders or Germany, garrison troops in Italy (which were always well trained) were called upon and replaced by a newly recruited troops, taking their place garrisoning the Italian fortresses and cities, thus beginning a new training process, until they in turn were required elsewhere.

The use of the Spanish Road gained momentum when the hostility of England and France led to a succession of wars, because despite the sea route through the North Sea being the fastest route, enemy fleets were always waiting to pounce on and sink vulnerable troop transports.

It was for that reason that it was better and safer to send troops to Italy first and then have them march on towards Flanders by land. Since the western Mediterranean was dominated by the galleys of Spain's allies (Genoa, Sicily and Sardinia), this revolving system of troops was usually started at the ports of Barcelona and Valencia, where the units were destined for Genoa or Naples, where they joined the garrisons. When it was necessary for the Tercios to march on Germany or Flanders, they congregated around Milan before beginning the march to the Alps.

From Milan there were possible several routes, depending on the destination or the presence of allies or enemies in the vicinity. Thus, one route passed through Savoy, Franche-Comté and Lorraine, to reach Brussels by passing through Burgundian territories under Spanish sovereignty or allies, such as Luxembourg, and the Episcopal Principality of Liege. Another option was through Lake Como, in the Valtelina Valley, along the shores of Lake Constance, via the Upper Rhine, Alsace and Strasbourg and finally Brussels. On the occasions when the destination was Bohemia or Austria, after reaching Lake Constance, the road followed the Rhine and Danube basins to Vienna and beyond.

This military route was at the same time commercial one, used by Italian, French and German merchants. However, it was the Spanish military that conceived the route in its entirety, from beginning to end. In fact, in order to assist in the passing of so many troops, some sections of the commercial route were adapted and provided with shelter and depots. If the army used this route when political circumstances dictated, merchants used it all year long, and precisely because of this everyday use, travellers needed food and shelter along the way.

But feeding dozens of merchants was not the same as feeding thousands of soldiers, and the Spanish military conceived a system of sectors along the route, from city to city, to guarantee accommodation and support for the troops. This system, known as the *etapas* (stages) was improving over time. It was established so that at the end of a day's march a population centre was reached that would provide lodging and food for the troops. To this end commissioners were sent to the cities on the route to agree with their authorities and merchants the quantities and prices of the provisions that would be needed, thus avoiding excessive price increases and a shortage of supplies among the civilian population.

Between 1567 and 1620, Spain sent more than 123,000 men by this route, and in the same period only 17,600 soldiers were sent by sea. The 1,000km that separated Milan from Brussels could be covered on an average of 23km per day.

'Pikeman and a Woman with a Child Holding a Spear', by Rudolph Meyer (ca. 1615–1638). It is a collection of engravings with the name 'Soldiers and Nobles' in which Meyer describes various types of soldiers (pikemen, musketeers) and their officers. Each plate presents two figures of the same type, but in different positions and different dresses. On this occasion, a veteran soldier with his partner and his little boy, and the author indicates that during the war, many civilians accompanied the army. This was not only a problem for the provision of supplies, but could also create conflict between the troops and with the population centres they passed through. (Rijksmuseum, RP-P-2011-83–16)

But in 1633, as much of the Spanish Road was occupied or threatened by the presence of Protestant or French armies, it was considered necessary for an army to leave in advance of the Cardinal-Infante, with the aim of clearing the route and to secure it by leaving garrisons in major cities.[46] Hence, Cardinal-Infante's lieutenant, Gómez Suárez de Figueroa, IV Duke of Feria, left Milan with an army to guarantee the route against any threats. However, as the spring of 1633 passed, and with the news of the successes of the Swedes and French, the objectives assigned to this army increased significantly, and it not only had to secure the Rhine route, but it also had to collaborate with the Imperial armies, defend the Franche-Comté and Tyrol, and also be able to divide its forces and return to Italy if the Protestants crossed the Alps to attack Spanish Italy.[47]

When Feria's army was ready to leave, a mishap delayed its march further north. Wallenstein, jealous of the presence of another Catholic army in the Empire, pushed for Emperor Ferdinand II to deny it passage through Alsace. This refusal, from the Spanish point of view, was unheard of and an affront, causing Olivares to become hostile and mistrusting towards Wallenstein. It was incomprehensible that the Emperor would refuse to allow the Spanish Army to enter his territory, because those Spanish troops were intended to collaborate with the Imperial army in clearing the Rhine of Protestant troops![48]

---

46 For an exhaustive analysis of this army and of its time in Alsace: De La Rocha, Carlos y Cañete, Hugo A.: *El Ejército de Alsacia. Intervención española en el Alto Rihin (1633/34)*. Sátrapa Ediciones, Zaragoza, 2010.
47 Elliot, *El conde-duque de Olivares*, p.510.
48 The number of troops that this army had to count on was continuously changing as new military objectives were added to address along its path down the Rhine. In addition, supposedly troops

THE BATTLE OF NÖRDLINGEN 1634

Imperial permission was finally obtained and on 22 August the Duke of Feria began his march with 1,300 cavalrymen and 10,568 infantrymen. His troops consisted of one Spanish tercio, with 221 officers and 2,343 soldiers, under the command of the *maestre de campo* Juan Diaz Zamorano; three Spanish companies, under the command of Juan Marin, with 32 officers and 355 soldiers; one Lombard tercio, with 114 officers and 1,476 soldiers, under the command of the *maestre de campo* Juan Bautista Paniguerola; one Neapolitan tercio, of 153 officers and 2,028 soldiers, under *maestre de campo* Marquis of Torrecusa; one German regiment, of Colonel Schamburg, with 198 officers and 2,102 soldiers; and one further German regiment, of Colonel Salm, with 134 officers and 1,414 soldiers. The 1,300 cavalry were grouped into 25 companies, under the command of Geraldo Gambacorta, while the field artillery was commanded of Giovanni Maria Serbelloni.[49]

By 5 September, this expedition had already crossed the Alps.[50] It was agreed that once in Germany, the Spaniards would be reinforced by Imperial troops. But events on the Eastern Front and Wallenstein's refusal to collaborate meant that the Imperial reinforcements were insufficient, as the rest of the Catholic forces in the area were trapped in Constance and Lindau. To relieve the pressure on those cities, the Duke of Feria sent them a relieving force of 1,000 infantry.

The Protestant army had also besieged Breisach, which was the largest fortress on the Rhine, and Wallenstein did nothing to collaborate here either. The young King of Hungary, Ferdinand, followed by Johann von

Reinforcing breastplate (c1625–1630), from Italian, probably Milan. This piece is made by steel and silver, and it was intended to be worn on top of a Cuirassier's armoured cuirass. It was designed to be bulletproof. These pieces were extremely heavy, so they were removed from the main breastplate if the wearer was not engaged in combat. In this cuirass we can see a dent, made by a bullet or a strong blow from the mace. As for its decoration, it has a pentagram, the letter F and a crown that surrounds a pair of crossed palm branches: they are the personal emblems of the Duke of Feria, Gómez Suárez de Figueroa and Córdova. It is thought that while he was governor of Milan (1618–1625 and 1631–1633) he ordered the construction of a set of armour (preserved in the Royal Armoury of Turin). This reinforcing breastplate and a pistol are both preserved in the Metropolitan Museum of Art from New York. This piece was held in the Real Armoury of Madrid until 1836. Its dimensions are: height 40.6cm, width 41.9cm, weight 6.662kg (Metropolitan Museum of Art, 14.25.867)

recruited in Germany were to be added, but never materialised (De La Rocha, *El Ejército de Alsacia*, pp.35–38).

49   Mesa, *Nördlingen*, p.13.
50   Elliot, *El conde-duque de Olivares*, p.514.

THE WAR IN GERMANY

'The Liberation of Brisach', by Jusepe Leonardo (1635). This is another of the paintings housed in the Hall of the Kingdoms. The canvas represents the liberation of the city of Brisach, on 16 October 1633, from the siege to which it was subjected by the Protestant Rhingrave Otto Ludwig. In the foreground is the Duke of Feria, Gómez Suárez de Figueroa, who wears a 'three quarters' armour, and a luxurious shirt collar over his gorget. He wears the Spanish red sash and a baton in his right hand. Next to him is a detachment of caballos-celadas, a light cavalry unit, similar to the Men-at-Arms, also armed with heavy lances, but without protection for the horses. In the background, the arquebusiers walk, preceded further by the halberdiers, who guard the flags and the ammunition carts. Between them and the city is a burned-out redoubt and, in the background, Brisach, into which the Spanish troops penetrate. The flags that are shown all have the Burgundian Cross, but the backgrounds are of different colours (blue, yellow and white). (Museo del Prado, P000859)

Aldringen, Wallenstein's general, formed an independent army. Aldringen's force met with Duke of Feria's Army on 1 October, near Ravensburg, with the immediate aim of relieving Constance and its surroundings. When this combined army arrived near Constance, the Swedish General Horn decided to lift the siege and retreat, which he did on 3 October.[51]

The next goal was to free Breisach. During their approach march the Spanish-Imperial Army conquered the cities of Waldshut, Laufenburg and Säckigen, without almost any resistance. But the Rheinfelden's defenders refused to surrender. Feria ordered an assault and the surviving members

---

51 Mesa, *Nördlingen*, p.13.

THE BATTLE OF NÖRDLINGEN 1634

'The Relief of Constance', by Vicente Carducho (1635). This is another of the paintings housed in the Hall of the Kingdoms. This painting celebrates the liberation of the Swiss city of Konstanz, from the siege to which it was being subjected by the Swedish troops of General Horn, who tried to cut off the communication of the imperial troops with the Spanish ones from Valtelina and Milanesado. Along with 'The capture of Rheinfelden' and 'The Liberation of Brisach', it is one of the three paintings that commemorate in the Hall of Kingdoms the victories of the Army of Alsace, commanded by the Duke of Feria, in 1633. The depiction of these acts of arms, which took place a few months before the paintings in the Hall were planned, are due to the fact that Olivares wanted to show the recent power of Hispanic armies (in the campaign of 1633), in a similar way to the victories of 1625 (Breda, Cádiz, Bahía), also painted in the Hall of the Kingdoms. On the canvas, the Duke of Feria appears in the foreground, on horseback, wearing armour and general's insignia. In the background appear various units of the Army of Alsace: cavalry, infantry, the baggage train, and in the distance, the Protestants can be seen as they flee over a bridge over Lake Konstanz. Since the Duke of Feria had died at the time the painting was painted, Carducho had to paint him according to the descriptions made of him at Court. (Museo del Prado, P000636)

of the garrison executed, in revenge for the Spanish soldiers executed by the Swedes at Oppenheim.[52]

The news spread like wildfire throughout the region, and when the Catholics arrived in front of Breisach, and when the Protestants lifted the siege, on 20 October the Catholic army entered the city.[53] Spaniards under

---

52   Mesa, *Nördlingen*, p.14.
53   Elliot, *El conde-duque de Olivares*, pp.514–517.

the Duke of Feria and Imperial and Bavarian troops continued to operate in Alsace and Brisgovia.

But the Swedes, having lost the campaign on the Rhine and around Lake Constance, directed their attention towards Bavaria. Their first objective was the free Imperial city (*freie Reichsstadt*) of Regensburg, a fortress that defended communications with Austria. The Emperor asked Wallenstein to mobilise his army, but again he refused. Days later Wallenstein changed his mind and moved his army, but with his own motives, against the Swedes and the Saxons to occupy Silesia. Wallenstein defeated his enemies at the Battle of Steinau, on the Oder River, on 18 October 1633.

Spain received contradictory reports from Wallenstein. While letters from Priest Quiroga, ambassador to Wallenstein, said that he could be trusted, despite his eccentricities, the ambassador to the Imperial court, the Marquis of Castañeda, reported just the opposite. Prime Minister Olivares continued to believe that Wallenstein could be trusted to support Spain in its war against the Dutch, if in return Spain agreed to his claim to be named sovereign of the Rhineland Palatinate.[54]

While this was being discussed, Protestants launched their next offensive and captured Regensburg on 13 November 1633. Horn and Bernard planned to join in an offensive that would secure south-eastern Germany for the Protestant caused and bring the war in the heart of Bavaria. Meanwhile, the Protestant army under Swedish Field Marshal Johan Banér was in Silesia regrouping for an attack on Bohemia.[55]

The combined Protestant strategy sought to put the Catholic command in serious trouble. Young King Ferdinand had to choose between defending Prague and Bohemia, or Bavaria. He decided on the latter option, which would allow him to free the Danube corridor and preserve the alliance between the two Catholic powers.

In December 1633, Emperor Ferdinand II ordered Wallenstein to begin a campaign to counteract the Swedish-German advance, but he refused to embark on a campaign during those harsh winter days. His response was received with great displeasure in the Imperial court. Not only was this insubordination, but it also opened up of the possibility that the enemy might gain the initiative to strike again. Then came the news of the death of Isabel Clara Eugenia and the Spanish requested the Emperor to authorise Cardinal-Infante's journey through western Germany. They also sought the collaboration of Wallenstein. Priest Quiroga was responsible for convincing Wallenstein to support the Cardinal-Infante's journey. It was not an easy task to convince the stubborn Duke, but he succeeded.[56]

But the harsh winter caused the operations to stop. Feria's army retreated into the devastated lands of Bavaria, and a typhus epidemic decimated the Spanish army, killing the Duke of Feria and more than half of his men.[57] The

---

54 Elliot, *El conde-duque de Olivares*, p.518.
55 Negredo, *Guerra*, p.173.
56 Negredo, *Guerra*, p.179.
57 A rumour circulated that claimed that the death of Feria – on 11 January 1634 – had been caused by poisoning ordered by Wallenstein himself, concerned about the victories of Feria and the

THE BATTLE OF NÖRDLINGEN 1634

Detail of the painting 'Siege of Aire-sur-la-Lys', by Peter Snayers (1653). The painter perfectly portrays the deplorable state of some Spanish soldiers who are besieging the city of Aire-sur-la-Lys. The action takes place during the French offensive in the Netherlands: the Cardinal-infante, had to stop the French advance on the province of Artois, whose capital, Arras, the French had just conquered. Don Fernando fell ill during the siege, due to a possible stomach ulcer, together with enormous fatigue due to exhaustion and stress to stop the enemy invasion. The young prince died on 9 November 1641 and the city surrendered on 7 December. We see here how the soldiers are dressed in rags, without any kind of uniformity, covering themselves from the cold with gnawed blankets, with torn hats; some wear gloves, others have torn boots. In the centre of the image, a dying soldier receives the last rites of a priest with a crucifix. (Museo del Prado, P001745)

survivors were found what quarters they could and awaited the advent of spring and new orders.[58]

General Wallenstein's unreliability, his physical and mental instability, and suspicions that he might change sides caused fear in Imperial court. Consequently, a plan was drawn up to eliminate him. In fact, when Wallenstein retreated with his soldiers to Pilsen in Bohemia in December 1633, it seemed to be confirming that he was about to change sides. It was then that Emperor Ferdinand II signed an order on 24 January1634, dismissing Wallenstein from his service, withdrawing him from command of his armies, and further

---

prestige and ascendancy the Spaniard acquired in the Imperial court for his actions together to General Aldringen. Wallenstein feared that his contract with the Empire might be in danger (Mesa, *Nördlingen*, p.14).

58   Elliot, *El conde-duque de Olivares*, p.521.

declaring him a traitor to the Catholic cause, condemning him to death. The Emperor wrote to the main commanders of the Imperial Army, taking precautions and avoid clashes with Wallenstein's troops. The Emperor did not want a civil war on the Catholic side, but he also needed Wallenstein's army intact to defend the Empire.

Imperial agents were convincing, and Wallenstein lost the support of part of his troops and on 23 February 1634, when, followed by only a few hundred soldiers, he left Pilsen for Cheb. Cheb authorities set a banquet for the illustrious general on the night of 25 February. All this was to save time for the Wallenstein assassination plan to be put into place. Irish Colonel Walter Butler, in command of a dragon regiment, in collaboration with Scottish Colonels Walter Leslie and John Gordon, executed Wallenstein's chief officers (generals Adam Trczka, Vilém Kinský and Christian Illov). Later, Imperial soldiers marched on Wallenstein's palace, knocked down his bedroom door, and Irish Captain Walter Devereux killed Wallenstein with a partisan.[59]

---

59 Negredo, *Guerra*, pp.180–181.

4

Fate Beats a Path to Nördlingen

The war in Germany for 1634 was marked by several active campaigns throughout the territory: Banér in Silesia, Arnim in Saxony, Duke George in Westphalia, the Rhinegrave and Birkenfeld on the Rhine, Horn in Swabia and Bernard of Saxe-Weimar in Franconia.[1]

It was Horn who became the most active of the Protestant commanders, launching a campaign in the spring to regain territory lost before Aldringen in 1633. He conquered Biberach (25 March), Kempton (31 March) and Memmingen (14 April).[2] Arnim advanced to Silesia and on 13 May defeated the army of Colloredo, who was tried and imprisoned for his defeat.[3]

Catholics were defending Bohemia, Silesia, the Rhine and Westphalia, focusing their efforts on an offensive that would allow them to control the Danube. The main field army was placed under Ferdinand, Archduke of Austria (1621), King of Hungary (1625) and King of Bohemia (1627), seconded by Lieutenant General Matthias Gallas. The army was made up of 15,000 infantry in 20 regiments, 9,000 cavalry in 18 regiments, 1,500 dragoons in four regiments, and 3,000 Croats in five regiments. The artillery train had four heavy cannon, 10 demi-cannon, 10 field cannon, four mortars and around 116 light cannon.[4]

In addition, in Bavaria was the Imperial corps under the command of Johann von Aldringen (with 5,000 infantrymen, 3,000 horse and 600 Croats) as well as the Bavarian Army (4,500 infantry in seven regiments, 3,000 horse in nine regiments, and 20 dragoon companies) and the Spanish Army of Alsace, the survivors of the Duke of Feria's expedition (3,300 infantry and 1,080 horse).[5]

King Ferdinand knew that Horn and Bernard's relations were far from cordial and that they operated independently. One of the reasons for the disagreement between the two commanders in the Swedish-German army was over who held the highest rank and, therefore, the supreme command,

---

1 Negredo, *Guerra*, p.179.
2 Guthrie, *Batallas*, p.368.
3 Guthrie, *Batallas*, p.367.
4 Guthrie, *Batallas*, p.367.
5 Guthrie, *Batallas*, p.367.

FATE BEATS A PATH TO NÖRDLINGEN

Map 1 Germany in 1634.

Horn was a Royal Marshal of Sweden while Bernard of Saxe-Weimar was commander in chief of the League of Heilbronn.[6] For this reason Ferdinand and Gallas planned a campaign aimed at defeating their opponents from the west individually. In early May the Imperialists set up camp at Pilsen and marched on Regensburg, defended by a Protestant garrison of 3,800 troops under the command of Colonel Kagge,[7] while the Bavarian Army advanced east to join the Imperial army.

On May 14, Bernard's scouts detected Croatians belonging to the Imperial army. The Bavarians, meanwhile, crossed the Danube over a bridge of boats they had built at Donauwörth. Aware of Catholic converging movements, Bernard mobilised his army to protect the town. He tried to block the passage of the Imperial army into Regensburg but was repulsed. His 10,000 men were outnumbered two to one by the Imperial Army, so he retreated to Kelheim.[8]

Gallas besieged Regensburg on 23 May. Bernard sought help from Horn, who had to lift the siege of Überlingen,[9] and march northeast to support the Duke of Franconia. The differences between the two Protestant commanders were obvious, but they could not risk losing a city as strategically important as Regensburg.[10]

While the siege of Regensburg lasted from June to July, Horn and Bernard combined their forces at Augsburg on 12 July. Their plan was to invade Bavaria in order to divert the Imperial forces besieging Regensburg, while Banér and Arnim's forces would attack Bohemia. Over the following days, the Protestants captured Freising and Moosburg[11] and on 22 July attacked Landshut. Their assault was so devastating that they destroyed the Catholic defences and General

6 pound mortar with base plate. It is a piece captured from the Saxon army. It has the inscription 'GEORG PETSEUT 1602' and underneath it the coat of arms of Saxony. This piece of a mortar should be considered a great rarity, partly because mortars were generally less common then, and partly because base plate mortars were not introduced into European artillery until about 80 years later. Mortars, due to their high arc of fire, were used in siege warfare to destroy the fortifications and houses of a fortress. The downside was that their range was quite short, so they had to be closer to their targets. Armémuseum, AM.010201)

---

6 Guthrie, *Batallas*, p.368.
7 Guthrie, *Batallas*, p.368.
8 Guthrie, *Batallas*, p.368.
9 Despite the Catholic threat to their positions, both Bernard and Horn did not want to lose the initiative, so Bernard left a detachment for the siege of Forchheim, while Horn left troops in the area around Lake Constance and Breisgau. They kept the pressure in the west, but at the expense of having a weak combined army, which they later did not want to risk in a direct attack on Ferdinand's Catholic forces (Delbruck, *Dawn of modern warfare*, p.210).
10 Guthrie, *Batallas*, p.369.
11 Delbruck, *Dawn of modern warfare*, p.210.

FATE BEATS A PATH TO NÖRDLINGEN

Johan von Aldringen died in battle. It is unknown exactly how as he was either trampled on by his men's horses as he tried to contain the retreat[12] or drowned while trying to cross the Isar river.[13] But the Protestant victory was of no great benefit as four days later, on 26 July, the Catholics occupied Regensburg.

As the Protestant offensive in Bohemia of Banér and Arnim was unleashed, the Imperialists turned their attention to the east. Gallas went with his troops to Bohemia, but the Catholic League Army, armed with news of a Spanish Army coming from Italy, chose to shy away from combat and retreat to Ingolstadt to await its arrival.[14] With the Catholic forces now divided and moving apart, the two Heilbronn League generals separated again. The Cardinal-Infante's army was understood to already be in the Tyrol, so Horn moved his troops to observe their movements. Bernard positioned himself on the Danube to prevent any Imperial advance. According to Delbruck,[15] Bernard and Horn made the mistake of not attacking the Bavarians, perhaps the weakest link in the Catholic coalition, then as they were the only Catholic army in position to stop them overrunning Bavaria.[16]

But the Protestant threat to Bohemia was ineffectual and the invasion of Swedes and Saxons slowed down. Gallas ordered a counterattack and his troops turned west and besieged Donauwörth, a strategic crossing point on the Danube.

In the face of the new Imperial attack, on 16 August Bernard met again with Horn to the southwest of Donauwörth, near the free imperial city of Ulm. But that same day, the Imperialists captured Donauwörth and the next day marched northwest against Württemberg, Sweden's most important ally in southern Germany.[17] On their route was the Imperial free city of Nördlingen, defended by a garrison of 500 Swedes and 100 militia.

After traveling 30km to besiege Nördlingen, on 17 August the Catholic Army of about 12,000 to 15,000 Imperialists and 6,000 Bavarians camped on some hills south of the city and immediately laid siege to the city.

On the Protestant side, Horn and Bernard's soldiers may have become demoralised because they had lost the military initiative and had difficulty obtaining supplies. For this reason, they were slow to react to the Catholic move on Nördlingen and did not march on that city as rapidly as needed. On 23 August, the combined army of Bernard and Horn, some 16,000 troops, reached Bopfingen, a three-hour march west of Nördlingen on the Eger River. At Bopfingen they expected the troops of Otto Ludwig von Salm and Johann Philipp Cratz to join them, adding almost 10,000 additional Protestant troops to their army.[18]

The Protestant command was determined to stand up to the Imperials and reverse the situation. After the loss of Regensburg and Donauwörth,

---

12 Guthrie, *Batallas*, p.369.
13 Engerisser and Hrncirik, *Nördlingen*, p.78.
14 Delbruck, *Dawn of modern warfare*, p.210.
15 Delbruck, *Dawn of modern warfare*, p.210.
16 Guthrie, *Batallas*, p.369.
17 Hrncirik, *Spanier auf dem Albuch*, p.15.
18 Guthrie, *Batallas*, p.369.

Swedish pikeman's helmet (c1600–1650). It presents the classical form of the Nordic helmets, far removed from the style of the Spanish morions which were spread profusely throughout the Mediterranean and Central Europe. This type of helmet comes from Holland, and its use became widespread between 1620 and 1660. They are characterised by having a lower and rounded profile, with wider cheek flaps. A reinforced iron skullcap was added underneath the hat's crown, so at least to protect from a slashing sword. The rivets along the side of the helmet are clearly visible, as well as the longitudinal reinforcement of the upper part. It is made of steel. (Livrustkammaren, LRK 7330)

the Catholics could not be allowed to recover any more of their cities. The Protestants were losing initiative in this part of Germany meaning that one of their allies might be tempted to change sides if they thought the Swedes were losing the war.

Bernard carried out a reconnaissance of the Imperial siege lines, and he suggested sending reinforcements to the Nördlingen garrison from the north, since the Catholics there had not even built trenches and only maintained a network of Croatian light cavalry who patrolled the area. Thus, on 24 August, the Protestants marched towards Nördlingen from the north bank of the Eger, but then discovered that the terrain was marshland, not suitable for cavalry and infantry, and for this reason the city could not be relieved from the north,[19] although Horn did manage to slip 250 musketeers into the city across the river.[20]

On 28 August, the first reinforcements arrived at the camp at Bopfingen in the shape of 1,000 professional soldiers under Schaffelitzky and 5,500 Württemberg militiamen commanded Liebenstein's.[21] The rest of Cratz and Ludwig's forces were on their way, but since the Rheingrave had to lift the siege of Rheinfelden, they calculated that it would take a week before they arrived.

During the first two weeks of the siege, the Imperial army had besieged the city to the south. They located 14 demi-cannons and eight culverins, spread over three batteries, two to open a breach and the other firing at the walls, but the city had a deep wide ditch that protected it. The besiegers had not surrounded the city, nor dug approach trenches. In addition, the

---

19 Guthrie, *Batallas*, p.377.
20 Guthrie, *Batallas*, p.369.
21 Guthrie, *Batallas*, p.369.

FATE BEATS A PATH TO NÖRDLINGEN

'The Siege of Jülich', painting attributed to Sebastiaen Vrancx. In this painting we can see how a siege unfolded during the Thirty Years' War. In this case, the siege of Jülich was a siege that lasted from 5 September 1621 to 3 February 1622, as part of the Palatinate campaign of the Thirty Years' War. Ambrosio Spínola's Spanish army captured the German city of Jülich. Both the Spanish and the Dutch, throughout the Eighty Year's War, became masters of siege warfare. In the foreground we see various types of redoubts, as well as the huts where the soldiers lived. In the distance is the main camp of the Spanish besiegers, with tents and huts. On the plain, trenches, and soldiers launching an assault are visible. The city of Jülich has a walled outer defence, behind which is a moat with water, and then there are the main walls. (Rijksmuseum, SK-A-857)

Catholic artillery positions were too high, and they did little damage.[22] Despite these errors, the Imperial high command insisted on launching an assault, and on 2 September the town was bombarded intensively which had an adverse effect on the morale of the defending soldiers and the civilian population. However, when the assault was launched, the garrison succeeded in repulsing it.

This small Catholic defeat strengthened the morale of the Protestant defenders but was offset later that day by the triumphant arrival of the Cardinal-Infante into the Imperial camp, with 15,000 infantry, 3,000 horsemen, and 500 dragoons. These Spanish reinforcements raised the strength of the Catholic army to 33,000, while the Swedish-Germans now had only 22,500.

---

22 De Vera, *Victoria sobre Norlinga*, p.100.

5

The Path of the Cardinal-Infante

The Swedish advance of 1632–1633 into the south of Germany, on both the Danube and the Rhine, as well as the invasion of Bavaria, a strong supporter of the Empire, had set alarm bells going in Spain. The situation was extremely delicate as Swedes were in a position to cut the Spanish Road and link up with the Dutch rebels.

Meanwhile, in the Netherlands, the Duke of Aerschot's conspiracy was dismantled, preventing the Belgian nobles from signing a peace with the Dutch.[1] That however did not solve Flanders' instability and it became more necessary than ever for the Cardinal-Infante to reach Brussels in order to guarantee continuity of governorship of the province.

Since the Spanish Road was blocked by the Swedes and the French, the route traditionally followed from Milan to Flanders was now impossible, so the route had to move further east, through Bohemia and Saxony, and then to west to take the road north through Cologne.[2]

On 30 June 1634, the Cardinal-Infante left Milan, starting the long journey that would take him to Brussels at the head of 12,500 soldiers.[3] The

---

1   Elliot, *El conde-duque de Olivares*, p.528.
2   Elliot, *El conde-duque de Olivares*, p.520.
3   The young prince had a retinue according to his princely status; first, the so-called 'Gentlemen of the Chamber', which were: Diego de Silva and Mendoza (Marquis of Orani and Almenara and gentleman of the Alcantara military Order) that had the office of *Sumiller de Corps* (Sommelier of Corps) and Captain of the two cavalry companies of the Cardinal-Infante's Guard; Antonio Portocarrero Moscoso (Marquis of Villanueva del Frezno, gentleman of the Calatrava military Order); the Marquis of Este (knight of the Order of the Golden Fleece), who was his *Caballerizo mayor* (master of the Cardinal-Infante's horse); Beltrán Vélez de Guevara (gentleman of the Alcantara military Order, and son of the count of Oñate); Valeriano Sfondrato (count of the Rivera, Commander of Guadalcanal, gentleman of the Santiago military Order); Diego Sarmiento (gentleman of the Calatrava military Order), as his *Primer caballerizo* (Main equerry); Alonso Pérez de Bivero (count of Fuensaldaña, gentleman of the Alcantara military Order); the Duke of Nochera, as extraordinary ambassador to the King of Hungary; Luís Lazzo de la Vega (count of Puertollano, gentleman of the Calatrava military Order), as *Mayordomo* (seneschal); Manuel de Guzmán (gentleman of the Santiago military Order, and member of the Royal Council of Orders), as *Capellán*(chaplain) and *Limosnero* (beggar); Martín de Axpe (gentleman of the Santiago military Order) as Secretary of State and War. The Cardinal-Infante

Prince spent the first night in the town of Saronno, continuing the next day, reaching Como, on the shores of the lake of the same name, on 1 July. He remained there for five days, while his army sailed across the lake to the north, to begin their ascent through the Alps.[4] While in the Lake Como area, Cardinal-Infante received an Imperial lieutenant-colonel with a letter from the King of Hungary, anticipating his plan to take Regensburg, and asking for his help in defeating the Protestants in southern Germany.[5]

On 8 July, the Cardinal-Infante and his army paraded in front of Fuentes Castle on Lake Como, by the town of Colico. This fortress, erected by Pedro Enríquez de Acevedo, count of Fuentes de Valdepero, Governor of Milan, symbolised Spanish rule over Italy and over alpine routes.[6]

They were about to enter Swiss-dominated territory in the Valtellina Valley. It was then that to secure the prince's safety, the harquebusier company of his Guard put themselves at the forefront of his entourage and the lancer company in the rear, as the agreement with the Swiss cantons was for the Hispanic Army to traverse their territory in small and unarmed groups, with the exception of the Prince's escort.

Due to the heavy rains, the Adda stream, which flows through the Valtellina to the Lake Como, was in full flow, so the march of the army was very slow. The Cardinal-Infante stopped in the town of Morbegno, as his enormous entourage always travelled behind the last infantry detachment, and they had stopped there. While they were waiting to resume the march, the Cardinal-Infante designated Martín de Aragón Gurrea y Borja, son of the Marquis of Villahermosa, as *maestre de campo general*, and Filippo Spinola, II Marquis of the Balbases, as general of the cavalry. In addition, to increase his own personal protection in Swiss territory, he ordered that the Spanish

---

    had eight pages, all of them gentlemen of different military Orders. In addition, Fernando had a Secretary of the Chamber – who had been rewarded with entering the Santiago military Order, four Chamber aides, 25 reformed captains who were paid from the entourage, as military advisers. In addition, along with these nobles, the Cardinal-Infante had at his service a multitude of commoner servants: wardrobe, stables, servants, cooks, waiters, etc. Up to a total of 1,100 people. In total, 1,300 mounts (horses, mules and donkeys) – carriages apart – were needed to transport this entourage (Aedo, *Viaje del Infante-Cardenal*, p.81).

4 Aedo, *Viaje del Infante-Cardenal*, p.84.
5 Mesa, *Nördlingen*, p.19.
6 Since the Duchy of Milan was a fundamental part of the Spanish presence in Italy, for its economic power but also its strategic situation, the Spanish rulers were always extremely attentive in providing for its defense. In particular, that strategic zone was a centre of the intrigues of French and Venetians. The gateway from the north to the Duchy of Milan was Lake Como, at the border with the territories of the Swiss Canton of Grisons. So, from Milan the Spanish Road started and passed through the Engandina Valley and the Valtelina Valley, and this route had to be secured by all means, given its importance in communications between Spain, Italy and Flanders. The Count of Fuentes, the governor of Milan, considered erecting a fortress at a key point in Alps at Colico. This fortification was erected on a small, isolated mountain, which controls the Adda and Mera river valleys. The works on the 'Fort of Fuentes' began on 25 October 1603 and concluded in 1612. On its construction worked Gabrio Busca, as a designer of the fort, and Giusieppe Piotto da Vacallo, the engineer and military architect, as well as Ercole Negro and Cristobal Lechuga (Martínez Aragón, Lucio y Fior, Michela: *El Conde de Fuentes de Valdepero y el Fuerte de Fuentes en el Camino Español*. Glyphos Publicaciones, Valladolid, 2015).

THE BATTLE OF NÖRDLINGEN 1634

A view of the Battle of Liegnitz (May 13, 1634) between the forces of the Electorate of Saxony, commanded by Hans George von Arnim-Boitzenburg and the army of the Holy Roman Empire under Hieronymous von Colloredo, resulting in a Saxon victory. In the foreground we see part of the baggage train of an army from this period. The servants have unhitched the horses from their carts to feed them. We observe the various types of carts that were used to transport supplies, such as the light ones, with a horse and with a single axle, without cover, to carry barrels of drink and provisions. In the background we see a large group of wagons, pulled by two horses and four wheels, with a canvas cover to transport food and ammunition. (Theatrum Europaeum, period 1633, Edition 1670)

infantry companies of Captains Carlos de Padilla and Gabriel Cobo de la Cueva, both from Tercio of Lombardy, temporarily join his escort.[7]

On 10 July the princely entourage made the way from Morbegno to Sondrio, always one day behind the rearmost army detachment, and in the middle of a great storm. The Adda river had burst its banks and at some points it had flooded the bridges crossing it. In addition, the streams that flowed down the ravines were running so fast and deep that crossing them was a risky enterprise. In the town of Sondrio, Fernando was received by the authorities and the people, in great show of affection. As usual a triumphal arch of flowers had been erected and all the streets were decorated. The inhabitants of La Valtellina were grateful for the Spanish support against the domination of the Swiss Grisons cantons.[8]

On 11 July the army continued its march to the city of Tirano and the next day they arrived at Bormio, where they rested for a day. On 14 July the Spanish Army travelled to Glorenza, the first town in the Austrian Tyrol, where an escort was sent by the widowed Archduchess Claudia of the Tyrol, to welcome the Spaniards into her territory. On 15 July the Cardinal-Infante spent the night at Laces, the next at Merano, on 17 July at Bolzano, and the next at Bressanone. On 19 Jul the entourage arrived at Vipiteno and the next

---

7   Aedo, *Viaje del Infante-Cardenal*, p.87.
8   Aedo, *Viaje del Infante-Cardenal*, p.87.

day reached Mutters.[9] The troops were much weakened by the arduous alpine terrain, rains and thawing snow caused the streams to flow so fast that they not only made it difficult for the troops to cross but also more significantly for the carriages carrying their provisions, which resulted in many soldiers going hungry.[10] Fortunately for all the worst was over.

The 21 July the Hispanic Army arrived at the city of Innsbruck. Before arriving in the city, the seven year old child, Archduke Ferdinand, with the military command of Tyrol, was waiting to accompany the Cardinal-Infante to Innsbruck Palace, where Archduchess Claudia held the official reception.

Over the next two days, the Cardinal-Infante alternated conducting various conventional tasks such as receiving bishops, military officers and ministers from the allied German states with his passion for hunting. Meanwhile, the Marquis of Leganés, as Cardinal-Infante's second-in-command, was in charge of mustering the various units around Innsbruck.[11]

On 24 July, the Cardinal-Infante took a boat from Innsbruck to Hall in the Tyrol, arriving at Rattenberg at night, where he was detained some days, to finish gathering his entire army (rear-guard units, ammunition supplies and all the impedimenta of an army on the march, together with the sick). On 25 July, the Cardinal-Infante received a letter with the news of the loss of Landshut to Protestants, as well as the death of Aldringen in battle.

The next day, he sent the Marquis of Balbases to visit the King of Hungary and to arrange a meeting point for the two armies. In addition, the Cardinal-Infante wanted his cousin to give permission for several Spanish units to withdraw from their positions in Bavaria to join with the Cardinal-Infante's army. These were the surviving units of the army of the Duke of Feria, who were fighting with the Imperialists and Bavarians while they waited for the arrival of Cardinal-Infante. These troops were listed as the Burgundian Tercio of the Count of La Tour (15 companies, 840 men), the Burgundian Tercio of the Count of Alberg (11 companies, 720 men), the German regiment of Colonel Leslie (11 companies, 1,600 men) and the German cavalry regiment of Baron Sebach (10 companies, 712 mounted and 83 dismounted).[12]

Waiting for the Imperial response, the Cardinal-Infante wanted to transform 500 foot soldiers into mounted soldiers, forming five companies of dragoons.. In addition, given the huge baggage train that trailed behind the army, he ordered that from then on everybody carry only the most essential things. The rest of the baggage wagons and carriages continued marching on to Flanders.

On 2 August, the Cardinal-Infante received the news that the King of Hungary had recaptured Regensburg, as well as of the Protestant Army withdrawal from Landshut and march to Augsburg, pursued by the Imperial cavalry. In addition, the Imperial cavalry captured a part of the artillery and impedimenta of the enemy army during their pursuit.[13]

---

9   Aedo, *Viaje del Infante-Cardenal*, pp.90–91.
10 Mesa, *Nördlingen*, p.20.
11 Aedo, *Viaje del Infante-Cardenal*, pp.92–94. In the muster that taken made in this town, Spanish sources report that there was a force of 9,240 infantrymen, grouped in 123 companies, and 2,020 horsemen, in 23 companies (Mesa, *Nördlingen*, p.16).
12 Mesa, *Nördlingen*, p.17.
13 Aedo, *Viaje del Infante-Cardenal*, p.96.

On August 5, the Marquis of Balbases returned from his embassy with King Ferdinand of Hungary, with a request that the Hispanic Army join the Imperial one to campaign against the Swedes in Bavaria and Swabia.[14] Cardinal-Infante gathered his high command in a war council and agreed with the proposal to unite the two armies in the vicinity of Ingolstadt. The Hispanic army would protect the western flank of the Imperial army, which was located on the right bank of the Danube. The Spaniards wanted to help the Imperialists, but they also did not want to deviate far from their march to Flanders. It was decided that the two armies would operate no more than 10 to 15 kilometres apart. In this way they would provide each other with mutual support and would not overburden the villages they passed for food and provisions.[15]

During the following days, the Cardinal-Infante reorganised his troops. The army had 3,000 Spanish foot soldiers, and he ordered them to form one tercio of 1,800 Spaniards, under the command of Martin de Idiáquez, and a second of 1,200 commanded by Enrique de Alagón, Count of Fuenclara, to which were later added 250 Spanish infantrymen who had formed the escort of the army war chest.[16]

On 9 August the Cardinal-Infante and his entourage set sail in small boats along the River Inn to Rosenheim, where Baron Criveli, the Duke of Bavaria's emissary, was waiting to welcome them to his domains.

The Duke wanted to receive the Spanish Prince at his camp at Braunau am Inn, however, the Cardinal-Infante excused himself from meeting Maximilian. He had received a letter from his sister Maria Ana of Austria (1606–1646), who was married to the King of Hungary, and who he had not seen for 5 years. The two brothers met in Passau.[17]

On 14 August, the Cardinal-Infante and his entourage departed from Passau to return to Kufstein. On the way, near Braunau am Inn, they met the retinue of the Duke of Maximilian of Bavaria, who had gone to meet them. They both entered the city and went to the palace, where Duchess Renata of Lorraine, Maximilian's wife, was waiting for them. The three began to chat, the Cardinal-Infante in Spanish, the Duke in Italian and the Duchess in French, languages that they all were fluent in but none agreed to change to the language of their interlocutor. Fernando was the guest of the Duke of Bavaria for two days.[18]

Meanwhile, the last Hispanic units to cross the Alps, which were five cavalry companies and an Italian musketeer company, reached the town of Rattenberg. The Marquis of Balbases sent messages to all units scattered around the city, leaving for Kufstein on 16 August, where the general muster was due to take place on the 18th.

---

14 Mesa, *Nördlingen*, p.20.
15 Aedo, *Viaje del Infante-Cardenal*, p.97.
16 Aedo, *Viaje del Infante-Cardenal*, p.98.
17 Aedo, *Viaje del Infante-Cardenal*, p.99.
18 Aedo, *Viaje del Infante-Cardenal*, p.104.

Plate 1 Spanish arquebusier and Sargento Mayor Escobar
(Illustration by Sergey Shamenkov © Helion & Company 2021)
See Colour Plate Commentaries for further information.

i

Plate 2 Italian musketeer and pikeman, in the defence of the redoubts of Albuch Hill.
(Illustration by Sergey Shamenkov © Helion & Company 2021)
See Colour Plate Commentaries for further information.

Plate 3 German cuirasser and Croatian trooper
(Illustration by Sergey Shamenkov © Helion & Company 2021)
See Colour Plate Commentaries for further information.

iii

Plate 4 Imperial musketeer and Bavarian officer prior to the attack on Lachberg Hill.
(Illustration by Sergey Shamenkov © Helion & Company 2021)
See Colour Plate Commentaries for further information.

Plate 5 Swedish cavalry trooper
(Illustration by Sergey Shamenkov © Helion & Company 2021)
See Colour Plate Commentaries for further information.

Plate 6 Swedish Musketeer
(Illustration by Sergey Shamenkov © Helion & Company 2021)
See Colour Plate Commentaries for further information.

Plate 7 Two jubilant German infantrymen reach the redoubt at the top of the Allbuch.
(Illustration by Sergey Shamenkov © Helion & Company 2021)
See Colour Plate Commentaries for further information.

vii

Plate 8 The Cardinal-Infante
(Illustrations by Sergey Shamenkov © Helion & Company 2021)
See Colour Plate Commentaries for further information.

THE PATH OF THE CARDINAL-INFANTE

On a large esplanade, while it was raining a great storm, all the units of the Cardinal-Infante's army formed up.[19] The cavalry force of the Hispanic army had 700 riders in 10 companies of Neapolitan cavalry under the command of the count of Ayala, 587 riders in seven companies of Burgundian cavalry under the command of Count de la Tour, 500 men in eight companies of Lombard cavalry commanded by the Marquess Florencio, and finally the 230 men from the two escort companies of the Cardinal-Infante, commanded of Marquis de Orani. In addition, there were 500 dragons divided into five companies.

Turning to the infantry, there was a Tercio of Spanish infantry, under the command of the *maestre de campo* Martín de Idiáquez, with a total of 1,800 soldiers in 26 companies; a Tercio of Spanish infantry commanded by *maestre de campo* Enrique de Alagón, Count of Fuenclara, with 1,450 troops in 17 companies, from the Tercios of Naples and Lombardy; a Tercio of Neapolitans commanded by *maestre de campo* Prince San Sivero, which had 24 companies in 1,900 men; the Neapolitan Tercio of the *maestre de campo* Gaspar de Toralto, with 10 companies and 750 soldiers; the Neapolitan Tercio of the *maestre de campo* Pedro de Cárdenas, with 13 companies and 950 infantrymen; the Lombard Tercio of the *maestre de campo* Marques of Lunato, with 15 companies and 1,300 soldiers; a Lombard Tercio called Prince Doria, of which Carlos Guasco was the *maestre de campo*, with 12 companies and 1,000 troops, and finally, the company of Swiss and other nations, commanded by Captain Rafel Sachi, with only 90 men.

The Hispanic Army had 2,017 cavalrymen in 26 companies, 9,240 infantrymen in seven Tercios and 118 companies, and 500 dragoons, in five companies of 100 men each. When the muster was taken, the whole army was paid a month's wages, and 2,000 suits of clothes, shoes, ammunition and hats were distributed among them. Since the payments were made on a regular basis as well as being well fed, the Hispanic Army was always well stocked and no episodes of desertion or disorder were reported.[20]

The Marquis of Leganés was appointed the Lieutenant-General. The cavalry general was Filippo Spinola, Marquis of the Balbases and the artillery general was Giovanni Serbelloni, Count of Castiglione; the *maestre de campo general* was the Duke of Nochera, and the *tenientes de maestre de campo general* were Pedro de León, Juan de Padilla and Tiberio Brancacio.[21] The Hispanic Army was a small, but very experienced force, with highly qualified and very well-trained soldiers and officers.

On 19 August the Hispanic Army left Kufstein, stopped overnight in Flintsbach, where commissioners sent by the Duke of Bavaria were waiting to arrange their accommodation. News was received that King Ferdinand had recaptured Donauwörth, and the Protestant Army had retreated to the other side of the Danube. The Spaniards set off for Bad Aibling, where they stopped

---

19 Aedo, *Viaje del Infante-Cardenal*, p.104.
20 Aedo, *Viaje del Infante-Cardenal*, pp.100–102.
21 Moreover, Cardinal-Infante counted in his entourage former *maestres de campo* and reformed higher ranking officers, as well as 25 reformed captains, who served as liaison officers between the Cardinal-Infante's staff and the units of his army (Aedo, *Viaje del Infante-Cardenal*, p.103).

for three days to reorganise their troops. There they received news from the King of Hungary informing them that he had laid siege to Nördlingen. On 24 August, the Cardinal-Infante named the Neapolitan Paulo Dentichi as cavalry lieutenant general.

The Spaniards spent the next night in Putzbrunn, where an urgent message was received from the King of Hungary urging them to meet at Nördlingen, as Horn and Weimar's forces had joined forces and set out to liberate the city. For that reason, the King urged his cousin Fernando to march quickly and to meet him in Donauwörth on 29 August.[22]

On 25 August the Cardinal-Infante left Putzbrunn towards Munich and about 2 km from the city, was greeted by Duke Charles of Lorraine, accompanied by 200 *chevaliers*. Both princes rode to a great plain on the outskirts of the Bavarian capital, where the last units of the former army of the Duke of Feria awaited them, who had gathered a few days earlier to wait for the arrival of Cardinal-Infante. There were formed the cavalry regiment of the Prince of San Sivero, the Neapolitan Tercios of Gaspar de Toralto and Pedro de Cárdenas, the Lombard tercio of Paniguerola and the German regiments of Count of Salm and Wurmser. Across a bridge on an adjacent plain was the Neapolitan Tercio of the Marquis of Torrecusa.

The Cardinal-Infante's entourage entered the streets of Munich, decorated to receive a Prince of Spain, and in the city's main square a Bavarian regiment formed up and fired 3 musket salvoes in his honour.[23]

To summarise, the Hispanic Army in Munich had 3,250 Spaniards in two Tercios; 4,550 Neapolitans in four Tercios; 3,100 Lombards in three Tercios; 4,640 Germans in several regiments, adding up to a total of 15,540 infantrymen. The cavalry was divided into two detachments of 1,080 horsemen in 23 companies led by Lieutenant General Gerardo Gambacorta and 2,017 horsemen in 26 companies by Lieutenant General Paulo Dentichi, including the two companies of the Cardinal-Infante's Guard. To this were added 500 dragoons and 10 pieces of artillery (of various types including culverins, field cannons and falconets), as well as hundreds of powder carts, bullets and cannon shot, ropes, fuses, match, tools, pontoons, and everything needed for the artillery train, together with the gunners, engineers and sappers.[24]

On 26 August the army left Munich marching towards Dachau with provisions for five days. The next day a forced march took place, which placed the army eight kilometres from Augsburg, in the town of Blumendael. The whole region that the army was passing through had been ransacked by Protestant and Catholic armies alike, and the few people they encountered

---

22 Aedo, *Viaje del Infante-Cardenal*, p.107.
23 Aedo, *Viaje del Infante-Cardenal*, p.107. The detail of the forces was as follows: the Neapolitan Tercio of the Marquis of Torrecusa (15 companies, 950 men), the Lombard Tercio of the Count of Paniguerola (12 companies, 800 men), the German regiment of the Count of Salm (11 companies, 2,400 men), the German regiment of Colonel Wurmser (10 companies, 2,150 men), Neapolitan and Lombard cavalry of Lieutenant General Gambacorta (18 companies, 630 men) and Burgundian cavalry of the Count of Alberg (5 companies, 450 men) (Mesa, *Nördlingen*, p.17).
24 Aedo, *Viaje del Infante-Cardenal*, p.110.

THE PATH OF THE CARDINAL-INFANTE

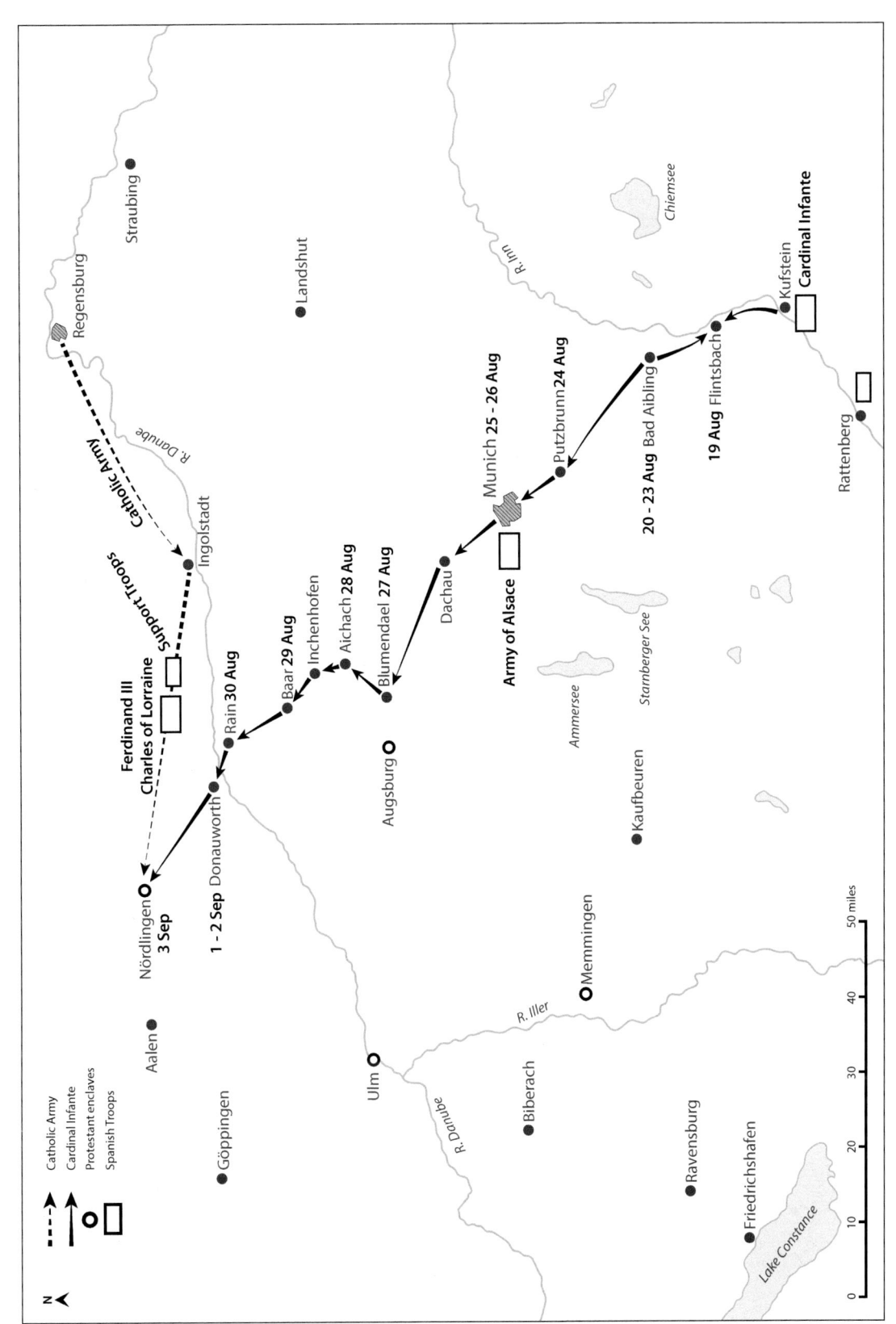

Map 2 The Cardinal-Infante's advance through Germany.

99

were 'starving and having no bones, such as shadows, and we were walking in a desert'.[25]

To prevent any Protestant attack, when the Prince's entourage was billeted, the infantry formed up on a nearby hill all night, with a thousand riders deployed as a protective screen between the camp and the town of Augsburg. An urgent message from the King of Hungary arrived that night informing the Cardinal-Infante that the enemy had retreated to a hill, about a two hours march from Cardinal-Infante's camp. The Protestants were entrenched and waiting for Cratz's and Württemberg's troops. The next day, the Hispanic Army marched ahead in case the enemy planned to attack.[26]

On August 29, Cardinal-Infante was visited by an emissary of the King of Hungary, the Spanish Colonel Contreras, with a message again emphasising the urgency that the two Catholic armies should meet. The next day Hispanic army marched north, parallel to the Lech River, across it at the town of Rain, and then also across the Danube through the town of Donauwörth. The Marquis of Grana, emissary of the King of Hungary, was waiting for them there, explaining that Württemberg's forces numbered 6,000 soldiers and Cratz had 4,000 men, and that Protestants had managed to get a 250 men into Nördlingen as reinforcements. The Marquis of Grana also provided a map showing the location of the two Catholic armies deployed in the vicinity of Nördlingen, so that they did not hinder each but were close enough to provide mutual supporting.[27]

The Marquis also reported the rumour that it was running around the Imperial camp, about an alleged Protestant prisoner who claimed he had heard how Bernard of Saxe-Weimar had disparagedly commented that 'in the King of Hungary's favour there were only four or five thousand Spaniards and barefoot Italians, and he, as a valiant general, requested that they be given a day to confront them, so that they could be beaten and not leave any alive'. Whether the allegation was true or not, the news spread throughout the Hispanic camp, and the outrage was so great that the Spanish soldier swore that 'they would become acquainted with General Weimar, and that the Spaniards would do with him and his army what he said he would do with them'.[28]

Despite the urgency, the Hispanic Army remained at Donauwörth for two days, because it was necessary to bake bread and distribute it among the troops as supplies had run low. Meanwhile, *maestres de campo* Martin de Idiáquez and Cheri de la Reyna marched on to Nördlingen to reconnoitre the terrain that had been assigned as camps for the Hispanic Army. They even went close to view the Swedish-German camp, which they found strong and well supplied.[29]

On 2 September, the Hispanic Army left Donauwörth, led by the cavalry and infantry to the rear. Halfway through the march, Sancho de Monroy y

---

25 Aedo, *Viaje del Infante-Cardenal*, p.112.
26 Aedo, *Viaje del Infante-Cardenal*, p.111.
27 Aedo, *Viaje del Infante-Cardenal*, p.112.
28 Aedo, *Viaje del Infante-Cardenal*, p.113.
29 Aedo, *Viaje del Infante-Cardenal*, p.113.

THE PATH OF THE CARDINAL-INFANTE

Zúñiga, Marquis of Castañeda and ambassador of Spain to Vienna, arrived to present his respects to the Cardinal-Infante and introduce the retinue of the King of Hungary, who was waiting for them at a kilometre before the Imperial camp.

Indeed, King Ferdinand was waiting for Prince Fernando, with Generals Picolomini and Matias de Medici, the great master of the Teutonic Order, Johann Kaspar de Stadion, as well as all the commanders and personalities of the Imperial Army. When the two Princes saw each other, at a distance of about 100 steps, the two simultaneously dismounted and hurried closer to embrace, between shouts of joy from those present. The two Princes were double cousins, that is, they were first-degree cousins, because Emperor Ferdinand II of Habsburg, the father of Ferdinand III, was the brother of Margarita of Austria, mother of the and Cardinal-Infante, wife of King Philip III of Spain; they were also cousins through the male line being descendants of Philip I of Castile and Joana I of Castile. In addition, they were brothers-in-law, since Ferdinand of Habsburg was married to Maria Ana of Spain, the sister of Cardinal-Infante and King Philip IV.[30]

Arriving near the main Imperial camp, one kilometre from Nördlingen, General Gallas received them. He had remained in command of the army, while the Imperial retinue marched to receive the Cardinal-Infante.

The two Ferdinand's were alone in a luxurious tent for a good while, having lunch with the two army commanders. Later, Cardinal-Infante and his entourage visited the area of their camp, from which the enemy camp at Bopfingen could be seen perched on a hill to the northwest, about two hours away.[31]

---

30   Aedo, *Viaje del Infante-Cardenal*, p.114.
31   Aedo, *Viaje del Infante-Cardenal*, p.115.

6

Movements around Nördlingen

At dawn on 3 September a heavy bombardment began on the city, with four medium cannons and eight culverins, distributed in three batteries. The King of Hungary sought out the Cardinal-Infante at the Spanish camp, wishing to see the Catholic army deployed and formed up by the trenches. The Imperial cavalry and infantry units were standing to arms, while the Catholic League troops waited a little further behind, also deployed in combat formation. While the King was telling the Cardinal-Infante where to deploy his army, Hispanic troops began to form up into squadrons with those of the League, so when he had finished reviewing the German troops, the Cardinal-Infante invited the King of Hungary to review the Hispanic Army.[1]

At the end of the morning, the Duke of Lorraine arrived at the Catholic camp, in order to assume the supreme command of the League Army.[2] In the afternoon, the main Catholic commanders[3] gathered in the Cardinal-Infante's tent to receive information on the total number of troops in the army and to coordinate their actions for the following days. It would not be an easy task, given the diversity and heterogenous nature of the units in the three armies. And, in addition, tensions between them existed, and there was rivalry when it came to deciding which regiments would lead the assaults and, therefore, be in a better position when it came to the distribution of loot.

Throughout the day and night, the Catholic artillery bombarded the town. The *fausse-brague* parapet was noted to be 20 feet high, so very tall ladders would be needed to overcome that obstacle. Hence, on the following day, 4 September, the Catholic artillery fired at the base of the *fausse-brague*, with the objective of causing a breach and collapsing the fortification.[4]

On the morning of 4 September, Imperial Lieutenant General Gallas sent a messenger to the city, commanding them to surrender, threatening that otherwise they would destroy them in 'fire and blood.' The Protestants

---

1 Aedo, *Viaje del Infante-Cardenal*, pp.115–116.
2 Aedo, *Viaje del Infante-Cardenal*, p.116.
3 The King Ferdinand, Generals Gallas and Piccolomini for the Imperial Army; the Cardinal-Infante, Leganés, Balbases and Serbelloni, for the Hispanic Army; Lorena, Fugger and Tiefenbach, for the Catholic League Army (Mesa, *Nördlingen*, p.23).
4 Aedo, *Viaje del Infante-Cardenal*, p.117.

signalled with smoke to notify the Swedish-German camp, telling them how much time they had to rescue them, and they answered with two cannon shots, thus indicating that they had to ask for two more days to gain time. But the Catholic commander did not grant two days but instead demanded to have the answer within two hours. The deadline passed, and the city's defenders did not respond, so the order to assault was given, to be carried out on three sides. Two were carried out by the Imperial troops and the Burgundian regiment of Count of Alberg,[5] while Catholic League soldiers attacked on the other side. The three assaults were repulsed after three hours of combat, which cost the Catholics 500 casualties.[6] The Catholics took their ladders and went down into the moat, then climbed the *fausse-brague*, but could not take it. During the assault, Burgundian soldiers were able to temporarily occupy a defence tower, but the Protestants set fire to it and the Burgundians had to retreat.[7]

In the Swedish-German camp they were aware of the events in Nördlingen. Their scouts reported the bombarding of the city and the furious assault on it. Furthermore, during the siege, on at least three occasions a messenger named Adam Jäcklin von Krauthausen (a native of the nearby town of Goldburghausen) managed to cross the Catholic lines and reach the Swedish camp. That is why on the night of 4 September the Protestant senior commanders held a tense council of war. Horn first spoke of the situation in the city and in the camp. He emphasised the numerical superiority of Catholic forces in a ratio of 3 to 2, accounting as well for the advantage of having fortified positions. According to his reasoning, if the Spanish Cardinal-Infante's troops left to march on Flanders, then the forces would become equal, and if their own reinforcements of Cratz (3,400 men) and the Rhinegrave (6,000 troops), then the Protestant Army could face battle with numerical superiority. They needed the city of Nördlingen to resist until their reinforcements arrived. The Swedish general preferred to preserve his army and to sacrifice the city if necessary.[8]

The Duke of Franconia did not agree with these arguments. Bernard asserted that it would be a cowardice not to fight and leave the city to its fate. According to him, they had already lost the strategic initiative, the Catholics had snatched from them two other important cities, and for that reason their cause would be lost, militarily and politically, if they withdrew from Nördlingen. Bernard despised the Spaniards,[9] saying that their small numbers (according to his intelligence there were about 7,000 troops, both infantry and cavalry), would not be as much of a threat that Horn claimed. Bernard agreed with Horn that they had to wait for Cratz but added that they

---

5   Mesa, *Nördlingen*, p.24.
6   A Spanish source indicates that the combats lasted until five hours and with 300 injured people and 'many dead men' (Anonymous, *Sucesos de 1634*, p.44).
7   Aedo, *Viaje del Infante-Cardenal*, p.118.
8   Guthrie, *Batallas*, p.377.
9   This is described by the English captain Sydnam Poyntz, who states that Bernard 'swore that he would send the proud Spaniards back to Spain with all their plagues' (Poyntz, *Relations*, p.109).

THE BATTLE OF NÖRDLINGEN 1634

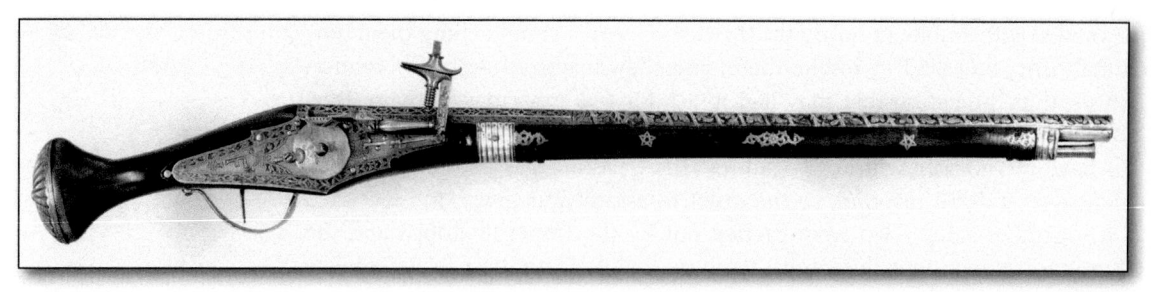

Wheellock Pistol (c1625–1630), from Italy, probably Brescia, made from steel, silver and wood. This pistol bears the emblems of the Duke of Feria, as was the previously mentioned reinforcement breastplate. Its dimensions are as follows: length 73.9cm; barrel length 55.7cm; weight 1.400kg. The wheellock was the next major development after the matchlock, developed in Europe around 1500, it was used alongside the matchlock and was later superseded by the snaplock (1540s), the snaphance (1560s) and the flintlock (c1610s). The operation of the wheellock consisted of a friction mechanism to fire it. This type of weapon was widely used by the cavalry of all armies, as well as more wealthy officers in combat. (Metropolitan Museum of Art, 14.25.1426)

could do battle without waiting for the Rhinegrave. After a vote, Bernard's plan was adopted.[10]

The Protestant operation plan was to cut through the Catholic supply line from Donauwörth, avoiding a frontal attack on heavily fortified siege positions south of the city.[11] They were confident that if the Imperial supplies were threatened, the Catholics would be forced to raise the siege to prevent their men from starving. To put this into practice, they would have to occupy the hills south of Nördlingen, so the Catholics would have to either retreat or charge up the hill to evict the Swedish-German Army.[12]

The surprise factor was essential, and Protestants wanted to convince Catholics that their intention was to retreat, so that they could move southwest of Nördlingen without being discovered. For this reason, the Protestant forces would march south, to the hamlet of Neresheim, where they would join Cratz and leave their luggage and supplies. Then they would turn north, towards one of the swamps in the Swabian Jura Range (*Schwäbischer Jura*), a wooded plateau locally known as Arnsberg, south of the Eger River.

To the east of the road, the path descended through a gorge, then up again towards the Nördlingen area. Much of this land was broken by streams and ravines, with a U-shaped mountain range perpendicular to the Eger

---

10   Guthrie, *Batallas*, p.370.
11   This is stated by Delbruck, who tells us that the plan was to hinder the Catholic supply route from Donauwörth, while ensuring the Protestant route on the Ulm-Nördlingen axis. In making this great flanking movement, the Duke of Franconia moved a little closer to the city than Horn had expected. Bernard had to consider that, if he got closer to the city and to the Catholic camps, the pressure on the Catholic Army would be greater. The subsequent battle of Nördlingen would have occurred unintentionally, if not because the Catholics positioned themselves in the Albuch, hindering the march of Horn's troops, who, to continue their plan to cut the enemy supply line, had no other option except to attack the hill. However, knowing Bernard's military temperament and skill, Delbruck maintains the hypothesis that Bernard deliberately provoked the battle by approaching so close to the Catholic camp, since his intention was to capture the hills that dominated the Nördlingen plain and fired the Catholic positions. According to Delbruck, Bernard 'was aware that in that way he would start the battle and forced his reluctant colleague in the high command to enter the battle against their will, because he knew that the situation in Nördlingen was already desperate and that the city could fall anytime'. (Delbruck, *Dawn of modern warfare*, pp.210–211).
12   Delbruck, *Dawn of modern warfare*, p.211; Guthrie, *Batallas*, p.377.

river about eight kilometres long and consisting of nine hills. From the western part of the U, there was, from north to south of Himmelreich, the westernmost hill, Ländle, the forest, and Lachberg. Further east, at the bend of the U, were the wooded hills of Heselberg and Albuch, and at the eastern apex, from south to north, were the Schönfeld Hills adjoining the Albuch, Adlenberg, Staffelberg and Galgenberg, the small hill, near Nördlingen. Of all these hills, there were three that had a prominent position in controlling the entire valley, the Heselberg, Albuch, and Schönfeld hills. In the centre of the mountain range was the Herkheimerfeld Plain, with the villages, from north to south, of Hohlheim, Ederheim and Hürnheim, both of the latter two on the banks of the Rezenbach River, and parallel to these, the hamlets of Herkheim, Reimlingen and Schmähingen. Finally, as a reversed 'V', were the roads from Nördlingen to Ulm, to the west, and from Nördlingen to Augsburg, to the east, with Nördlingen itself as the point of the 'V'.[13]

However, the Protestant Army's knowledge of the topography of the terrain was not entirely complete, so after the war council Horn ordered a cavalry detachment, at the command of the Chief of the Intendance General, Morschauser, to reconnoitre the ground. However, ignorance of the terrain,[14] darkness, and the presence of Croatian scouts and Imperial dragoons, hovering around the Arnsberg Massif and in the town of Uzmemingen, made it difficult for Morschauser to conduct a thorough reconnaissance. Upon returning to camp, Morschauser informed Bernard and Horn that the terrain south of Nördlingen was 'a large hill,' when in fact there were several parallel hills, which encircled the plain.[15]

---

13   Guthrie, *Batallas*, p.378.
14   The Swedes believed that the zone of the Arnsberg was much more extensive of that really it was, and that spread much more to the north and to the west. They did not identify the hills placed in the southwest of Nördlingen, thinking that it was about only one mountain, either correctly. As a matter of fact, in the relation of the battle, Horn referred to the Albuch as if it were the Arnsberg (Guthrie, *Batallas*, p.378).
15   Guthrie, *Batallas*, p.378.

7

The Battle

As is usual in the study of any battle, the sources available to historians are often incomplete, or biased or generally unreliable, either because they are indirect sources, or because the witnesses were only able to narrate what they little observed and were unable to comment on the 'big picture'.

To describe the Battle of Nördlingen, I will mainly follow the narrative by William P. Guthrie,[1] reinforced by accounts from Spanish[2] chronicles and other authors.[3]

Movements of 5 September

On the night of the 5th, the Swedish-German army struck camp and began their march.[4] Meanwhile, in the morning, the besieged garrison sent a messenger to Gallas requesting a parley and asked for two days to wait for the Swedish-German force to relieve them, or else they would agree to surrender.[5] Gallas answered by giving them only one hour to surrender. The messenger left and after a while returned with the response that the city would not surrender, so the makeshift truce was concluded and the bombardment of the town began.[6]

In the morning there was a council of war in the tent of the King of Hungary in which the commanders of the three armies participated. The experience of the Spaniards in siege warfare influenced the decision to continue working on the construction of batteries and trenches, with the

---

1 Guthrie, *Batallas*, pp.363–404.
2 Aedo, *Viaje, suceso y guerras del Infante Cardenal de Fernando de Austria*; Cánovas, *Estudios del reinado de Felipe IV*; De Vera, *Victoria sobre Norlinga*.
3 Engerisser, *Von Kronach nach Nördlingen*; Hrncirik, *Spanier auf dem Albuch*; Mesa, *Nördlingen 1634*.
4 Cánovas, *Estudios*, p.427. Approximately, 5 a.m. (Guthrie, *Batallas*, p.378).
5 The burgomaster of Nördlingen, Johannes Mayer, left evidence of the facts experienced by the inhabitants of the town. He reports that they had to cook bread made with a mix of whatever cereals they could find and that they ate cats and dogs. He himself recognised that he had to eat from the piles of cow manure. (Rucker, *Die Entscheidungsschlacht bei Nördlingen*, p.11).
6 Cánovas, *Estudios*, p.419.

THE BATTLE

Battlefield (1659), by Peeter Snayers, the great master of battle painting. The observer notes the harsh realities after the battle, with the victors stripping the bodies of the dead, undressing them without any shame. They finish off the dying to steal their belongings and sometimes disputes arose over taking the best loot with the result that those who were previously friends fought over boots, a coat, or a sword. (Kunsthistorisches Museum, Gemäldegalerie, 773)

intention that they should reach the ditch surrounding the city and once there, the sappers would bridge it with fascines to facilitate the assault.[7]

King Ferdinand ordered the Cardinal-Infante to send 1,000 Spanish infantrymen assault one side of the city walls, while the Imperial troops attacked on the other. These troops, under the command of the *teniente de maestre de campo general* Pedro de León,[8] would consist of 100 Spaniards of the Tercio of Idiáquez, 100 Spaniards of the Tercio of Count of Fuenclara, 100 Neapolitans of the Tercio of the Prince of San Sivero, 100 Neapolitans of the Tercio of the Marquis de Torrecusa, 300 Germans of Count Salm's regiment and another 300 of the German Wurmser's regiment.

However, because all that was needed for the assault (fascines, earthbags, stone, gabions) could not be made available for that afternoon, the assault was postponed until the following day and the bombardment of the city continued for another day.[9]

---

7 The Spanish commanders recommended that the trenches reach the ditch to prevent the infantry, as had happened in the previous attack, from crowding into the upper edge of the ditch before crossing it to assault the walls, so they would not be easy targets for the guns and muskets of the garrison. The Spaniards proposed that mobile parapets (called *espaldas*, 'backs') be available to cover the advance through the ditch until they reached the other side (Anónimo, *Sucesos de 1634*, p.44).

8 Aedo, *Viaje del Infante-Cardenal*, p.120; Cánovas, *Estudios*, p.419; De Vera, *Victoria sobre Norlinga*, p.102.

9 Aedo, *Viaje del Infante-Cardenal*, p.120.

THE BATTLE OF NÖRDLINGEN 1634

In the morning the regiments which the Cardinal-Infante had asked for as reinforcements, joined the Hispanic camp in the shape of the two Burgundian Tercios of the Counts La Tour and Alberg, the German regiment of Leslie, as well as the cavalry of Baron Sebach. The Cardinal-Infante now had around an army of 17,000 infantry, 3,900 cavalry and 500 dragoons.

At about 11.00 a.m. during preparations for the Catholic assault on Nördlingen, news came from Croatian scouts that the Protestants were on the move, but the messages were contradictory as some claimed that the Protestants were preparing to do battle, others claimed that they were preparing for to march away or even moving by force into the city.[10]

The news caused the preparations to attack the city to be halted. The Catholics did not know what the Swedish-German objectives were, if their plan was to outflank the Catholics and attack the besieging army outside Nördlingen, or to leave the area and withdraw towards Ulm, this latter being the option supported by many officers.[11]

When a new message from the Croatian scouts reported that the enemy was coming down from the hills, Gallas ordered a general alarm to be sounded at all the camps, including that of the Imperial cavalry which was dispersed in a more distant camp. All units were formed up at their muster points. Meanwhile, the Catholic high command held another council of war[12] headed by Count Gallas, as Commander-in-Chief of the Imperial Army and by the Marquis de Leganés, as *maestre de campo general* of the Spanish Army. The council decided that the army would be divided into three blocks, the left under the Spanish, the centre commanded by the Catholic League and the right made up of Imperial troops.[13]

More messages came from the Croats, saying that the Swedish-German Army had left the road to Ulm and turned into some woods, in the direction of the Hispanic Army's camp.[14]

The Duke of Lorraine, Gallas, the Marquesses of Leganés and Balbases and the rest of the other major commanders went to reconnoitre the place where they supposed the enemy army would deploy.[15] The Catholic commanders were surprised that the Swedish-German army advanced toward them, with the intention of engaging in battle. In the words of the Spanish chronicler Aedo, this was due to the pride of Duke Bernard of Saxe-Weimar:

> But they still did not believe that the enemy wanted to come to battle, by the great forces together, King Ferdinand, His Highness Fernando and Duke Charles. But the arrogance of Saxe-Weimar was so great, that he thought the Imperial Army was very little and inexperienced, as it had been shown on previous occasions

---

10 Aedo, *Viaje del Infante-Cardenal*, pp.119–120. The Croatians interrogated two enemies that they had captured in a skirmish among scouts and they confessed that the intention of the Protestant command was to attack the Catholic army (Mesa, *Nördlingen*, p.24).
11 De Vera, *Victoria sobre Norlinga*, p.104.
12 De Vera, *Victoria sobre Norlinga*, p.104.
13 De Vera, *Victoria sobre Norlinga*, p.104.
14 Aedo, *Viaje del Infante-Cardenal*, p.121.
15 Aedo, *Viaje del Infante-Cardenal*, p.121.

and about the army which carried His Highness Ferdinand also spoke with great contempt.[16]

On their way back to Catholic camp, the generals deployed the army taking into account the terrain and their mustering points. As a result, Imperial and League troops deployed on the plains closest to Nördlingen, around the Galgenberg hill. The Hispanic army marched onto the hills (Landle, Lachberg and Heselberg) at the front of its camp.[17] The Imperialists made us of the time to dig trenches in certain parts of the plain to better protect their infantry. Many warnings came from the Croatians scouts, which did not however specify the exact place where the Protestants would attack.[18]

The King of Hungary and the Cardinal-Infante embraced one another and headed for their respective forces. Accompanied by his entourage, the young Fernando de Austria arrived at the place where the Tercios and cavalry squadrons of the Hispanic army were formed. The troops, seeing the young Prince, burst into tears of joy. The Cardinal-Infante, in silver armour, with a red sash and the baton of a Spanish general, addressed his men with these words:

> The day has arrived, valiant Spaniards, Italians, Walloons and Germans, to fight against those whom we have sought so gallantly. Many facts have caused this formidable army to be in Germany. I have no time or need to refer your exploits, as I see them written on your faces and I look forward to seeing them practiced from your swords.
>
> I just remind you that in you the Heaven is entrusted to fight for the defence and glory of his Church. God knows that none of us does not seek to prevail Catholic glory, even if it costs us all our blood.
>
> I remind you to defend the hereditary states[19] – the birthplace and origin of our King and also the dignity and grandeur of the Empire. Now you have the opportunity to help the Empire. The value of the Spaniards was admired by Germania in 1617,[20] and many of you demonstrated it in 1633 and now you will prove it again,[21] because you will do it for me, commanding you on the battlefield.[22]

---

16 Aedo, *Viaje del Infante-Cardenal*, pp.121–122.
17 Aedo, *Viaje del Infante-Cardenal*, p.122; Guthrie, *Batallas*, p.378.
18 Aedo, *Viaje del Infante-Cardenal*, p.122.
19 It was about the *Erbländer*, the hereditary territories, the patrimonial provinces of the Habsburg family (Parker, *Guerra*, p.5; Borreguero, *Guerra*, pp.63–67).
20 It refers to the conflicts experienced during the War of the Uskoks and the conflict over the succession of the Monferrato. For the Uskoks' conflict: Borreguero, *Guerra*, pp. 132–140; Bracewell, *The Uskoks of Senj*; Caimi, *Guerra de Friuli*; Nider, *Relación verdadera*, pp.43–159; Parker, *Guerra*, pp.53–56; Reberski, *El duque de Osuna*, pp.45–46 y pp.300–351; Tenenti, *Venezia e i corsari*; Todesco, *Gli Uscocchi*; Tordesillas, *Relación verdadera*; Vigato, *Guerra Veneto-Archiducale*; Wilson, *The Thirty Years War*, pp.193–196. For the Monferrato's conflict: Merlin, *Monferrato* pp.15–30; Perez, *The Question Of Monferrato*; Wilson, *The Thirty Years War*, pp.131–136.
21 It refers to the campaign of the Duke of Feria.
22 Young Fernando refers to the fact that for his soldiers, fighting at the orders of the brother of the King of Spain should be a source of pride. That is why Fernando expected his soldiers to fight as bravely as they had done a few months earlier, during the Duke of Feria's campaign.

On our part is justice, there is the strength and there are the merits of the most religious Emperor, who is my uncle.[23] And God has sometimes placed the Emperor in extreme situations, but God has always rescued him, proving that he has the support of the Divine.

The army you have to fight begins to appear there, at the exit of the forest in front of you; I do not deny that most of those troops are soldiers from valiant nations. But you are used to defeating this kind of man and these are the descendants of soldiers who your parents have overcome in other conflicts. And now they are trying to take away from you the prestige of being the best men in the Orb.[24]

But the deeds of the dead King of Sweden in this war may seem very successful. But I will tell you the truth and I will tell you that this king, who was indeed very skilled in war and his very brave person,[25] but he was really fortunate as some traitors helped him during his campaign and he was helped by some subjects of the Empire who were forced to oppose him. Those traitors were German subjects of the Empire and also people of France. And I tell you that I know that cities and fortresses surrendered treacherously in just 10 days, because they were traitors, because they had weapons and supplies that would help them endure a siege for 10 years. So, what glory should the Swedish armies deserve?

The reality is that the Swedish King was discouraged and could resist because he had many, many mercenary soldiers. And I tell you, people are confused: you cannot say that there is a great victory when there has been no defence. And with that there is no glory. Keep in mind that when the Swedes faced the brave 'Popenaynes',[26] and others like them, see how the Swedes got scalded and wanted to negotiate. Remember how the Swedish King, when he knew that 1,500 Spaniards marched to help the defence of Mainz, was frightened.

From your experience you will know, my dear soldiers, that many victories were achieved not so much by self-worth as by alien weakness. This is the day that Protestants must taste your pikes and swords. And these will be your tools with which you will make known to the world the value of each nation. So, show your courage, soldiers who have crossed with me in the Alps.

And if anyone is scared, I remind him that when someone wants to save his life, he actually risks it more when he turns his back on the enemy to retreat. And if you seek remedy in cowardice to save your life, then you will find danger in the escape. In a battle like this, the humble soldier only gets on the path of life when he is not afraid of death; because the wounds he receives in the back, as well as being infamous, are more dangerous. Yes, because the sword wounds on his back, because it has no opposition, even if it wields a weak arm, has no resistance and is even more cruel.

---

23 Cardinal-Infante's mother was Margarita, sister of Emperor Ferdinand II.
24 Thus, the Cardinal-Infante alludes that the Swedes have a reputation for invincibility and thus have displaced the Spaniards from the heights of military hegemony.
25 In spite of the ideological differences and the victories won against the Catholic armies, Gustavus Adolphus was a King and, therefore, deserving of the honour and respect that any sovereign was due.
26 He refers to Gottfried von Pappenheim (1594–1632), who fought in White Mountain, Breitenfeld and Lutzen, where he met his death. His operations on the Rhine and the Wesser damaged the Swedes communication lines.

THE BATTLE

The Cardinal-Infante Ferdinand of Austria, by Jan van der Hoecke (c1634–1635). The young Fernando wears 'three quarters' armour, which protects his body and legs, was bulletproof and expensive. He wears high cavalry boots, a rapier sword, the typical red sash of the soldiers of the Hispanic monarchy and a general's baton. Before Nordlingen, Fernando had never participated in battle, but since childhood he had dreamed of emulating the actions of his ancestor Charles V, the last of the Habsburg rulers who had fought in person. Since then, the Spanish kings left their generals to command in battle. (Kunsthistorisches Museum, GG_699)

Think that through my eyes the King, my Lord and my brother, are seeing you and that for you and the families you leave in Spain and Italy, you will immediately receive a reward for your actions. Do not doubt that I know you all and that by your names I will encourage you in the heat of battle. And who is a coward, who is more afraid of my sword than that of the enemy. God forbid, that from the columns of Hercules[27] we have brought our honour and prestige to bury them and lose them in the fields of Nördlingen.

Finally, in front of us, we have a great army against whom to fight. And here, next to us, the troops of the King of Hungary, my cousin, with whom you have to compete for glory.

You are Spanish and Italian and I don't need any order to give you. You are very expert. Attack and tear down the Swedish standards. And fight in a friendly rivalry with the Imperial soldiers and try to precede in value the soldiers of the Emperor, my uncle.[28]

But, despite the apparent imminence of the battle, the Protestants did not appear. The Catholic army was formed up in combat formation for a few hours, but by late morning, reports from the Croat scouts indicated that the Protestants had marched further south. In response to this news the Catholic units broke ranks and went to rest and to find food lunch.[29]

Horn and Bernard's troops had continued south, arriving in the town of Neresheim at about 11.30 a.m.[30] There, according to plan, Cratz's detachment was waiting for them. Confident in their victory and because they needed to travel fast to move between the hills and forests, the Protestant command ordered their wagons with baggage to be sent around Neresheim. Half of the Württemberg militia companies were left behind to protect the baggage

---

27 The Columns of Hercules was the classical name for Straits of Gibraltar and symbolised the edge of the world since the Atlantic Ocean meant 'the unknown'.
28 De Vera, *Victoria Sobre Norlinga*, pp.108–120.
29 Cánovas, *Estudios*, p.428; Guthrie, *Batallas*, p.378; Poyntz, *relations*, p.109.
30 Guthrie, *Batallas*, p.378.

wagons, as they were considered to be unfit to take their place on the battlefield.[31]

The vanguard of the Swedish-German Army was led by Bernard, while Horn was at the centre and rear. They followed the route linking Neresheim with the villages of Kosingen and Schweindorf. There they changed course, beginning their approach march to Nördlingen to the northeast. Initially they were not detected by the Croats, as the Protestants marched through a forest-covered terrain that prevented the enemy scouts from discovering the exact path they were taking.[32]

The Marquis of Leganés had taken the precaution of setting up a protective screen of dragoons and harquebusiers. Gallas did the same in the other areas, where Croatian scouts and Imperial dragoons continued to patrol.[33] At about 3.00 p.m.[34] the vanguard of the troops of the Duke of Saxe-Weimar, formed by the Cratz Cavalry Regiment, was sighted by Imperial scouting parties,[35] and there were continuous skirmishes with the enemy involving the various scouting detachments (Butler and Pedro de Santacilia's dragoons; Croatian light cavalry and Imperial cuirassiers, commanded by Prior Aldrobandino, of the Order of Malta).[36]

These first exchanges became more intense as more units of both sides were committed, but the Protestant advance guard was gaining the upper hand due to its superior numbers. For the next hour or so the Catholics delayed their enemies, but gradually lost ground. The combat shifted from the woods of the Arnsberg to the Himmelreich hill. It was around 4.00 p.m. that the units of the Protestant army appeared in the woods near the Ulm Road,[37] west of Ederheim and near the Himmelreich hill. Following confirmation of the presence of the Swedish-German army, a general alarm was again sounded at all Catholic camps. The commanders and senior officers of the three armies – Imperial, Spanish and Bavarian – conferred on what actions

---

31 Guthrie, *Batallas*, p.378.
32 Cánovas, *Estudios*, p.419; Guthrie, *Batallas*, p.378; Poyntz, *Relations*, p.109.
33 Poyntz reports that while the infantry and cavalry returned to the camps, Colonel Butler ordered that his dragoon regiment remain in position, on guard, at a distance of half an English mile from the initial battle line of the Imperial army and that, in addition, he ordered Captains Poyntz and Burke to advance to a promontory to try to get visual contact with the enemy (Poyntz, *Relations*, p.109).
34 Cánovas, *Estudios*, p.428; Guthrie, *Batallas*, p.378.
35 Poyntz states that he and Burke left the regiment's formation and rode west. They reached a promontory and went down into a forest. There they located the tracks of a cavalry detachment, but they didn't know if it was from friends or enemies. They followed the trail and when they had been riding for 15 minutes, they heard the sound of drums and trumpets. They deduced that it was the enemy. Therefore, they advanced with caution until they reached the edge of a forest. There they saw, advancing through a large meadow, the vanguard of the Protestant army. The two captains rode swiftly to find their Colonel and explain the news. When they returned, the Colonel sent them to the tent of King Ferdinand to inform him first hand. The two officers arrived and explained to the Catholic high command what they had seen, but it seems they were not believed. It seems that the Catholic generals believed that the Protestants were marching towards Ulm. But after a while, another scout arrived informing them that the enemy was attacking Butler's dragoon regiment, confirming the truth about the route that Protestant army was following. (Poyntz, *Relations*, p.109).
36 De Vera, *Victoria sobre Norlinga*, p.124.
37 Poyntz, *Relations*, p.109.

THE BATTLE

to take and decided to redeploy, much as they had in the morning upon receiving the first news of the Protestant approach.[38]

The Cardinal-Infante and the Spanish generals, led by the Marquis of Leganés and the Marquis of Los Balbases, examined the terrain surrounding the Spanish camp. They seized on the importance of a grove in front of the Albuch hill and the Cardinal-Infante ordered that strategic position be defended.[39] It was the hill of Heselberg. The Marquis of Leganés, fulfilling his orders, sent Sergeant Major Escobar with 200 musketeers of the Tercio of Fuenclara, to take position in the woods.[40] Escobar took advantage of the little time he had to distribute his men through the woods, improvise parapets and familiarise himself with the surrounding terrain to ascertain where the enemy could attack him.[41]

Escobar found that the position of the forest was very likely to be the front line. But it was also a position of major importance, as it prevented the Protestants from storming the hill directly. Escobar requested reinforcements,[42] and Leganés sent him 200 Italian musketeers from the Tercio of Toralto, another 200 Burgundians and two dragoon companies.[43] At the same time the Count of Salm's regiment and 700 horse under the command of Gerardo Gambacorta was sent to occupy a 'hooked hill in the woods', as the Spanish chronicler initially described the Albuch hill.

Realising that the Catholics were preparing to face Himmelreich with their cavalry regiments, Bernard had to change the deployment of his vanguard. Thus, he deployed from march to battle formation. Cratz and Sattler's cavalry regiments deployed and immediately attacked their Catholic opponents on Himmelreich Hill, who retreated to Landle Hill. To delay the Swedish advance, the Imperial command sent more cavalry regiments (full units of Butler's Imperial dragoons, Aldobrandini's and Nicola Strozzi's cuirassiers regiments, as well as the harquebusier regiments of Colonels Saint-Martin, Tornetta and Binder.[44] The total number of Catholic horsemen approached 3,000 men, under the command of Piccolomini. In the hills a bloody battle was gaining momentum so more and more cavalry squadrons were being committed.[45]

The advance of Cratz's Protestant horse was stopped and broken by the Imperialists, but Cratz's men were rescued by the Courville cavalry regiment, which charged successfully at the Imperialists, causing them to withdraw in confusion. Bernard wanted to take advantage of this victory and, as his cavalry reached the front line, sent them immediately into battle. These were

---

38 Cánovas, *Estudios*, p.428; Guthrie, *Batallas*, p.378.
39 Aedo, *Viaje del Infante-Cardenal*, p.123.
40 Cánovas, *Estudios*, p.421.
41 Cánovas, *Estudios*, p.423.
42 Aedo states that it was the Cardinal-Infante himself who, valuing the strategic position of the forest, ordered Escobar to be reinforced (Aedo, *Viaje del Infante-Cardenal*, p.123).
43 Aedo, *Viaje del Infante-Cardenal*, p.123; Cánovas, *Estudios,* p.421. In the official Spanish account of the battle, it is recorded that they deployed 100 Spanish musketeers, 100 Italians and 200 Burgundians (Cánovas, *Studies*, p.429). One of the officers was the Englishman Poyntz (Poyntz, *Relations*, p.110) in command of the Imperial dragoons.
44 Hrncirik, *Spanier auf dem Albuch*, p.17.
45 Aedo, *Viaje del Infante-Cardenal*, p.122.

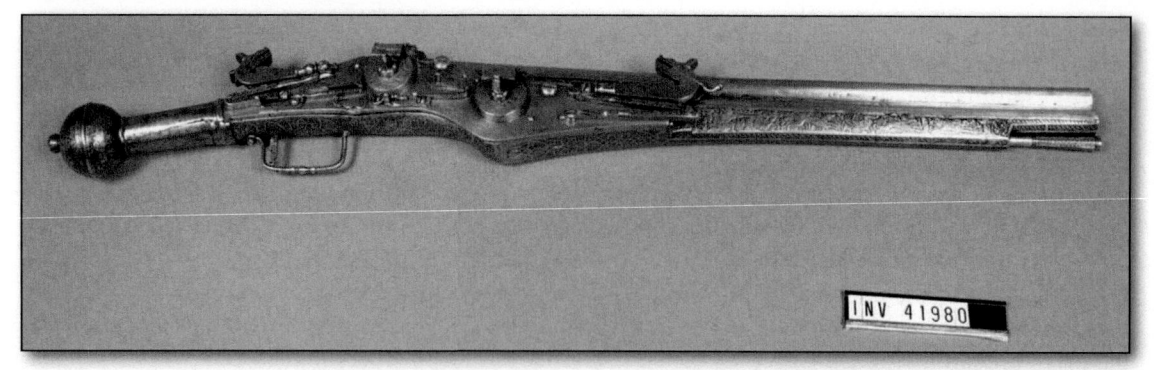

Cavalry pistol, with two wheel locks. Dating from the early seventeenth century, in Germany. The pistol is made entirely of iron with a front and rear facing wheel lock that has a single common trigger. The upper barrel is round with an octagonal chamber piece 18.8cm long. The lower barrel is completely round. The body is made of iron and is completely covered with engravings. The measurements are as follows: length 704mm; calibre 14.5mm; length 486mm; weight 2,880g. (Armémuseum, AM.041980)

the Öhm, Hofkirchen and Bodendorf cavalry regiments.[46] But Bernard had a problem. The hills and other terrain limited his ability to deploy in a coherent and continuous line. As they gained ground, the Protestants deployed the new units to their right to widen their front.[47] The Protestant cavalry were accompanied by musketeers, who fired on the retreating Catholic horsemen to speed them on their way.[48]

The battle between the cavalry was unusually violent and in the heat of the combat, Escobar left his cover with 80 musketeers to attack the Protestant cavalry, causing to them the 'loss of more than a hundred men'.[49]

Half an hour before sunset, the cavalry on both sides retreated, leaving dozens of dead and wounded on the field.[50] In total, more than 6,000 riders participated in this gigantic cavalry battle.[51] Bernard's Germans vanquished the Catholics on Landle Hill and later the Lachberg, but they took three hours to conquer these three westernmost hills.[52]

At around 6.30 p.m. the Protestant Army attacked again and began the battle for Heselberg. To assess the strength of the resistance of the Catholic position, the Duke of Franconia sent a musketeer detachment to reconnoitre the field.[53]

Bernard was determined to take that position and he ordered Major-General Johann Vitzthum von Eckstädt to capture Heselberg Hill. Von Eckstädt had to wait to move his infantry units into the front line and then ordered a joint infantry and cavalry attack against the forest.[54] Seeing the

---

46 Hrncirik, *Spanier auf dem Albuch*, p.16.
47 Cánovas, *Estudios*, p.428.
48 Aedo, *Viaje del Infante-Cardenal*, p.123.
49 Cánovas, *Estudios*, p.422.
50 The cavalry Colonels Aldobrandini and San Martín lost their lives in the cavalry battle (Aedo, *Viaje del Infante-Cardenal*, p.124) and Colonels Tornetta, Blinder, Strozzi and Devreux were seriously injured. (Poyntz, *Relations*, p.110).
51 Aedo, *Viaje del Infante-Cardenal*, p.122.
52 Guthrie, *Batallas*, p.379.
53 Hrncirik, *Spanier auf dem Albuch*, p.17.
54 Hrncirik, *Spanier auf dem Albuch*, p.18.

approach of enemy horsemen, Escobar made the decision to go back out into the open to harass and hinder its march.[55] However, the numerical pressure of the Germans was overwhelming and the Hispanic musketeers withdrew in good order to the tree cover.

As the Protestants marched on the woods, they were harassed by the effective fire of Hispanic muskets and arquebuses. According to Escobar, successive Swedish attempts were aborted by Spanish firepower. Bernard ordered his light artillery to be placed near the forest to bombard it. They placed nine pieces of artillery in three detachments,[56] but while the sappers were placing their batteries, Escobar attacked these positions and in his words, surely exaggerated, 'killed 200 enemies'.[57]

By 7.30 p.m. Bernard had committed most of his units by capturing the first hills of the mountain range. Nerves in the Swedish-German army began to fray as progress had been delayed. The Protestants needed to secure a position to rally their army. For that reason, Horn decided to get involved his units relieved those of Bernard in order to take the Heselberg Hill. However, Horn's forces were lagging behind and they were not ready even long after dark.[58]

Indeed, the Swedish troops could not deploy as they wished. The darkness and rain made it difficult for the infantry to march, but it was especially difficult for cavalry and artillery. In addition, the march was made more difficult by the destruction caused on the way by Bernard's troops, who had gone too fast to get into combat.[59]

While fighting in the woods and taking advantage of general alarm throughout the Catholic camp, and with most units being deployed to the west, a sortie was made from the garrison of Nördlingen against the siege lines. They slipped into the approach trenches and burned whatever they could find. Panic spread initially among the Catholic companies on guard, which were apparently newly raised and low quality troops since the veteran units were on the battlefield, but when the sortie tried to go further afield, they were repulsed and forced to return to the city. Material damage as a result of the sortie was insignificant.[60]

The fight in the Heselberg forest subsided temporarily with the first shadows of the night, as both sides needed to recover. Since that part of the battle was concentrating all the efforts of the enemy, the Cardinal-Infante sent an urgent command to *sargento mayor* Escobar to defend the forest 'until death'.[61] Escobar's men fortified their position as best as they could, as the slackening enemy fire and darkness made it possible. The Protestants again launched an assault on the forest, testing the resistance of Escobar's detachment, which finally lost the tip of the forest within an hour of nightfall.

---

55 Cánovas, *Estudios*, p.422.
56 Aedo confirms that there were 10 pieces (Aedo, *Viaje del Infante-Cardenal*, p.124).
57 Cánovas, *Estudios*, p.422.
58 It got dark about 7.00 p.m. (Guthrie, *Batallas*, p.379).
59 Guthrie, *Batallas*, p.379.
60 Aedo, *Viaje del Infante-Cardenal*, p.127.
61 Aedo, *Viaje del Infante-Cardenal*, p.124.

One of the Spanish captains and a Neapolitan one, plus several dozen soldiers died in the fighting.[62]

The Cardinal-Infante was traveling all over the Spanish front line, gathering information on Protestant moves, so in view of the fact that the Heselberg was the only place where fighting was taking place, he ordered that Escobar be strengthened with 500 more musketeers.[63]

Between 9.00 p.m. to 10.00 p.m. Horn's first infantry were able to reach the front line but were not able to complete their deployment until well after midnight, when the cavalry arrived to begin the assault on the Heselberg. Despite not having deployed all their units, the pressure of Protestant numerical superiority had been noted. At 10pm news coming from the forest indicated that Protestants had managed to gain a foothold, but it appeared that Catholics could not be forced out. However, it seemed that the Protestants would soon take the forest and that the new focus of the battle would move to the Albuch Hill. which would be the next critical point in the battle. For that reason, Cardinal-Infante ordered Count Giovanni Maria Serbelloni,[64] commander of the Spanish artillery, to join him, as he had been delayed transporting the Hispanic artillery from their camp towards the hills. The Cardinal-Infante ordered Serbelloni to lead the defence of the hill. The German regiments of Wurmser and Leslie, a total of 3,250 troops, were sent to support him and once they had arrived began digging fortifications.[65]

Despite the lack of picks and shovels and the stony terrain, the Germans managed to dig two trenches, about three feet deep that partially surrounded the hill to the front and flanks. They did not have time to protect the rear. It was possible to deploy 10 pieces of field artillery which were located between the two redoubts,[66] with two pieces on the left side and two on the right.

---

62 Aedo *Viaje del Infante-Cardenal*, p.124.
63 Poyntz recounts the moment when the 500 musketeers entered the forest and his dragoon unit was relieved to return to the main body of the army. Protestant units surrounded the grove and it was very dangerous to try to cross to their own lines, but Poyntz was determined to leave the forest. He ordered his men to have their weapons ready, but forbid them to use them until he gave the order. They advanced as quietly as they could, but some enemy lookouts stopped them and demanded the password. They kept moving forward, a fact that made the sentinels doubt that they were friendly forces. The Imperial dragoons did not respond until they were in the middle of an enemy detachment, then Poyntz gave the order to shoot, generating such confusion that it allowed him and his men to run towards the Catholic line. Pursued by the enemy, Colonel Butler appeared with his regiment and fled. (Poyntz, *Relations*, p.110).
64 Serbelloni was true veteran. In addition to being an expert artilleryman and engineer, his appointment as director of the fortification works and the batteries that defended the hill was decisive for the development of the battle.
65 Aedo, *Viaje del Infante-Cardenal*, p.125.
66 The Spanish sources mention the existence of three defensive positions, called generically called 'redoubts'. Such definition included a fortification with a parapet made of soil or wood that gave protection on three or four sides, with a fire-step for the musketeers to position themselves along and generally with a ditch in front. Hrncirik agrees, based on German sources and various excavations carried out in the nineteenth and twentieth centuries that they were *media-lunas* (in German, *halbmond-schanzen*, or lunettes). Initially only evidence of two of the three redoubts was found, but later the third one was located. Hrncirik concludes that its location was ideal, being built on the highest levels of the hill, at around 528 to 534 metres, with at least one flank protected by the rugged slope of the hill (Hrncirik, *Spanier auf dem Albuch*, pp.31–38).

	Menos tira.	1	2	3	4	5	Mas 6
Falconete de dos libras.	320	704	1408	2112	2640	2970	3200
Falconete de quatro libras.	400	880	1760	2640	3300	3712	4000
Sacre de feis libras.	420	990	1980	2970	3742	4176	4500
Mediaculebrina de ocho.	500	1100	2200	3300	4125	4640	5000
Mediaculebrina de diez.	550	1210	2470	3640	4537	5104	5500
Mediaculebrina de doze.	600	1320	2640	3960	4750	5346	5600
Culebrina de quinze.	650	1430	2860	4290	5150	5720	6180
Culebrina de diez y ocho.	700	1487	2974	4759	5944	6604	6800
Culebrina de veinte.	720	1560	3120	4994	5986	6584	7022
Culebrina de veinte y dos.	800	1738	3466	5546	6469	7115	7355
Culebrina de veinte y cinco.	900	1980	3960	5940	6622	7127	7369

Illustration from the military treatise 'The perfect gunner: theory and practice' by Julio César Firrufino (1648). In this illustration, we see a table of ranges of the various types of minor artillery pieces: falconets, sakers, demi-culverins and culverins. The steps are equivalent to about 70cm although it is not an exact measurement. The first column ('tira menos') indicates the level shot, with the barrel parallel to the ground, while the last column ('más 6') indicates the barrel at an angle of 45°. (Author's collection)

This artillery was directed by the Jesuit priest Gamassa,[67] of the entourage of the Marquis of Leganés. Gamassa was a mathematician and artillery expert, well acquainted with the rules and calculations necessary to apply them with good effect in the field.[68]

During this time, the Protestants continued to attack the Spaniards in the Heselberg forest. After so many hours of combat, Escobar's troops were already exhausted. Count Serbelloni already had the defensive work on the Albuch to quite an advanced state, so at around 10.30 p.m. he tried to regain possession of the whole of Heselberg, at the head of a detachment of 200 musketeers from the German regiment of Count of Salm.[69]

Meanwhile, the position of Albuch Hill was further strengthened by the presence of the Tercio of Toralto, with 900 men, strengthened by 200 musketeers of the Prince San Sivero's Tercio.[70] These Italians stood on the right flank of the hill, digging a trench about two feet deep a hundred metres from the foremost German positions.[71]

---

67 Jesuit priest Francesco Antonio Gamassa (1588–1646) was a professor at the prestigious Imperial College of Madrid, where he held the chair of 'Military Mathematica'. In 1633 Gamassa published the book 'Tabla universal para ordenar en cualquiera forma esquadrones' ('Universal table for ordering squadrons in any form'), a practical manual with detailed tables for squadron formation based on the number of available troops and the terrain, in a clear example of what at that time was known in Spain as *Arte de Escuadronerar* (Art of Squadrons). The Marquis de Leganés required his services for the Cardinal-Infante's campaign in Germany and when Leganés was appointed governor of the Duchy of Milan (1635), Gamassa was serving him as engineer and military architect (Hrncirik, *Spanier auf dem Albuch*, pp.112–113).
68 Aedo, *Viaje del Infante-Cardenal*, p.125.
69 Aedo, *Viaje del Infante-Cardenal*, p.126.
70 Aedo, *Viaje del Infante-Cardenal*, p.125.
71 Aedo, *Viaje del Infante-Cardenal*, p.125.

Serbelloni's efforts resulted in the recovery of the forest, with the Spaniards advancing in the woods almost to the edge of the trees at the clearing. But the Protestant command was determined to recapture the position and from 10.45 p.m. the Protestants launched several simultaneous attacks on the forest from several directions.

Escobar sent his assistant, Felipe de la Maza, to brief the Marquess of Leganés on the perilous position they were in, requesting material from sappers (axes, picks and shovels) to better fortify themselves and resist the assaults of the enemy, as well as a hundred pikemen to defend against cavalry, but none was forthcoming. General Piccolomini came up to the front line and promised to send the requested material, as well as powder and shot.[72] Aware of the pressure the Protestants were exerting on his men in the forest, Serbelloni brought in another 200 musketeers, this time from the Tercio of Toralto. These new reinforcements held the Protestant's attack for another half hour.[73]

Around the Albuch Hill the Burgundian cavalry companies of La Tour and Alberg arrived to position themselves on the left flank of the infantry, while the Neapolitan cavalry of Gambacorta formed up on their right. General Piccolomini, acting as a liaison officer between the separate Imperial and Spanish high commands, assisted Serbelloni in fortifying the Albuch and transferred a further 1,000 Imperial cavalry and 4 guns to that sector.[74]

At around 11.00 p.m. the Protestants decided to launch a devastating and final assault and between 3,000 and 4,000 of their soldiers assaulted the forest.[75] The Spaniards ran out of ammunition, so they had to give ground. The fighting was intense in the darkness and among the trees and the bushes and the Protestant assault force managed to push the Spanish, German and Italian survivors up the hill.[76] Thus, finally, the Protestants, at 11.30 p.m. managed to expel the Hispanic troops from the hill of Heselberg, but at great cost. Many of the Hispanic soldiers were able to retreat in good order to the positions on the next hill, the Albuch.[77]

Guthrie describes the resistance of these Spaniards in the Heselberg as 'of extreme value' 'gaining by their performance the admiration of friends and enemies'. There are those who consider this small action the defining moment of the battle'.[78]

Sergeant Major Escobar was taken prisoner[79] and questioned by Bernard of Saxe-Weimar. The Spanish officer, who had defended his position for five hours, he had no problem with proudly reporting the numbers and experience of the Cardinal-Infante's army, but it seems that Bernard, who despised those 'ruthless Spanish soldiers', did not believe the warnings that

---

72 Cánovas, *Estudios*, p.423.
73 Aedo, *Viaje del Infante-Cardenal*, p.126.
74 Aedo, *Viaje del Infante-Cardenal*, p.128.
75 Aedo, *Viaje del Infante-Cardenal*, p.126.
76 Mesa, *Nördlingen*, p.29.
77 Cánovas *Estudios*, p.423.
78 Guthrie, *Batallas*, p.379.
79 Other officers and non-commissioned officers were likewise captured and some of them were executed the next day (Poyntz, *Relations*, p.110).

Escobar issued. In fact, Bernard threatened to hang him if he did not tell the truth, but Escobar insisted that there were 15,000 infantry and 3,500 horsemen,[80] again provoking the anger of Bernard, who ordered that he be taken to a prison tent. However, after a while, the Duke of Franconia invited Escobar to his tent with Horn and they chatted amicably – with the Spaniard closely watched by Bernard's personal guards.[81]

Serbelloni reported to the Cardinal-Infante that he had succeeded in withdrawing the defenders from the woods to the positions of Albuch, but not without the capture of Escobar and the musketeers' captain of the Tercio of Toralto and other soldiers. Serbelloni stated that it was impossible to recover the forest and that the next stage of the fight would be for Albuch Hill. Cardinal-Infante thanked him for his services and ordered him back with his men on the hill to defend it, as its tenure was vital to the victory of the Catholic army and assured him that reinforcements would be sent.[82]

Swedish cabasset (circa second half of the sixteenth century – early seventeenth century). The term cabasset comes from the Spanish 'capacete'. This type of helmet is an evolution of the medieval 'Kettle hat' and predecessor of the morion. It was used in Western Europe, especially in Spain and Italy, from the middle of the fifteenth century to the end of the seventeenth century. It was used by infantry and pikemen and also by mounted troops who handled firearms, such as arquebusiers, argulets and pistoleers. The crown of the helmet was shaped like a bowl, or an almond or a pear (hence the nickname of the pear headpiece). It was provided with a narrow rim and ended in a protruding point at its upper edge (like the stalk of a pear). Most of the helmets were plain, although they were sometimes decorated with engravings or piping. This Swedish helmet maintains the same morphology as the other continental helmets, with a high profile, without yet evolving into the Swedish type which were low profile and rounded. It is made of steel, iron and leather. Its dimensions are: length: 276mm; width: 242mm; height: 200mm; weight: 1.334kg (Livrustkammaren, LRK 22423)

80　Bernard had been informed by his spies in Venice that the strength of the Cardinal-Infante's army was about 5,000 foot soldiers and 2,000 horsemen (Aedo, *Viaje del Infante-Cardenal*, p.127)

81　Escobar tells us that he spent the next day in a prison tent and when at the end of the morning of the 6th the Protestants fled after the battle, he saw Duke Bernard riding near them. When Bernard recognised Escobar, the Duke fired his gun with the intention of killing him, but that he missed. Then Bernard shouted at the guards to slaughter Escobar, who, sensing what was going to happen to him, seized the sword of one of his guards and ran into the forest, in the direction of the Catholics advance. Escobar was afraid that he would be mistaken for an enemy and that his own comrades would kill him, so he tried to stay calm and appear as harmless as possible. According to his testimony, the Catholics (he does not indicate from which country) identified him as a friend yet in spite of that, they robbed him of everything that he had. But at least he was safe. (Cánovas, *Estudios*, p.423).

82　Aedo, *Viaje del Infante-Cardenal*, p.127.

Dawn on 6 September

In the early hours Horn's troops had occupied the hill of Heselberg and rested before the battle to come. Horn and Bernard decided their troops needed to rest as after more than 20 hours of marching and combat over a continuous succession of hills, with each fight more bitter than the previous one. Guthrie wonders if that pause decided the outcome of the battle, because if the Protestants had continued their fight, they probably would have captured Albuch Hill and if it had fallen on 5 September the whole battle would have been very different. However, it is questionable whether Bernard's Germans or Horn's Swedes would have been able to take the hill due to their extreme exhaustion.[83]

Albuch Hill was the tactical key to the battlefield.[84] Its dominant position would allow the Catholics to repel the Protestant attacks across the whole front, but if the latter managed to take it, they would be able to bring up cannons and dominate the entire Catholic army with their fire, forcing them to retreat from the battlefield.

In fact, the Catholic commanders were aware of the importance of the hill from the beginning of the first fighting, when it became clear to them that the Protestants intended to advance through the hill line to the Albuch, although Protestants continued to believe that it was a single hill. This Catholic decision to move the epicentre of the battle onto its left flank was paramount to the outcome of the battle.[85] According to Guthrie, it was Gallas who shortly after sunset ordered the hill to be heavily defended.[86] However, Spanish sources say it was the Cardinal-Infante and the Marquis de Leganés who, while Escobar's men continued to fight in the forest, gave orders to fortify the hill, due to its importance to the entire Catholic deployment.[87]

After receiving the news of the fall of the Heselberg, the two Catholic princes assembled their generals in another council of war. Gallas reproached the Spaniards for the loss of the forest, as he had previously suggested that the Spaniards reinforced the position more effectively, but Spanish commanders had ignored him. Seeing how this speech could undermine the mutual trust and cooperation that had existed until then, the Cardinal-Infante urged Gallas to stop talking about past events and focus on providing solutions to the crisis they were experiencing. The Cardinal-Infante wanted all the officers to help decide what to do in the face of the approaching sunrise and not to be discouraged by the previous events. Gallas remained angry and declared that nothing could be done now the forest had been lost. The Cardinal-Infante

---

83 Guthrie, *Batallas*, p.379.
84 Delbruck reasons that the battle occurred because the march through the gorge lasted too long and the 'Swedes' did not reach the position foreseen by Bernard in time, so they engaged in a series of skirmishes that ended in a battle. In his systematic analysis of the battle, Delbruck identifies the battle of Nördlingen as a 'meeting engagement' and not a formal 'pitched battle' (Delbruck, *Dawn of modern warfare*, p.211).
85 Rucker, *Die Entscheidungsschlacht bei Nördlingen*, p.12.
86 Guthrie, *Batallas*, p.379.
87 Mesa, *Nördlingen*, p.29.

THE BATTLE

was angered by the Imperial general's attitude and rebuked him for his lack of collaboration.[88]

The Marquis de Grana, the officer in command of the Imperial artillery, intervened to calm the atmosphere, indicating that the defence of Albuch was the key to the Catholic plans. Grana reasoned that out of the four Tercios positioned there, one was made up of newly raised troops, which led him to think that their effectiveness in combat would be low. He called for the position to be strengthened by a Spanish Tercio and that the reserves were adequate to relieve the troops in the battle for this crucial position.[89]

The Cardinal-Infante accepted his advice and ordered the Tercio of Martín de Idiáquez to take up position at the Albuch. Some Spanish commanders considered the choice of Idiáquez was inappropriate, but the Cardinal-Infante did not change his mind.[90]

Hispanic officials agreed the battle plan, including the number of Tercios and regiments that should strengthen the Albuch defences and the order in which the reinforcements should intervene; even the composition and planned moments of the arquebusier *mangas*, which as mobile reserve would have to go into combat whenever required.[91]

Protestant commanders were also gathering together to plan the day's coming battle. Horn, supported by other officers, stated that it was inadvisable to go ahead with the action and better retreat, but Duke Bernard's opinion prevailed, insisting that the Catholic line be broken at dawn.

At around 2.00 a.m. the Duke of Nochera set out to inspect the situation on the front line and to see how far the Protestant forces had come and where they would be likely to attack. After a while he returned, reporting that numerous enemy troops were preparing to attack the Albuch Hill.[92] Aware of the importance of the hill, the Cardinal-Infante considered the importance of strengthening the hill with more men and sent the Lombard Tercios of Paniguerola and Guasco. Captain Manuel Sanchez de Guevara was responsible for guiding them to take positions on the nearby Schonfeld Hill beside the Imperial Webel Brigade. The Lombards were joined by an Imperial battalion.[93]

Catholic infantry company flag, with the Burgundian Cross in its centre. On the flag is a monogram believed to belong to Archdukes Alberto and Isabel Clara Eugenia, who ruled as regents of Flanders from 1599–1621, the date of Alberto's death. Isabel remained in power, as governor until her death in 1633. Thus, it could be the flag of a Walloon or Burgundian unit in service in the Army of Flanders or of the Duke of Feria. (Armémuseum, AM.084274)

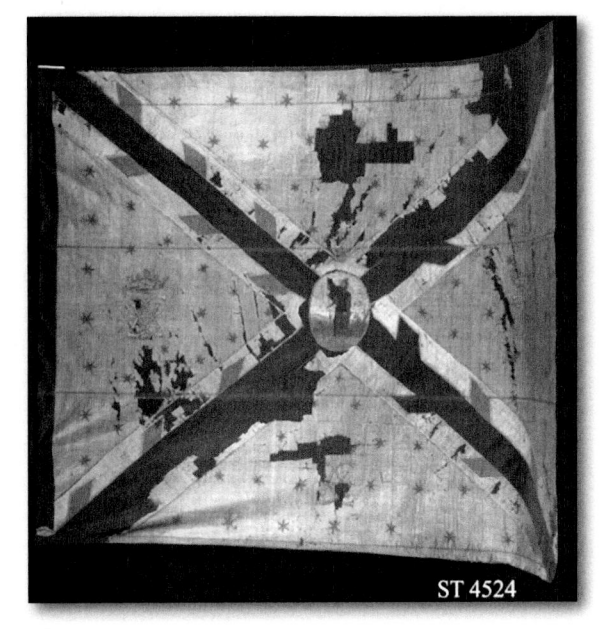

ST 4524

---

88   Aedo, *Viaje del Infante-Cardenal*, p.128.
89   Mesa, *Nördlingen*, p.33.
90   Martín de Idiáquez enlisted at 16 years of age, serving in Africa and Europe in several units and conflicts. For his distinguished military service, Cardinal-Infante named him on 25 July 1634 as *maestre de campo* of the Tercio of the deceased Juan Díaz de Zamorano. Some officers were opposed to his recent promotion to command of a Tercio.
91   Mesa, *Nördlingen*, p.33.
92   Mesa, *Nördlingen*, p.33.
93   Guthrie, *Batallas*, p.380.

While the positions around the Albuch were being strengthened, fortification work continued on the mountain. While they were working on fortifying the Albuch, the Germans were well-stocked with gunpowder, rope and bullets by Captains Manuel Sanchez de Guevara and Juan de la Cueva, who talked with German Colonels Salm and Wurmser about the delicacy of the hill's position. From the top of the Albuch they could hear the noise of Protestants preparing to launch an attack on the hill at dawn. Indeed, the German colonels thought that hill was of great importance and that they – with two regiments – were too few to defend it, because if the Protestants took hold of the forest where Escobar's detachment was, in the morning they would attack that hill with all their might and once captured, they could easily bring up their artillery and bombard the Catholic camp.[94]

Captain Manel Sánchez de Guevara reported again to Cardinal-Infante, who was with King Ferdinand, the Imperial staff and the senior Spanish commanders – the Marquises of Leganés and Los Balbases. The Cardinal-Infante arranged to send another two Tercios to the hill and so gave the order to Lieutenant-General Pedro de León Villarroel who led Colonel Leslie with his German regiment and *maestre de campo* Gaspar de Toralto with his Tercio towards the fighting. Captain Manel Sanchez de Guevara was again in charge of guiding the two Tercios to their position and again gave valuable intelligence to the Catholic commanders.[95]

The Cardinal-Infante, following the comments of the war council about the newly-raised German regiments, gave orders to Lieutenant-General Pedro de León Villaroel to go to Albuch and personally deliver to Colonel Wurmser the order to have his troops removed from the hill and be relieved by the soldiers of Idiáquez;[96] but the veteran German colonel refused, claiming that he had been serving the King of Spain for 30 years and that with the honour he had gained for his services it was not fair to relieve him of the responsibility of defending the position. León Villaroel insisted that it was a direct order of the Cardinal-Infante and that he, as an officer and friend, recommended that he obey. More infuriated, the German colonel replied that it was not for friends to advise him of such a thing and that if the Cardinal-Infante did not trust in his men, he preferred that, when the Spaniards of the Tercio of Martin de Idiáquez occupied his position, he would obey Fernando's order, but when his men retreated, he personally would join in the front rank of Martín de Idiáquez's Tercio, serving his King as a simple pikeman.[97] León Villaroel returned to the Cardinal-Infante's tent, who, content with the brave response of the German Colonel, consented to the Wurmser regiment remaining in the front line and ordered that Idiáquez's Tercio be placed in reserve in a second line, ready to intervene.[98]

The Cardinal-Infante ordered Captains Manuel Sánchez de Guevara and Juan de la Cueva to join with the Marquis of Leganés and Gallas and to offer

---

94　Cánovas, *Estudios*, p.429.
95　Cánovas, *Estudios*, p.425.
96　Cánovas, *Estudios*, p.430.
97　Cánovas, *Estudios*, p.426.
98　Aedo, *Viaje Del Infante-Cardenal*, p.130.

THE BATTLE

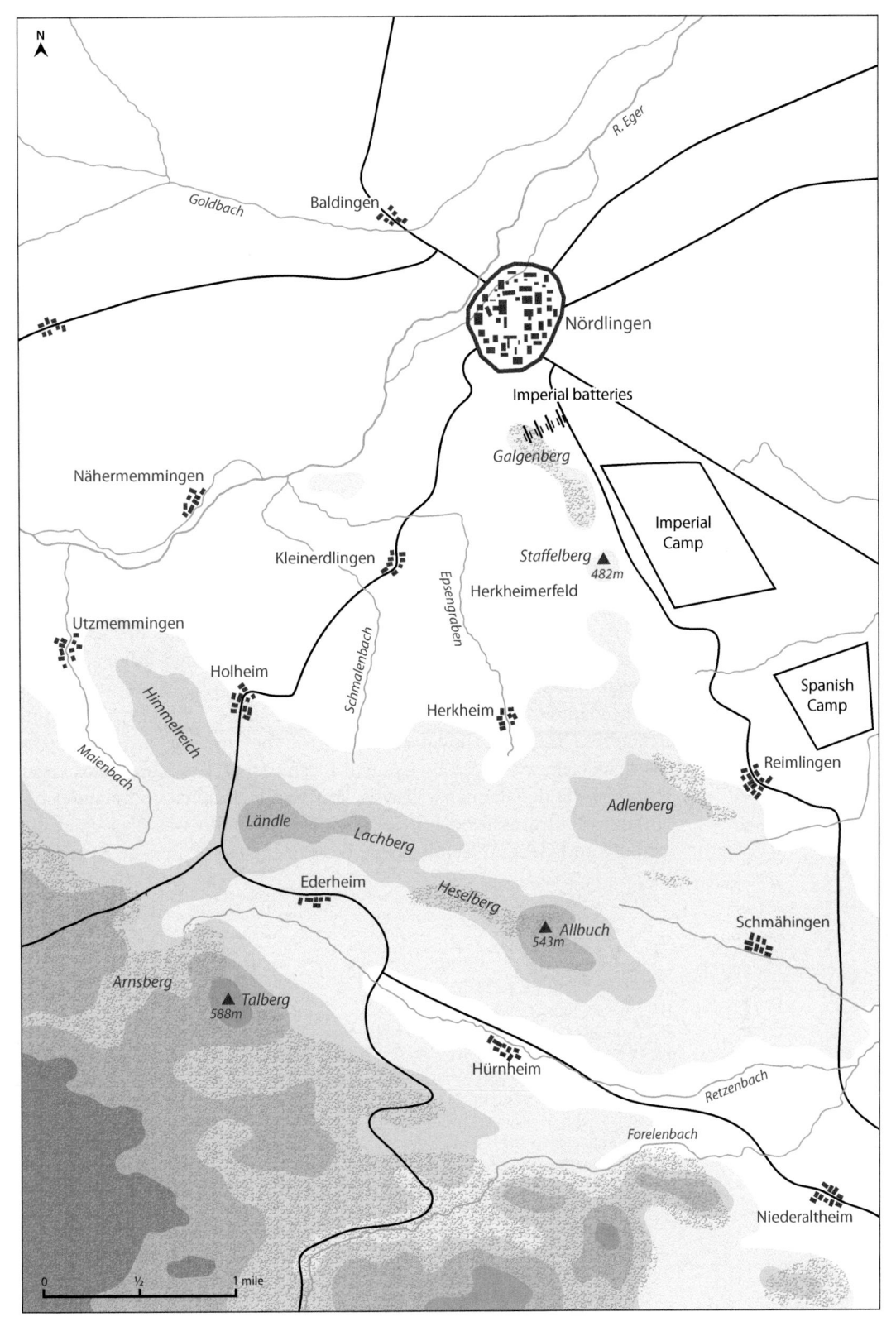

Map 3 The area of the battlefield.

them their advice, as they were veteran officers and to serve them as they directed. The two captains informed Gallas of the fortification work that Spaniards had done at Albuch.[99]

With all this information, Gallas reasoned that the decisive combat would be on the plain outside Nördlingen and that there would be no exit from the city for the garrison. That is why he ordered the removal of all the artillery they had placed in batteries around the town, as well as all the infantry and cavalry they had in the besieging trenches, to deploy them to the battle front.[100]

The rest of the night, actually just a couple of hours, the troops of the two armies remained tense, on alert; as chronicler Aedo recounts 'all armies being ready to fight'.[101]

Perhaps some soldiers were lucky and could contain their nerves and sleep; most of the soldiers were probably awake, wondering what would happen to them on the new day and if they would still be alive the following night.

The Deployment of the Armies

At the start of 6 September 1634, the Catholic Army had about 23,000 infantrymen, 13,000 cavalrymen and 65 cannons. The supreme commanders were Archduke Ferdinand, King of Hungary, son and heir of Emperor Ferdinand II of the Holy Roman Empire and Cardinal-Infante Fernando, younger brother of King Philip IV of Spain.

The Catholic force was composed of three armies with separate command structures. The operational command of the Imperial army rested with Matthias Gallas, assisted by General Piccolomini. The Marquis of Leganés, Diego Mexía de Guzmán y Davila, was the operational commander of the Hispanic Army, assisted by Count Serbelloni, who was also chief of the artillery and General Gambacorta, head of the cavalry.[102] The Bavarian and

---

99 Cánovas, *Estudios*, p.428.
100 Cánovas, *Estudios*, p.430.
101 Aedo, *Viaje del Infante-Cardenal*, p.129.
102 In his book *The Road to Rocroi*, Fernando González de León brings up the hypothesis that the Hispanic Army was phased out, in part, the aristocratic origin of its senior officers, who did not have knowledge or experience of the war and who would only be in command because of their social status as members of the nobility. It is true that in the last years of the government of the Archduchess Isabel Clara Eugenia there was discontent among the generals of the Flanders army. But these struggles between Álvaro de Bazán, Carlos Coloma and Gonzalo Fernandez de Córdoba were not due to their lack of experience, but to the lack of a clear chain of command and the rivalry between them, as they were reluctant to fulfil the orders of other nobles they considered as equals, but not superior. This caused communication errors between them, which resulted in failures in military operations. But as was demonstrated in Nördlingen, the Spanish leaders – all of them aristocrats – fulfilled the orders of the Cardinal-Infante and the Marquis de Leganés. And when Prince Fernando arrived in Flanders, the 'wayward' generals obeyed him perfectly, given that the chain of command was perfectly clear and the authority of the Cardinal-Infante unquestioned.

THE BATTLE

Catholic League contingent was led by Duke Charles IV of Lorraine, assisted by General Fugger.[103]

The Hispanic Army occupied the left flank, south of Nördlingen. The centre was defended by the Catholic League troops. The Imperial army defended the right flank, closer to Nördlingen.

On the left flank, the Spanish army occupied the strategic Albuch hill, under Serbelloni's command. This general had ordered that the left, southern redoubt, which overlooked the Rezen Stream, be protected by Leslie's Imperial Regiment, mixed with the Bavarian Fugger Regiment.[104] The central redoubt

Photo G.2 (see Appendix I). Erected in 1896, in the shape of a pyramid, this commemorative monolith atop Albuch Hill commemorates the battle. It was built by the Verschönerungsverein Nördlingen (VVN). A replica of the engraving of the battle by Matthäus Merian was attached to the memorial stone in 2009. (Courtesy of Tobi Merk)

---

103 Guthrie, *Batallas*, p.370.
104 Guthrie reverses the deployment of the defence: he states that the redoubt facing south was defended by the Tercio of Toralto (750 troops); the centre by the Salm and Wurmser infantry regiments (1,500 in total) and the bastion to the far right was defended by the Leslie infantry regiment and the Fugger Bavarian battalion (1,650 in total). Idiáquez's Tercio (1,800 troops) was behind, a short distance away as an immediate reserve, with the Tercios of Paniguerola and Guasco (1,800 soldiers in total) slightly more to the rear. The open left flank was covered by the regiments of Burgundian cavalry of La Tour (587 troops) and Alberg (450 soldiers). The 1,830 Italian horsemen of Gambacorta were on the right (Guthrie, *Batallas*, p.380). The explanation of the investment in the order of Hispanic battle in the redoubts is profusely explained by Hrncirik, who reports that the Central European sources were based on the battle report of Marshal Horn, who attributed the northern position to the men of Leslie and Fugger; on the contrary, the Spanish and Italian sources, logically better informed of their own deployment, agree that

Photo G.1 (see Appendix I). This image is taken from the Battlefield Memorial looking towards the central redoubt and the 'Otto Rehlen's' hut. This is roughly where the southernmost redoubt, held by Leslie and Fugger's units, was located but the traces of the defences are no longer visible. (Courtesy of Daniel Staberg)

was defended by the German regiments of Salm and Wurmser, in the service of Spain. The redoubt on the right, to the north, in front of the Heselberg Hill, was held by the Italian Tercio of Toralto, reinforced with a manga of 200 arquebusiers of the Italian Tercio of San Sivero.[105] As the entrenchments were not completed because of the rocky terrain, most of the infantry on the Albuch were deployed in the open, in *escuadrones*, without any protection.

Further back, Idiáquez's Tercio was on the left, flanked to the right by five Neapolitan cavalry squadrons (around 1,800 riders), under Gambacorta's command, while the left flank was covered by five to seven squadrons of Burgundian cavalry (La Tour and Arberg) and Imperial cavalry (about 1,200 troops), under the command of Piccolomini, covering the southern part of the Albuch.[106]

The defence of the hill included eight to 14 light artillery pieces – four to eight pounders – according to various sources[107] in three batteries,

---

the Tercio of Toralto occupied the northern position and the Germans the southern redoubt (Hrncirik, *Spanier auf dem Albuch,* p.113).

105 Aedo, *Viaje del Infante-Cardenal,* p.130; Cánovas, *Estudios,* p.430; Hrncirik, *Spanier auf dem Albuch,* p.21.

106 Formed by the cavalry regiments of cuirassiers of Alt and Neu-Piccolomini, Piccolomini and Aldobrandini regiments (Guthrie, *Batallas,* p.380). However, the exact make-up of the cavalry present in the defence of the Albuch, in its vicinity and in the Schonfeld is impossible to know with certainty (Hrncirik, *Spanier auf dem Albuch,* p.113).

107 According to Cánovas, between eight and 10 cannons (Cánovas, *Estudios,* p.430); Guthrie indicates a maximum of 14 (Guthrie, *Batallas,* p.380). The pieces on the Albuch could have been Imperial, or Spanish, since they had a minimum of 10 pieces (Mesa, *Nördlingen,* p.17) although Guthrie doubts that they were Spanish (Guthrie, *Batallas,* p.402).

THE BATTLE

supporting the defence of redoubts. Cavalry units were placed between the infantry, especially on the flanks, to give them better support.[108]

The Albuch Hill defence was a corollary to the dominions of the Hispanic Monarchy, its three main Nations – Spanish, Italian and Burgundian – and German mercenaries.[109] In total, on the Albuch Plateau on 6 September before dawn, the Hispanic defenders had about 5,400 infantry, 2,700 cavalry,[110] and up to 14 light cannon.[111] In addition, a force of 1,000 Imperial musketeers, from the Tieffenbach Regiment, at the command of Lieutenant Colonel Teutschvoll, deployed to the right of the Tercio of Toralto, on the slope of the hill, descending between the Hispanic encampments and the forest.[112]

In the centre-left of the Catholic line, around the hills of Schonfeld and Albuch, were about 3,000 troops, commanded by the Marquis of

Photo D.2 (see Appendix I). This image is taken inside the central redoubt looking down on Hürnheim. It shows how the slope combined with the raised earthwork would have protected the men inside the redoubt, but not those actively on the firing step from Swedish infantry fire. From the Spanish point of view, the shooters defending the redoubt would have had a large field of fire, although some areas would be protected by the slight unevenness of the terrain. We can see just how exposed the Swedish infantry was as they advanced up the hill and why the Albuch was a strategic position. (Courtesy of Daniel Staberg)

---

108 Aedo, *Viaje del Infante-Cardenal*, p.130.
109 The multinational nature of the Army of the Hispanic Monarchy in the defence of the Albuch Hill is evident: 51 percent of the force was German, 29 percent Italians, 11 percent Spaniards and 9 percent Burgundian (Hrncirik, *Spanier auf dem Albuch*, p.94)
110 The numbers for the defenders of the Albuch – as in most battles – do not match between sources. Guthrie (Guthrie, *Batallas*, p.402) states that there were about 7,500 foot soldiers, 3,000 cavalry and 14 light cannon, while Hrncirik states that there were about 5,400 infantrymen and 12 cannon (Hrncirik, *Spanier auf dem Albuch*, p.113). The difference in the figure can be derived that in the first case, it also includes the nearby units (Paniguerola and Guasco), while the second scholar is limited to the units of Toralto (900 men), Salm and Wurmser (1,500), Leslie and Fugger (1,500) and Idiáquez (1,500), as a reserve behind the central redoubt; however, the figures are always approximate.
111 Hrncirik, *Spanier auf dem Albuch*, p.22.
112 Hrncirik, *Spanier auf dem Albuch*, p.25.

THE BATTLE OF NÖRDLINGEN 1634

Photo D.3 (see Appendix I). Looking west towards Ederheim. In 1634 this would be the position of the northern redoubt, defended by Toralto's Tercio, which researchers have not been able to find traces of. Beyond that, he would have deployed the rest of Spanish Tercios (San Sivero, Torrecusa, Cardenas, Fuenclara, La Tour, Alberg and Lunato Tercios), Santacelia Dragoons and the two Cardinal-Infante guard companies. (Courtesy of Daniel Staberg)

Leganés, with the Lombard Tercios of Paniguerola and Guasco, assisted by a detachment of 500 Imperial musketeers (from the Tiefembach Regiment) and the Imperial Webel Brigade.

Above the Schonfeld was the Hispanic Army Reserve: 1,500 cavalrymen and 7,000 infantrymen, with three Neapolitan Tercios (San Sivero, Torrecusa and Cardenas), the Spanish Tercio of Fuenclara, two Burgundian Tercios (La Tour and Alberg), the Lunato Lombard Tercio, the Santacelia Dragoons and the Cardinal-Infante's guard companies.

The centre-right was commanded by Duke Charles of Lorraine, with the bulk of Bavarian troops, with the Hartenburg and Ruepp infantry regiments – as well as other unidentified infantry units – and 11 cavalry squadrons under the command of Jean de Werth. In total, around 2,000 infantrymen and 3,000 horsemen.

The right flank was commanded by Mathias Gallas, commander-in-chief of the Imperial army,[113] consisting of three infantry brigades, deployed in two lines. In the first, the regiments of Suys, Diodati, Pallant-Moriame, Tiefembach, Alt Aldringen, Neu Aldringen and Neu Breuner. In the second line, seven cavalry squadrons – commanded by Louis de Gonzaga – and the infantry brigade of the two Guards regiments of the King of Hungary. Behind them, in support, was also a grouping of seven cavalry squadrons

---

113 Taking the records described in the *Krieglisten* – text written at the end of 1634 or start of 1635 – into account, the Imperial Army had the following regiments of infantry of whom their presence was highly probable in Nördlingen: Alt-Breuner, Baden, Kehraus, Gallas, Beck, Venian-Lafosse, Strassoldo and Neu Waldstein (Guthrie, *Batallas*, p.401).

Photo A.2 (see Appendix I). In this photo we see the geography of the terrain behind Herkheim town in more detail. We can see the current Reimlinger cliff and from there and along the entire ridge, towards the forest on the right, the Imperial troops of General Gallas would be deployed. Thus, from left to right, near Reimlinger, stood the Croats of Issolano's Cavalry, then the rest of the Imperial units of Gallas, Billehe and Werth's Cavalry in front of the Staffelsberg and Adlerberg in a line stretching to Herkheim. On the hill above Herkheim, the infantry of General Gallas, the army of Duke of Lorraine and some of Leganes' troops would be visible as well along the ridge. On the hills behind the battleline would have been the sprawling Imperial-Spanish camps. Bernhard Saxe-Weimar Protestant cavalry squadrons would have been hidden from view by the line of trees in the middle of the photo. (Courtesy of Daniel Staberg)

under the direct command of Gallas. And at the end of the Catholic line, at its far right, several Croatian cavalry detachments, around 1,000 to 2,000 men, were near the town of Kleinerdlingen, under the command of Issolano. Various sources indicate that, formed on the battlefield, the Imperial units would have numbered about 5,000 foot soldiers and 5,000 cavalry.[114]

Gallas had 50 cannon of various sizes[115] spread across the front, mainly in the Galgenberg and Schonfeld hills, with others in the siege works around Nördlingen.[116] In addition, around 2,000–3,000 Bavarian infantrymen (Reinach, Alt-Pappenheim and Back regiments) occupied positions to prevent any sortie from the Nördlingen garrison – or to prevent any Protestant force from circumventing the city blockade, around the city, backed by hundreds of Croatian scouts. The two Ferdinands positioned their command post near

---

114 Guthrie, *Batallas*, p.380; Piccouet, *Armies*, p.237.
115 The *Krieglisten* indicates that the Imperial army had 140 pieces of artillery of every type on that front; in other sources, there are 30 demi-cannons, without specification of the smallest pieces (Guthrie, *Batallas*, p.402). So, depending on the source, the figures vary greatly. And to this we must add that some authors only compute certain types of cannon, while other authors compute other types.
116 Guthrie, *Batallas*, p.380.

Adlerberg Hill. The Catholic slogan was *Viva la Casa de Austria* (Long Live the House of Austria).[117]

The Swedish-German army had 16,300 infantry, 9,300 cavalry and 62 guns, divided into two wings, commanded by Horn and Bernard respectively. Meeting at a war council, Horn and Bernard planned the battle that was about to take place. The key to victory was the possession of the Albuch Hill, which they erroneously identified as 'Arnsberg'. If they captured the hill, they would threaten the entire Catholic position, forcing them to either recapture the summit or to retreat, resulting in the relief of the besieged Nördlingen. As Horn occupied the Heselberg, he would be responsible for launching the attack, while Bernard's troops at the Lachberg would protect their left flank and fixed the majority of Catholic units.[118]

The summit of the Albuch was so important that, as long as Bernard held his flank, Horn would focus on the hill, 'though for this he had to occupy the last man in his infantry'.[119] That is why, to reinforce the Swedish offensive, Bernard reinforced Horn's 2,300 troops, giving to him 600 men from the Schaffelitzky regiment, 2,600 from Cratz's regiment, 3,000 from Württemberg's Army – at the command of Philipps II von Liebenstein – and 900 from his own contingent (infantry regiments of Vitzthum and Palsgrave).[120]

Horn's detachment stretched from the Heselberg to the Rezen stream, with five infantry brigades and 19 cavalry squadrons, deployed in four lines, with the cavalry on the right and behind the infantry. In the first line were the Scottish and Pfuhl brigades, supported by three cavalry squadrons under the command of Witzleben. In the second line were seven cavalry squadrons under the orders of Colonel Goldstein. In the third, the brigades of Horn, Rantzau and Wurtemberg, with a cavalry squadron. In the last line were eight cavalry squadrons under the command of Margrave von Brandenburg. The infantry brigades, except the Württemberg militia, had six regimental guns.[121] Saxon General Johan Vitzhum von Eckstadt would lead the first wave of the assault, consisting of the Scottish and Pfuhl brigades[122] while Horn would command a second assault wave and the reserves.

On the left flank were the Germans of Bernard of Saxe-Weimar, extending between the hills of Landle, Lachberg and the Heselberg. They were deployed in two lines, with about 4,000 foot soldiers and 5,500 cavalry and dragoons: a first line with the Thurn, Rosen and Weimar infantry brigades and eight cavalry squadrons, under Colonel Courville and four dragoon companies under the command of Colonel Taupadel, with order to fix the Catholic

---

117 Guthrie, *Batallas*, p.380.
118 Guthrie affirms that, given the character of both commanders, so opposed: 'They would have done better by exchanging the papers, but it would have taken them too long to change their respective army corps' (Guthrie, *Battles*, p.380). However, as the fight developed, it is not certain that Bernard had emerged victorious against the Spanish defence of their positions in the Albuch Hill.
119 Guthrie, *Batallas*, p.381.
120 Guthrie, *Batallas*, p.381.
121 Guthrie, *Batallas*, p.381.
122 Poyntz, *Relations*, p.111.

THE BATTLE

Photo C.1 (see Appendix I). Side view of the start of the Albuch ascent, looking west. Throughout this panorama, Horn's units are deployed to launch the unsuccessful assaults on the redoubts. The town of Hürnheim would be on our left, out of the image. Pfuhl 's brigade would have been closest with the Scots' brigade further away. The slope is not particularly steep, but it is long, while the ground is flat enough for a brigade to advance without disorder, the men would feel the exhausting effort of going uphill with musket and pike. Numerous craters run through the hill, probably as a result of cannonballs. (Courtesy of Daniel Staberg)

line and take the Galgenberg; the second line with seven cavalry squadrons under the command of Colonel Beckerman and the six cavalry squadrons of General Cratz, located at the Lachberg. The infantry brigades had six regimental guns each, while heavy guns deployed in battery along the front of the infantry, in order to target the centre and right of the Catholic battle line, but not to support the assault on Albuch Hill.[123]

Horn positioned himself behind his brigades to oversee the deployment, while Bernard did the same in the vicinity of the Heselberg. The war cry was *Gott mit uns* (God with us!).

The Protestant army was more homogeneous, with better quality and more standardisation in its troops – especially in the Swedish army – whose infantry brigades had an average of 1,750 to 2,000 men, in addition to six field guns per unit.

Conversely, the Catholic army was composed of a conglomerate of three armies: the Imperial, the Bavarian and the Spanish. Each had different doctrines and tactics, as well as a different composition, quality and staff. Thus, the Italian regiment of Toralto, in the Hispanic army, had about 800

---

123 Guthrie, *Batallas*, p.381.

THE BATTLE OF NÖRDLINGEN 1634

Photo A.1 (see Appendix I). Photo taken from the Riegelberg area, looking northwest. Close to this position the left flank of Bernhard of Saxe-Weimar's army corps would deploy. In the distance we can see, following from the left to the right, the city of Nördlingen; the 'Daniel' tower of the Church of St. George stands out, 90 metres high. A little closer we can see the municipality of Kleinerdlingen and a little further behind, the wooded hills of Galgenberg, Staffelberg and Adlenberg. The little town on the right is Herkheim. (Courtesy of Daniel Staberg)

soldiers, while the German regiments in the service of Spain could have 2,500 troops. The Bavarian and Imperial regiments were generally larger, but some of them were quite weak.

By contrast, the Italian, Burgundian and Spanish troops in the Cardinal-Infante's army were all veterans of conflicts in the Netherlands, against the Turks, in Italy, or in the German conflict. In fact, along with the experience of the Tercio's soldiers, it was possible to consider the presence of many 'reformed' soldiers in the ranks, meaning that within the Spanish companies there were experienced commanders who could direct, coordinate or advise their colleagues, in perfect harmony with the orders of their senior officers.

Once the Imperial troops were formed up, King Ferdinand spoke to them with these words:[124]

> The danger we have created against this city, forces the enemy army to present us the battle; they risk losing the battle, in fear of losing more cities, which will surely leave them if they cease to help Nördlingen, because no one wants to be next to soldiers who whom somebody does not expect to help them.[125]

---

124 De Vera, *Victoria sobre Norlinga*, pp.146–156.
125 King Ferdinand agreed with the fears of Horn and Bernard that the loss of Nördlingen could cause the disintegration of their Protestant German alliances.

THE BATTLE

18 pound cannon model (c1600). According to the 1888 catalogue this cannon was from the mid–nineteenth century and 'badly made'; later investigations revealed that it was not badly built but was much older. The barrel is decorated with various ornaments. The gun carriage was built in later times. (Armémuseum, AM.089028)

I inform you, my very faithful Germans, that you do not believe that if our enemy seek us, it is because they are very brave, but because of the need that you have caused them. And it has no bravery to attack us, given its inability to retreat. And to beat them, you only need to dig in your feet and wait for them.

In all this wartime that the King of Sweden and his allies had attacked Germania, or at least since the Battle of Leipzig, which Tilly lost, more by overconfidence in his army than by the value of the Swedes, our Religion has not been successful in saying that this fight it is for the benefit of the freedom of the Empire. But now, all the German cities will know about the consequences of our victory today. We will now begin the judgment that must be sentenced today.

Oh, valiant soldiers, how much we advance is there already to beat them! At least, the cause we stand for is the most just, being God's cause.

At this time in this part of the world, the sacrifice required by the Lord of Victories is immeasurable and the angels are begging him to grant it to us. But if you doubt Him, He will deny you.

The act of valour of this day must purge the German nation of external enemies and of their own infamy. And your hand will be the one who will open this grace to restore honour to the Empire and the Fatherland. This honour lost because of some Germanic rebels and it will be precisely the incomparable fidelity of the Germans themselves, those who follow the orders of Caesar, my father and Lord, which will bring back German honour.

The Spaniards, who have sought our friendship for so many centuries and more rightly since their Kings have our blood, Germanic like yours. And just as they have accompanied us in lesser dangers, they have now come with a mighty force. And its army is so imposing that it could only be commanded by a person as high as the Most Graceful Prince, my cousin.

But this is not the greatest relief we have. I assure you, valiant Teutons, that the religious and virgins of four thousand houses of God, which the Protestants have expelled from Germania since 1630, will invisibly help us. Yes, by the detestable impiety of the Protestants and the malice of their actions!

I want you to believe in these Holy Spirits. They will wield, in our defence, their heavenly weapons, the weapons with which they were killed. And the angels and virgins will lift up in your honour the palms of their martyrdom. And these palms will also be the crowns for our victory.

Captains and soldiers of Holy Church and Empire! Fight for the exaltation of the first, the stability of the second, my honour and yours. It's up to you today to defend them. And this cannot be accomplished in only two ways: either by dying in glory or by gaining an overwhelming victory. And I say to you, that today, those of us who are left alive, we can only be proud when we have plenty of wounds. If not, we will be dishonoured.

I acknowledge that I am not a captain as skilled as Hannibal, but at least I tell you that I am your commander and I will never say, 'Go fight', but 'Come fight with me'.[126]

The fighting on Albuch Hill

The battle for the Albuch Hill began at 5.00 a.m. on 6 September 1634, when the Swedish artillery began a bombardment of the hilltop positions followed by counter-battery fire along the whole line.

Vitzhum ordered the deployment of his brigades in the southern part of the Heselberg along the creek. When they began their march, the forested slope provided them with partial cover for a while, but as they approached the open area below the Albuch, they were received by the deadly discharge of the 14 guns which the Catholics had arranged in the fortified line on the hill.[127]

Vitzhum's advancing infantry had the support, to its right, of three cavalry squadrons under the command of Lieutenant Colonel Witzleben. The Leib Horn Cavalry Regiment formed the spearhead. But the riders of the Leib Regiment charged too enthusiastically, getting too far ahead of the foot soldiers. When the horsemen were south of the Albuch, they encountered a small ravine, which ran south from Albuch to Rezen. This made them reduce speed and they were severely punished by fire from the musketeers of Leslie's regiment and Fugger's Bavarians in the southern redoubt.[128]

Despite the enemy fire, Witzleben was not intimidated and ordered his bloodied and exhausted riders to deploy into line and charge the Catholic trenches, but his advance was cut short when La Tour and Arberg's cavalry regiments charged him in the flank. The Leib Regiment was shattered but was saved from annihilation when the other two cavalry squadrons arrived in support. All the surviving cavalry turned back, leaving the Vitzthum Protestant infantry alone to continue their advance.[129]

---

126 With these words, the young Ferdinand recognised his military inexperience, but also that, instead of sending the soldiers to fight, he impelled them to fight with him, because he would be by his side, just as it really happened, since the two Ferdinands were touring the battlefield (De Vera, *Victoria sobre Norlinga*, p.156).
127 Guthrie, *Batallas*, p.382.
128 Guthrie affirms that it was the Tercio of Toralto (Guthrie, *Battles*, p.382).
129 Guthrie, *Batallas*, p.382.

THE BATTLE

Photo B.1 (see Appendix I). From the town of Hürnheim a road leads us to the top of Albuch. The assaults by Horn's brigades came from our left, heading for the summit. The battlefield memorial is visible next to the tree. (Courtesy of Daniel Staberg)

Photo B.2 (see Appendix I). Looking east it is possible to see the area which saw the Swedish attempt to outflank the redoubts with cavalry. The attack of the cavalry, under the command of Witzleben, was easily beaten back and there was little fighting in that section for the rest of the battle. (Courtesy of Daniel Staberg)

Now, the Scottish and Pfhul brigades had to advance unprotected in the final stage of their attack – the Scots from the northwest and the Germans from the southwest – making a convergent movement towards the central redoubt.[130] Spanish sources[131] however, mention that the Protestant attack was brought simultaneously against the three Catholic redoubts. This makes sense because in the early stages the Protestants had sufficient numerical superiority to launch a general assault on the entire hill.

Thus began a fierce struggle for possession of the redoubts, in which valour and blood ran on both sides. The pressure put on them by the Protestants forced the German regiments of Salm and Wurmser to withdraw. Wurmser's soldiers withdrew first, followed by Salm's, despite their veteran colonels trying to hold them.

Having won part of the Catholic line, the Protestants took up positions to rally their forces and continue the attack, but lost order and mixed up some units in the process. While this was happening, the fleeing Germans of Salm and Wurmser were attacked by a lone Protestant cavalry detachment,[132] which provoked panic among Catholic Germans. It was a critical moment for Catholic resistance in the Albuch. Two redoubts resisted the attack, but the centre had given way. Serbelloni ordered a counterattack with Gambacorta's horsemen, who broke the aforementioned cavalry detachment and chased it into the central redoubt. The Germans of Wurmser and Salm regiments had been hastily rallied and regrouped by the Spaniards of the Tercio Idiáquez, who executed those who refused to return to combat.[133] Officers from the two German regiments managed to reform them and led them down the hill to support Gambacorta's horsemen and together they recaptured the fort.[134]

From his observation post at the Heselberg, Horn analysed the situation. His men had conquered the redoubt, but misfortune had led to their loss. Reasoning that a new and rapid assault could lead to victory, the Swedish marshal ordered that his second wave of the Horn and Josiah von Rantzau's brigades to advance,[135] while ordering the rest to reinforce the exhausted Pfuhl and Scottish brigades.[136]

The target of the attack was the redoubt occupied by the Tercio of Toralto. The defenders first suffered the attack of a number cavalry squadrons and since the fort was not wide enough to accommodate the entire Tercio, most Italians were formed by *escuadron*, deployed in the open. Protestant riders stubbornly charged against the infantry but being well positioned and maintaining their discipline, the Italians managed to withstand the charges

---

130 Guthrie, *Batallas*, p.382.
131 Aedo, *Viaje del Infante-Cardenal*, p.132.
132 Aedo, *Viaje del Infante-Cardenal*, p.133.
133 De Vera, *Victoria sobre Norlinga*, p.158.
134 Aedo, *Viaje del Infante-Cardenal*, p.133.
135 There is a discrepancy in the information given between the sources: Aedo indicates that those who attacked in Toralto on this occasion it was the Scottish regiment, 'the one appointed Yellow' (Aedo, *Viaje del Infante-Cardenal*, p.133), who was defeated. Perhaps it can be inferred that was the case, or Aedo related the initial attack of the squadron of Vitzthum as a separate attack, or that he was wrong in the name of the attacking unit.
136 Guthrie, *Batallas*, p.382.

of the riders. Both from the garrison of the redoubt and from the *escuadrons*, musketeers and arquebusiers fired on the horsemen, who 'struggled so hard to break the *escuadron*, that many of the riders died by pikes'.[137] The combined action of pikes and shot disrupted the attack by the cavalry, which fell back, leaving the assault in the hands of the Protestant infantry.

In the short time between the cavalry's withdrawal and the infantry's attack, several *mangas* of Toralto's arquebusiers and musketeers left the formation and advanced to the front. The combined action of these men and those who remained in the fort against the advancing Protestant infantry caused an intense duel between the shot of both sides, 'with great effect from both sides in a fight less than 50 steps away'.[138]

While this was taking place at the Toralto Neapolitan redoubt, the Swedes launched a new fierce cavalry assault that caused the Wurmser and Salm regiments to collapse again, worn out by so much fighting and they fled. Colonels Wurmser and Salm, next to their personal staff and a few soldiers, resisted until the end, surrounded by Swedish. Wurmser died in combat, Salm received several mortal wounds that resulted in his death the following day.[139] The Germans of the Wurmser and Salm regiments sought to escape up the hill but again met with the Tercio of Idiáquez.[140] The Spaniards were

Photo C.2 (see Appendix I). Here we see a wide view from almost the top of Albuch, just to the front of where the Spanish redoubts were. We can see how exposed the advance of the Swedes was to the Spanish fire. The town that can be seen is Hürnheim. (Courtesy of Daniel Staberg)

---

137 Aedo, *Viaje del Infante-Cardenal*, p.133.
138 Aedo, *Viaje del Infante-Cardenal*, p.133.
139 Mesa, *Nördlingen*, p.35.
140 Aedo, *Viaje del Infante-Cardenal*, p.133.

instructed to *calar las picas* (close the pikes), that is to keep those pikes levelled in a defensive pose to prevent the fugitives from disordering their formation, which is why some Germans were trapped on the Spanish pikes.

The situation was critical, as if the Catholics lost the central fort, they could lose the entire Albuch hill, which was the anchor for the Catholic left flank and was to be the defining point of the whole battle.

Serbelloni ordered that Idiáquez's 1,800 Spaniards recover the position lost by Salm and Wurmser.[141] As they advanced down the hill, they were fired on by musket fire and the artillery in the redoubt, which had already been turned around and begun firing on the Spaniards. Several *mangas* of musketeers and arquebusiers from the Tercio of Idiáquez advanced, under the command of Captains Francisco de Aragon, Diego de Contreras and Lope Ochoa de Oro, who returned fire on the Protestants to protect the advance of the pikes. The Spaniards then continued to advance and stormed the redoubt. A cannonball struck Captain Ochoa's arm and killed his sergeant, who was on his side. A bloody hand-to-hand fight began and after an hour of intense fighting, the Spaniards cleared the fort, driving the Protestants down the hill.[142]

As the rest of Idiáquez's men took up positions in the redoubt, Protestants launched a furious counterattack to try to regain their lost prize. According to the chronicler Aedo, these were the Blue and Black regiments.[143] At the sight of the Protestant flags, Idiáquez instructed his men that while the Protestants fired on them, they should kneel or lie down so that the bullets passed over their heads. This they did and then immediately stood and fired their arquebuses and muskets at the Protestants, causing them many casualties in the front ranks and forcing them to retreat.[144] In the meantime, survivors of the Salm and Wurmser regiments had been reformed and remained in the second line.[145] Horn sent his cavalry to try to regain the fort, but was repulsed yet again.[146]

It was then that a stray shot caused a Spanish wagon loaded with powder to explode, causing ammunition to run low on the hill.[147] The Protestant forces were perhaps aware of the weakness of the Hispanic defence, because

---

141 Aedo, *Viaje del Infante-Cardenal*, p.134; De Vera, *Victoria sobre Norlinga*, p.160.
142 Aedo, *Viaje del Infante-Cardenal*, p.134.
143 Aedo was wrong (Aedo, *Viaje del Infante-Cardenal*, p.134), since the Black regiment was not in that brigade, but was part of the Thurn brigade, which at that time was on the flank of Bernard's troops. Minutes later this unit would attack the Toralto redoubt – perhaps this is the reason for the confusion. In any case, it is also not certain that the Blue Regiment was present, since the unit was garrisoned in Augsburg. However, a detachment of up to 600 men of this regiment may have been present in the battle, but it is not entirely certain. Perhaps the most plausible explanation was that the attacking unit carried flags or banners in which the blue colour prevailed, hence Aedo's error (Hrncirik, *Spanier auf dem Albuch*, p.116).
144 Aedo, *Viaje del Infante-Cardenal*, p.137; Guthrie, *Batallas*, p.383.
145 De Vera, *Victoria sobre Norlinga*, p.164.
146 Mesa, *Nördlingen*, p.35.
147 The incident of the explosion of a gunpowder wagon is told in a different way in the Protestant sources, which say that the explosion was came moments after the troops of the Scots and Phufl's brigades took the redoubt expelling the regiments of Salm and Wurmser. The explosion would have caused many casualties among the attackers and caused enormous confusion and chaos, weakening them before the Spanish counterattack of Idiáquez's tercio. The Spanish sources, on

THE BATTLE

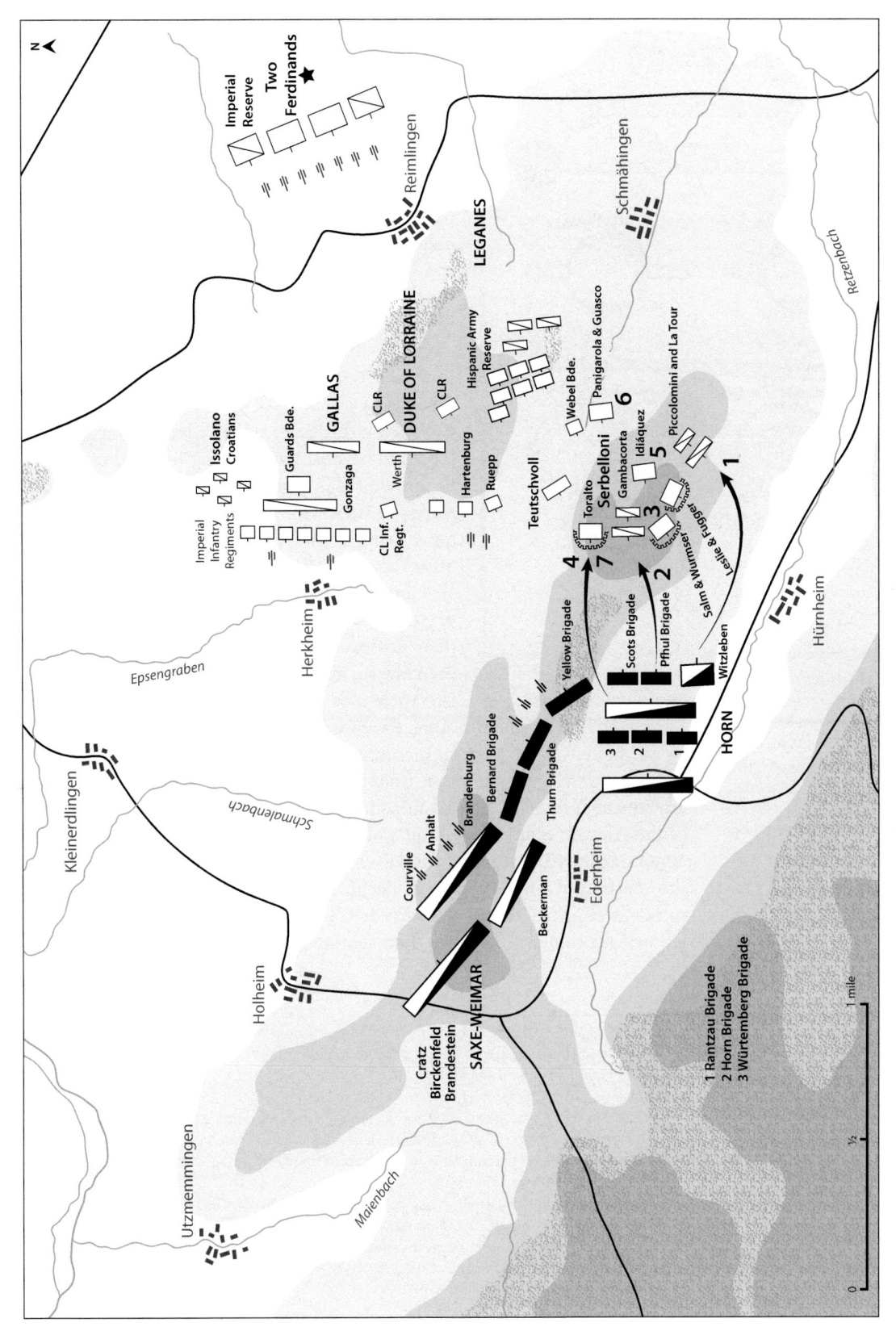

Map 4 The first phase of the battle. For further notes on the map, see Appendix II.

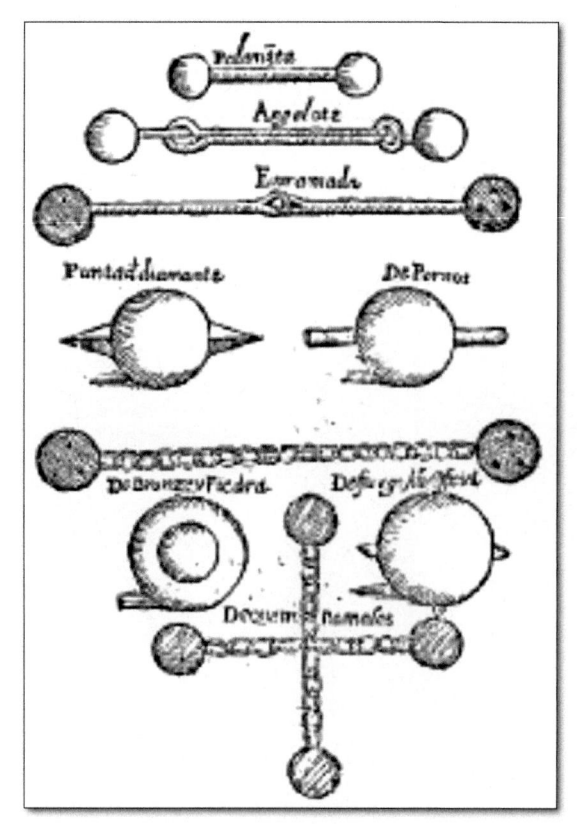

Illustration from the military treatise 'The perfect gunner: theory and practice' by Julio César Firrufino (1648). In this illustration, Firrufino drew various types of projectiles, each more deadly than the last: they are double cannon balls, linked by an iron chain, which fired at the compact infantry blocks, wreaked havoc, mutilating the bodies. (Author's collection)

they launched yet another assault, first by infantry and then cavalry, but were again thrown back by the fire of Idiáquez's shooters and the guns in the redoubt.[148]

Aedo states that the success of the actions of Idiáquez's troops was due to the experience of his soldiers and the presence of 'many private people, veteran sergeants, reformed captains and lieutenants, a lot of nobility[149] and chevaliers, being the first ranks being full of them'.[150] Sometime later, when Horn wrote his report of the battle, he described that the possibility of beating Albuch virtually disappeared when the Spaniards of Idiáquez consolidated their defence of the central redoubt.[151]

During this time, Horn ordered some artillery pieces to be positioned facing in the direction of Schonfeld Hill, causing great harm to the Catholic ranks, to which they responded by placing more guns firing at the Protestant regiments, causing great mortality.[152]

General Serbelloni, worried that the defenders of the Albuch might end up succumbing to their losses and exhaustion, gradually sent in the reserves of the Italian Tercios of Paniguerola and Guasco. In addition, he sent a message to Leganés requesting further reinforcements. In fact, noting the Swedes' continued assaults on the and as the fight was gaining momentum as the hours went by, the Cardinal-Infante ordered that the other units positioned on the Schonfeld also send arquebusier's *mangas* and cavalry squadrons to act as reserve in the defence of the Albuch. Since the Marquis of Leganés seemed to Horn to direct his attacks against the Toralto's Tercio, now weaker than that of Idiáquez due the continuous combat, Leganés decided to send two reinforcing *mangas* of musketeers of the Tercio of Pedro de Cárdenas. These reinforcements were led by four captains. Leganés then sent another *manga* of the Tercio of the

---

the other hand, do not mention this event, but just the explosion of the wagon in the rear of the Tercio of Idiáquez (Hrncirik, *Spanier auf dem Albuch*, p.116).
148 Aedo, *Viaje del Infante-Cardenal*, p.134.
149 In recognition of the services rendered to the Spanish crown, the King granted the privilege of a 'habit' to those courageous subjects. Such honorary recognition entailed the right to receive a life pension (Álvarez-Coca González, María Jesús: 'La concesión de hábitos de caballeros de las Ordenes Militares procedimiento y reflejo documental (s. XVI-XIX)' in *Cuadernos de historia moderna*, 14, 1993, pp.277–298).
150 The reformed officers as well as the particular gentlemen who had served previously in the Tercios formed up in a place of honour, but an extremely dangerous one, in the first rank. The first ranks were those that suffered the most enemy fire and the clash of pikes but if they stood firm, the unit would maintain its cohesion (Aedo, *Viaje del Infante-Cardenal*, p.134).
151 Hrncirik, *Spanier auf dem Albuch*, p.117.
152 Aedo, *Viaje del Infante-Cardenal*, p.135.

Photo D.1 (see Appendix I). Perspective from the second Spanish line, located behind the redoubts. Here were the Tercios of Idiáquez, Paniguerola and Guasco and 'mangas' that were to reinforce the main defensive line. The remains of the redoubts are barely perceptible. The traces of the earthworks are so faint that the grass effectively hides it from view. At most you would see a shadow on the ground or actually feel the outline of the entrenchment with your feet as you walked the field. (Courtesy of Daniel Staberg)

Marquis of Torrecusa, led by two captains. Gallas sent another 1,000 Imperial horse, under the orders of Picolomini, to strengthen the position between Albuch and Schonfeld.[153]

In the face of the new failure, Marshal Horn ordered the infantry of the Württemberg, Pfuhl and Scots' brigades to advance, while reorganising the survivors of the previous assault.[154] In fact for hours, Horn regrouped his soldiers again and again to launch them back into the assault, always looking for a decisive moment – which was ever more remote and never came – to break the Catholic defence of Albuch.[155]

Horn ordered a new charge of cavalry however, as Aedo describes, the Protestant riders changed the direction of their attack. Due to the strong

---
153 Aedo, *Viaje del Infante-Cardenal*, p.135.
154 Guthrie, *Batallas*, p.382.
155 Several chronicles declare that the Swedes launched seven, 13 or even 15 assaults against the Albuch Hill. Guthrie questions whether so many assaults could actually be carried out, as the later ones would be carried out by exhausted units accumulating more and more casualties, to the point where they would succumb and disintegrate under enemy fire (Guthrie, *Batallas*, p.383). In addition, although the various sources mention assaults located against a particular position, they had to be part of the coordinated attacks on the entire front line, so in reality the number of assaults must have been lower.

defence of the redoubts with the Tercios of Idiáquez and Toralto, the Protestant riders passed by the redoubts and concentrated their charge on the units located in the hollow between Albuch and Schonfeld. Seeing this enemy attack, the well-coordinated cavalry led by Gambacorta and Piccolomini charged the Protestants. Thus began an intense battle in which Gambacorta was injured. Eventually the Catholics prevailed and the Protestant cavalry retreated. But while retiring they were fired on by all the muskets and arquebuses of the infantry located on the Schonfeld and Albuch, who had returned to their positions. The ground was filled with dead and wounded riders.[156]

The two Princes Ferdinand were marching along the entire Catholic line to encourage their troops. At one of these stops, they observed this charge of cavalry against the Schonfeld and halted. As they were on the hill, they were a very visible target, so the Protestant artillery managed to fire at the royal entourage, killing Colonel Ayasso and wounding in the thigh[157] Pedro Girón.[158] The officers of the entourage begged the Princes to leave the front line, but the two cousins, showing their cool blood and courage,[159] they each refused to be the first to leave the dangerous location. Thus, the King of Hungary wanted his cousin Fernando to be the first to 'flee' and the Prince Fernando, for dignity's sake, did not wish to go before the King.[160]

By about 7.30 a.m. Horn was aware of the failure of his frontal assaults, with his men exhausted and after launching his fourth assault, he sent a messenger to Bernard asking for reinforcements, as Bernard's flank had barely fought. Indeed, from 5.00 a.m. until then, the action of the Duke of Franconia's troops had been limited to an artillery duel and a cavalry skirmish. When the Catholics advanced a few light cavalry squadrons to skirmish on the Herkhimerfeld Hill and a contingent of Croatian auxiliaries explored Bernard's left flank, between the Landle and Eger, the Duke sent Taupadel's dragoons to block them. Indeed, along the entire battle front virtually nothing had happened except for the fighting on the Albuch.[161]

Bernard was also aware that the battle was not proceeding as expected. The resistance on the Albuch was more determined than he had supposed and moreover, their own inactivity had contributed to the failure. His only plan was simply to wait for the conclusion of the fight for the Albuch, forcing Catholics to retreat, after which the troops under his command would attack the retreating enemy.

---

156 Aedo, *Viaje del Infante-Cardenal*, p.135.
157 Aedo, *Viaje del Infante-Cardenal*, p.135; De Vera, *Victoria sobre Norlinga*, p.168.
158 The illegitimate son of Pedro Téllez-Girón y Velasco Guzmán y Tovar (1574–1624), III Duke of Osuna and his Flemish lover Elena de la Gambe.
159 Guthrie is sceptical that such an episode would occur: 'Catholic testimonies emphasize the personal danger of princes and members of their high staff to being hit by cannonballs and their royal serenity under fire. But, at two kilometres, the danger was not great, although Tilly, Mercy and Turenne finished their days in this way' (Guthrie, *Batallas*, p.384).
160 De Vera, *Victoria sobre Norlinga*, p.170.
161 Guthrie, *Batallas*, p.384.

The Battle of Nördlingen, by Peter Snayers (1634). From an imaginary position, the painter presents us with the defence of Albuch and the deployment of Spanish troops behind that hill and in neighbouring Schönfeld. The three redoubts are perfectly distinguished, as well as the squadrons of the Tercios formed for their defense. We also see various cavalry units and the other infantry squadrons, with their flags in the centre, then the pikemen and the garrisons of musketeers and arquebusiers. In the foreground we have various servants carrying supplies into battle. In the distance, the Herkheimerfeld plain, with the gigantic cavalry battle. (Nationalmuseum, NM 277)

So, resolving to reverse the situation, he ordered Thurn to take his Black and Yellow regiments and reinforce Horn's contingent.[162] Bernard would launch an assault with the rest of his troops, thus distracting the enemy's front and forcing Catholic reserves to be used in their sector and not in the Albuch's, allowing Horn to launch a new assault, reinforced with Thurn troops.[163]

Assuming correctly that the Protestants were planning a new assault, Leganés ordered the Tercios defending Albuch to be strengthened by 1,000 musketeers and that the Tercios of Guasco and Paniguerola advance from the Schonfeld Hill and approached the forest standing at the foot of the

---

162 The veteran Count Thurn had served on all theatres of war and had succeeded the Swedish Major General Lars Kagg in command of the brigade, who had returned to Sweden after the fall of Regensburg. Thurn assumed joint command of the Yellow Regiment, until then under the orders of Kagg, and of his own Black Regiment, so since July 1634 that corps was known as Thurn Brigade (Hrncirik, *Spanier auf dem Albuch*, p.118).
163 Guthrie, *Batallas*, p.384.

THE BATTLE OF NÖRDLINGEN 1634

Battle of Nördlingen. Interesting view from Bernard of Saxe-Weimar's point of view. The city appears incorrectly to be besieged on all sides. From the viewer's perspective, located on Lachberg hill, one can observe how the Swedes and Germans charge towards the top of a mountain, supposedly the Allbuch, on which three defending units can be distinguished and the viewer might suppose that this refers to the three strongholds. However, the other hills where the Catholics were positioned, or the battle of Herkheimerfeld Plain, do not appear. (RCIN 722080)

Heselberg, with orders to open fire on the enemy units that were climbing past that sector.

While waiting for Bernard's reinforcements, Horn again sent his cavalry to attack, but was repelled once more by Catholic horse.[164]

The Final Assault

The Swedes and Germans had been carrying out fruitless assaults on the Albuch hill all morning. How many attacks is open to debate but there were many, be it four, seven, or 10 times, they threw themselves up the hill.[165] The infantry and cavalry attacks had all been countered, all had failed and

---

164 Aedo, *Viaje del Infante-Cardenal*, p.136.
165 Aedo writes that the Swedes-Germans attacked the hill of the Albuch at least 15 times, continuously for six hours, 'with the most trained and numerous of its best troops' (Aedo, *Viaje del Infante-Cardenal*, p.137).

more and more dead and wounded had been lost, on top of which, morale was falling fast. This is why Horn received a message from Bernard sent by the Thurn Brigade,[166] consisting of the magnificent Black Regiment under the command of Colonel Hans Jakob von Thurn and the Yellow Regiment commanded by Lieutenant Colonel Wulf von Schönbeck to take the hill and on the arrival of these troops the morale of the assault force went up again. These units formed the elite of the Swedish-German army and had about 3,350 experienced, fresh and highly motivated men. They hoped that by their efforts the hill would fall and the victory for their side would finally be settled. Like the Swedish units of Count Kaspar von Eberstein in the Battle of Lützen, they trusted that the Thurn brigade could dislodge the Catholics from their trenches and fortified positions. As Thurn's troops approached, Horn ordered his cavalry to prepare to support them.[167]

At about 7.45 a.m. Thurn's force marched from Bernard's flank to Horn's position. On his march from Heselberg to the south, where Horn's command post was positioned, General Thurn saw the fort defended by Toralto's tercio.[168] As he thought this was what Horn expected of him, after the Swedish Marshal had asked for his presence in that sector, or because Thurn decided to take his own initiative, the fact is that Thurn ordered an immediate attack on that position.[169] His reasoning was faulty, because they initiated the assault without protection of the cavalry and without co-ordinating with Horn's forces. Overestimating his own forces – some 3,350 soldiers against 1,650 defenders –[170] Thurn ordered his men to advance up the hill to confront the Catholics.[171]

Toralto's Italians were exhausted, but well positioned and most were veteran soldiers. They systematically fired their arquebuses and muskets at the Protestants,[172] causing them to lose many in the front ranks of the Yellow and Black regiments, who were unable to approach the Catholic parapets. But Thurn wanted to encourage his men, ordering them to stay in position, to move neither forward nor backward. Instead of acknowledging defeat and saving his men with a timely retreat, Thurn did the opposite and forced his men to continue on up the hill,[173] hoping that the fire of his muskets and the

---

166 Hrncirik, *Spanier auf dem Albuch*, p.24.
167 Guthrie, *Batallas*, p.384.
168 A discrepancy is produced here among the several stories about the battle: Aedo affirms that the troops of Thurn attacked the redoubt of the Tercio of Idiáquez (Aedo, *Viaje del Infante-Cardenal*, p.137), while Guthrie indicates that Thurn attacked the redoubt of the north, occupied according to him by the regiments of Leslie and Fugger (Guthrie, *Batallas*, p.384). These units, according to Hispanic sources, were in the redoubt to the south, the Tercio of Toralto being the one that occupied the north redoubt. Hrncirik affirms that the Thurn's brigade attacked the Italians of Toralto's tercio (Hrncirik, *Spanier auf dem Albuch*, p.24).
169 Hrncirik, *Spanier auf dem Albuch*, p.119.
170 Guthrie, *Batallas*, p.384. Hrncirik informs of the strength of the Thurn's unit being more modest: just 1,200 soldiers, of whom 750 belonged to the Yellow regiment and 450 to the Black regiment. Also, the strength of Toralto was considerably minor, about 900 foot soldiers. In any case, the attackers were superior in numbers to the defenders (Hrncirik, *Spanier auf dem Albuch*, pp.117–119).
171 Guthrie, *Batallas*, p.384.
172 Aedo, *Viaje del Infante-Cardenal*, p.137; Guthrie, *Batallas*, p.383.
173 Guthrie, *Batallas*, p.384.

THE BATTLE OF NÖRDLINGEN 1634

Photo F.1 (see Appendix I). This photo is taken in the North Redoubt area, looking west with Ederheim partly visible. This is probably the general area where Thurn's brigade advanced from the Heselberg only to be halted and defeated by the Spanish counterattack. The modern-day woodland effectively hides the Heselberg from view and covers a good part of this section of the battlefield. (Courtesy of Daniel Staberg)

determination of his men would be enough to break the will of their Catholic opponents; soldiers positioned inside redoubts, with supporting artillery and plenty of ammunition.

In case the situation was not dire enough for the brave men of Thurn's command, in remaining in that position, at the foot of Albuch Hill, they were exposed on their north side to the crossfire between the Schonfeld and Albuch, from artillery and the musketeers of Tiefembach. And to unbalance the situation, not having Protestant cavalry to support the infantry, they were too desirable a prey for Generals Gambacorta and Piccolomini to resist and they instantly led their cavalry units in a charge against the Protestant infantry.[174]

Horn watched in horror as Thurn's troops were shot at from both the front and the flank and decided to send his cavalry to assist them. Swedish Marshal Horn decided to send it between Heselberg and Albuch. Protestant cavalry engaged in melee against the 1,830 men of Gambacorta and the 1,200 of Piccolomini. However, despite their numbers, the Protestants were beaten by the Catholic cavalry and retired. Thurn's infantry was left alone again, holding on in an unspeakable and deteriorating position for the next hour and a half.[175]

---

174 Guthrie, *Batallas*, p.384.
175 Guthrie, *Batallas*, p.384.

Photo E.1 (see Appendix I). This photo looks south and shows the shallow depression between the middle and northern redoubts. In this area the Swedish cavalry attacked in the last stages of the battle only to be repulsed. Hürnheim and Ederheim are visible in the photo, although in 1634 they were much smaller towns and the panorama would be different. (Courtesy of Daniel Staberg)

Then the Spaniards of Idiáquez, emboldened by having stopped the invincible 'Swedes', understood that their position was extremely precarious and left their positions with the battle cry of *Santiago y Cierra España* ('Santiago and Spain attacks!' that they always shouted when they started an assault).[176] This was another of the critical moments of the battle for the hill. The Spaniards recklessly threw themselves out of the protection of their parapets, which had served them well, to stop the succession of attacks of the enemy. But if the Protestants had reserve units available, or they had been fresh, they could have counter charged and defeated the Spaniards. But by Fortune's design, the charge was effective for the Spaniards and terrible for the Germans. Idiáquez's men came into close combat with Protestants who, although demoralised, continued to fight like lions but had to withdraw. The Tercio of Idiáquez lost its sergeant major, Diego de Bustos and Captains Juan Negrete and Juan Losada injured, as well as several dozen soldiers.

Pressed by Idiáquez's attack, Thurn gave the order to retreat to Heselberg Hill and it was carried out in the best possible way, under agonising circumstances. In this unsuccessful attack, the elite Swedish brigades lost more than half of their men. The Catholics captured five Swedish field guns, but Protestants launched a local counterattack and recovered them.[177]

---

176 Mesa, *Nördlingen*, p.38.
177 Cánovas, *Estudios* p.431.

Horn then turned his gaze again to the position of the Tercio of Toralto. The assault started with light cannon fire and was then followed by an infantry and cavalry attack. But the Neapolitans, despite the previous fighting, remained calm and stopped the attack, which was not as fierce as on previous occasions, fully understandable after so many hours of combat and so many casualties.

It was then that Serbelloni agreed to advance the Catholic line. First, the *mangas* of Torrecusa's arquebusiers advanced, who had just arrived to reinforce Toralto's tercio. In this way the Catholic line moved forward adding a few tens of metres to the defensive perimeter and relieving the pressure on the redoubt of Toralto. The Protestants sent some musketeers to slow the movement of the Italians, but they were unable to do so.[178]

Leganés reinforced the redoubt on the hill, sending two *mangas* of musketeers of the Tercio of San Sivero, under the orders of his sergeant major and two captains, who integrated themselves with the Tercios of Paniguerola and Guasco. Then came up to seven companies from the Tercios of Cárdenas, Lunato and La Tour, to reinforce the Albuch sector.[179]

Horn's men appeared reluctant to launch a new attack, and at around 9.30 a.m. Serbelloni ordered the Tercios of Paniguerola and Guasco to move forward to support the advanced detachment of Torrecusa. The *maestre de campo* Paniguerola was shot dead with a bullet in the neck, being replaced in command by his sergeant major, Juan de Orozco. Guasco was wounded in the right thigh with two gunshots and he continued to advance, but when a third shot struck his left thigh, his men pulled him up the hill, being relieved by his sergeant major Alejandro Campi, who was also wounded by a bullet. Orozco assumed the control of both Italian Tercios.[180]

The Struggle at Herkheimerfeld

While these events were taking place on the Albuch Hill, at around 8.00 a.m. and according to the plan drawn up by Bernard and Horn, Bernard's troops were ordered to begin their assault, while Taupadel led a flanking attempt on their left on the Catholic right flank, on the town of Kleinerdlingen, where they were repulsed by Issolano's Croatians.[181]

However, the main attack of the Protestant cavalry was yet to come. Its first wave was made up of eight squadrons, mainly cuirassiers, advancing from the Lachberg[182] to charge against the Catholic positions at Herkheimerfeld.

Bernard's 2,000 horsemen ferociously charged down the Lachberg, breaking onto the Herkheimerfeld Plain, easily sweeping away groups of skirmishers positioned there. No doubt psychological success was achieved, sweeping away any resistance with its charge. However, on arriving in the

---

178 Aedo, *Viaje del Infante-Cardenal*, p.138.
179 Aedo, *Viaje del Infante-Cardenal*, p.138.
180 Aedo, *Viaje del Infante-Cardenal*, p.139.
181 Piccouet, *Armies*, p.241.
182 Guthrie, *Batallas*, p.384.

THE BATTLE

General Georg Christoph von Taupadel, by Raphael Custos (before 1651). At the age of 25 he enlisted in Bernard of Saxe-Weimar's Regiment in the service of Denmark (1625). It was the beginning of a relationship of service and friendship with Bernard and he participated in all the battles with him. Taupadel was captured in August 1638 at the Battle of Wittenweiher. He was liberated in 1640 and took command of Bernard's former army and fought in the service of Sweden and France against the Imperialists and Bavarians until 1646, when he retired to his estate at Sundgau, near Basel, where he died in 1647. (Herzog Anton Ulrich-Museum, R. Custos AB 3.73)

vicinity of the village of Herkheim, where the advanced Imperial infantry companies were posted, the Protestant cavalry was stopped by repeated volleys of Catholic muskets and arquebuses. In addition, taking advantage of the confusion, several parties of Croatians hidden there also attacked the Protestant cavalry.[183]

Taking advantage of the confusion and disorganisation of the Protestant cavalry, Gallas ordered a counterattack by his own cavalry. Gonzaga and Werth's horsemen attacked Bernard's.[184] The cavalry combat was very intense and both sides lost heavily, but the greater numbers of Catholics prevailed and Bernard's cavalry were defeated.

From his prime position as observer on top of the Lachberg, the Duke of Franconia contemplated how his riders had could be losing, as the cuirassiers were being massacred. Then Bernard ordered his reserves to charge to rescue them. Cratz took command of these seven squadrons and galloped over the more than 1,200 metres that separated the Protestant line from the centre of the battle on the plain. Those minutes seemed endless, but at least Cratz contacted and rescued the cuirassiers. But upon seeing Cratz's movement, General Gallas ordered that the Imperial cavalry reserve, consisting of nine squadrons and located to the front of the centre, to gallop north to contain the new Protestant attack.

Bernard then sent his last five reserve squadrons. The Catholics sent more regiments to support Gonzaga and Werth's riders.[185] In addition, the Marquis of Leganes sent 400 musketeers from the Tercio of the Count of Fuenclara[186] to support the action of the Catholic cavalry.

---

183 Aedo, *Viaje del Infante-Cardenal*, p.140.
184 De Vera, *Victoria sobre Norlinga*, p.170; Guthrie, *Batallas*, p.385. Poyntz took part in this clash at the head of his company of dragoons (Poyntz, *Relations*, pp.111–112).
185 Guthrie, *Batallas*, p.385.
186 Aedo, *Viaje del Infante-Cardenal*, p.140.

Photo F.2 (see Appendix I). The hill and fields behind Herkheim were the scene of Bernhard von Weimar's failed cavalry attack late in the battle with the Imperial counterattack coming down the slope of the hill and pushing the Protestants back to the ground just outside the right edge of the photo. (Courtesy of Daniel Staberg)

Such a large concentration of Catholic forces led to the final withdrawal of Protestant cavalry, though they did so in reasonable order, but Cratz himself was captured as he attempted to rally his men.[187]

While the battle was taking place on the Herkheimerfeld Plain and in the vicinity of Heselberg, Horn ordered a halt to any action on the Albuch and went to Bernard to discuss a general retreat.[188] At that time, Bernard's last five cavalry reserve squadrons were rolling down the hill to rescue the 15 squadrons of Cratz[189] from Werth and Gonzaga's horsemen on the Herkheimerfeld ridge.[190]

When Horn explained the failure to take the Albuch, Bernard – who was still contemplating the magnitude of the cavalry battle a mile away – believed that Horn was exaggerating. Perhaps Bernard believed that his men were now waging the real battle and could not afford to withdraw, because that would lead to the collapse of his attack.

The Swedish general, now discouraged by the casualties and defeat of his veteran brigades, called for a general retreat. Bernard refused to retreat, suggesting that in any case the army should take defensive positions and wait

---

187 Guthrie, *Batallas*, p.385.
188 De Vera, *Victoria sobre Norlinga*, p.180.
189 Guthrie, *Batallas*, p.385.
190 Guthrie, *Batallas*, p.385.

THE BATTLE

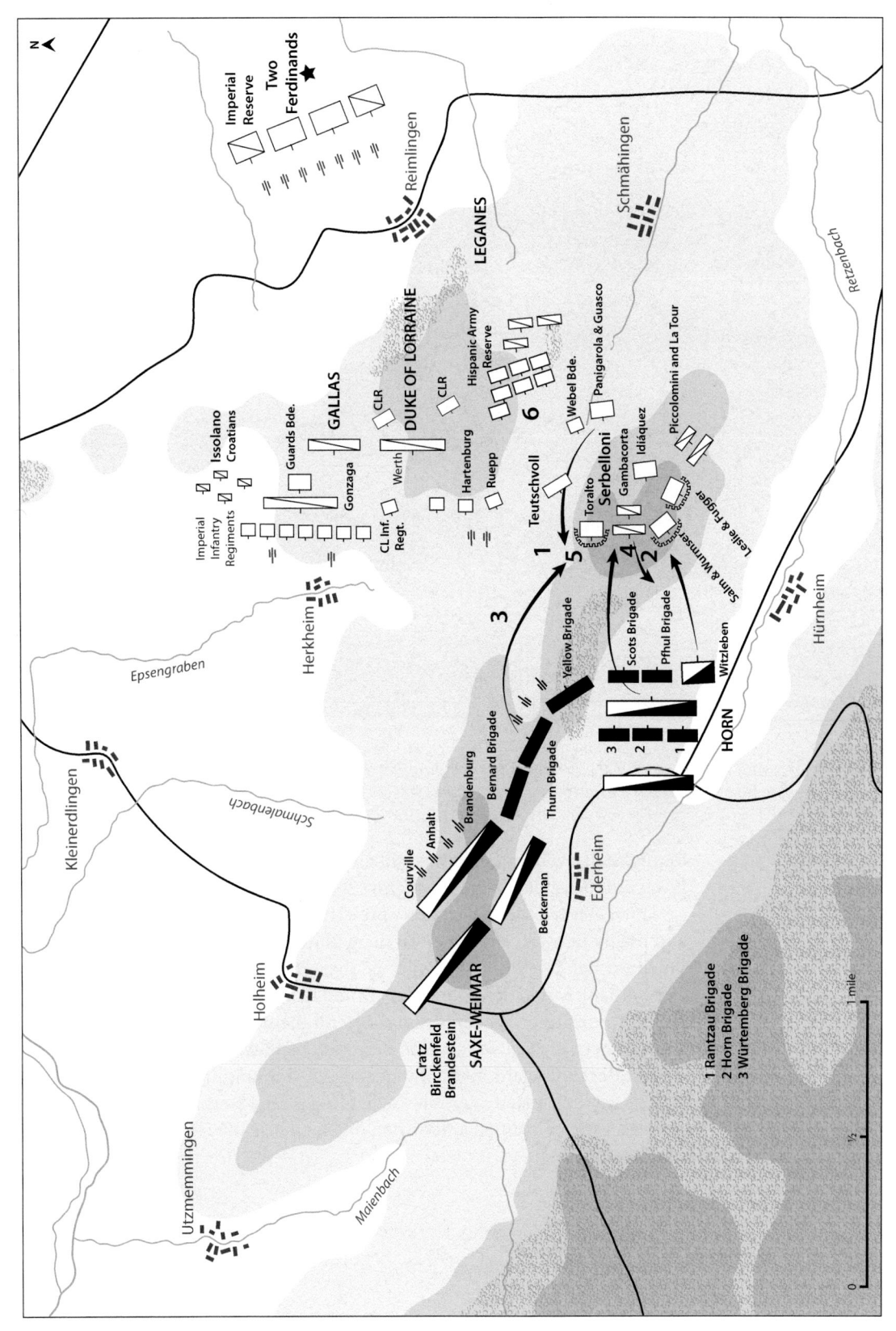

Map 5 The second phase of the battle (see Appendix II).

THE BATTLE OF NÖRDLINGEN 1634

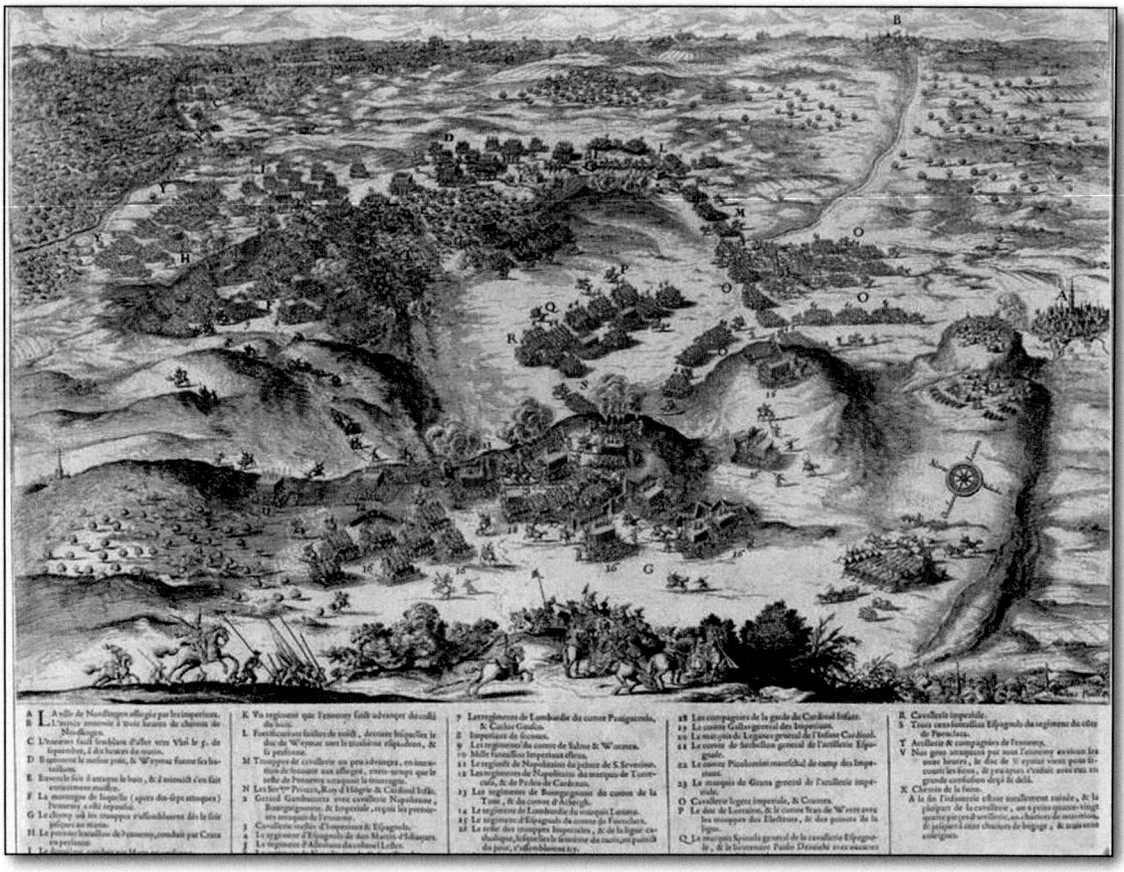

Battle of Nördlingen. Oriented with east-north-east to top (compass rose). In this engraving the three main elements of the battle take place, although they are captured in a single vision. In the foreground is the defense of the Allbuch by the Hispanic tercios. Further to our right we see the cavalry combat on the Herkheimerfeld plain. And finally, there is the flight of the Protestant army and the pursuit by the Catholic troops towards the Rezen stream. This print comes from Frederick Muller (1863) vol. I, no.1727, p.235, lists this view as an engraving by B.F. Berckenrode and cites the source as an atlas then belonging to J.T. Bodel Nijenhuis of Leiden.

for nightfall, even though it was still nine hours before it got dark and believed it was still possible for the *Rheingrave* to arrive and save the situation.[191]

Horn insisted that his troops were exhausted and that they should retreat and finally Bernard consented to the withdrawal,[192] since his Germans were much fresher and with better morale than Horn's troops. Bernard proposed that his flank would hold the Lachberg and Landle peaks long enough to allow Horn's troops to break contact and defend themselves in the woods around the Arnsberg area, at which time Bernard's flank would also withdraw.[193]

But Bernard again made the mistake of thinking too optimistically. His cavalry was exhausted after intense fighting on the Herkheimerfeld plain, his reserves were consumed and he had only one brigade remaining to hold the Lachberg.[194]

---

191 Guthrie, *Batallas*, p.385.
192 De Vera, *Victoria sobre Norlinga*, p.180.
193 Guthrie, *Batallas*, p.386.
194 Guthrie, *Batallas*, p.386.

The Catholics Counterattack

For more than five hours the Swedes and Germans had been launching repeated attacks one after the other on the Albuch. Horn was now fully aware of the slaughter his men had suffered. After the last attack on the Albuch, the Catholics had further strengthened their front line, so by 10.00 a.m. paradoxically, the defenders outnumbered their demoralised attackers thanks to the ordered and steady entry into action of several *mangas* and reserve Tercios throughout the morning.

Thus, the Imperial Webel brigade was sent forward[195] to occupy the right flank of the new Hispanic deployment. The Spaniards were getting closer and closer to the Heselberg. Webel was next to the Tercio of Guasco and close to Toralto's Tercio. General Toralto warned of the importance of their new position[196] and that it would be highly advisable to have artillery there. There was a Protestant unit firing on them from the woods, and if Catholics had placed cannons there, they could have neutralised it.[197]

Serbelloni informed Toralto that they had two light guns in the rear, but no horses to pull them. Toralto ordered his troops to search for the cannons and manhandle them down the hill to position the pieces. After the guns were in position, they began to shoot against the Protestant regiment located around the forest of Heselberg, destroying its regimental guns first and soon forced the regiment to retire with heavy losses. It was at that moment that Sergeant-Major Orozco ordered his two Italian Tercios to charge into the woods to evict the Protestants.[198]

The Marquis of the Balbases was alert to every movement along the battlefield. When he was in the Imperial sector, where the cavalry battle on the plain had taken place, he was informed of the Hispanic advance to the Heselberg and ordered Paulo Dentichi to take four cavalry companies and flank the enemy position at Heselberg to attack units there that opposed the Catholic advance. In addition, 400 musketeers of Fuenclara followed Dentichi.[199] Piccolomini also supported Leganés's order, sending two Imperial regiments up the hill. Also, the Duke of Lorraine with the cavalry of Gonzaga and Werth marched to attack the summit of Heselberg. The Protestant position in the vicinity of the Heselberg was thus virtually surrounded by Italian, Bavarian, Imperial and Spanish troops, who launched themselves into the assault. First the Protestants lost their artillery near the forest and then the other units fell. The Duke of Lorraine, in personal combat, captured a banner of Bernard's cavalry.[200]

---

195 Hrncirik specifies that the Italians were probably reinforced by the Imperial infantry regiments of Webel – under the command of Colonel Webel and Alt-Sachsen under Lieutenant Colonel Studnicky (or Studnitzki) and that they were in reserve until 6.00 a.m. near the Albuch (Hrncirik, *Spanier auf dem Albuch,* p.26).
196 Aedo, *Viaje del Infante-Cardenal,* p.140.
197 Mesa, *Nördlingen,* p.39.
198 Aedo, *Viaje del Infante-Cardenal,* p.141.
199 De Vera, *Victoria sobre Norlinga,* p.184.
200 Aedo, *Viaje del Infante-Cardenal,* p.141.

THE BATTLE OF NÖRDLINGEN 1634

The Battle of Nördlingen, by Jan van der Hoecke (1635). The two cousins march with their troops into the heat of combat. The pikemen are visible, who are protected only with a breastplate and helmet and the flags, with the ever present Cross of Burgundy, symbol of the Habsburgs. Behind are Catholic cuirassiers, with the red sashes. The Imperial heir wears a Hungarian-style cap, while the Cardinal-Infante wears a wide-brimmed Spanish hat and has the same appearance as in another Hoecke painting preserved in the Kunsthistorisches Museum. (Royal Collection at Windsor Castle, RCIN 400100)

The Beginning of the End

Optimism was noticeable in the Catholic ranks. Albuch's defences remained intact, the Heselberg had been won and the great battle of the Herkheimerfeld Plain had been favourable to the Imperialists. Gallas ordered a general attack to evict Bernard's troops from their position at Lachberg. He was almost certain that the decisive moment of the battle had arrived. The fighting in Albuch had ceased through the exhaustion of the Protestants and the Spaniards had firmly established their position on that hill and had won the Heselberg. If Bernard did not send troops to retrieve it, that would have been because he did not have them and therefore, he was also in a difficult situation.

Indeed, despite the withdrawal plan establishing that Bernard should resist as the right flank retreated, the truth was that with the Catholic attack ordered by Gallas, the Weimar infantry brigade, formed by the Bernard, Hodiagowa and Limbach regiments,[201] with a total of just 1,250 troops,

---

201 Guthrie, *Batallas*, p.398.

was totally overwhelmed by the Catholic cavalry and infantry. A short and intense battle took place. Bernard himself was on the verge of capture since unarmed, with his horse dead and wounded twice, a captain surrendered his own horse, allowing him to flee.[202]

As Bernard's flank collapsed rather than holding to allow Horn's troops to retreat in some order the Swedish Marshal was planning how to withdraw and save his men. According to his initial plans, they would retreat along the narrow valley between the Heselberg and the Rezen, to reach a fork and continue towards Ederheim. Once there, Horn believed that his vanguard and artillery could take position there and that they could then defend the withdrawal of his rear, with the supporting fire of the guns. Horn even imagined that if their deployment was successful, they could help the Duke of Weimar's contingent withdraw.[203] Horn relied on that plan, leaving a large number of musketeers in Ederheim so that they could contain the Catholics. The rest of the army in that part of the Rezen, could entrench themselves in the hills of that area and resist until the arrival of the relief army of Rhinegrave Otto Ludwig of Salm and Landgrave William of Hesse-Kassel.[204]

Pfuhl lead the vanguard and the valuable Swedish artillery was located immediately afterwards to avoid capture, but their reduced mobility slowed down the rest of the formation. The rest of the survivors of the Horn's forces covered the retreat.

Serbelloni sent part of the troops who had been defending the Albuch to follow the Protestant retreat closely, but without engaging in any combat.[205]

Horn's column approached Ederheim and was about to cross the Rezen stream, when Bavarian cuirassiers[206] appeared riding from the Lachberg and Heselberg, followed by Gambacorta's horsemen and other Imperial cavalry units; there were even some Croatians.[207] They were followed by 400 Spanish musketeers of the Tercio of the Count of Fuenclara.[208] Behind them came the reserve of the Hispanic army – the Burgundian Tercio of Alberg and the Lombards Tercios of San Sivero and Lunato – all fresh because they had not participated in the Albuch and Heselberg battles.[209]

Horn's cavalry offered barely any resistance, dispersing in a thousand directions taking advantage of their speed. The Catholic cavalry seized the artillery and cut off the Protestant column, leaving the bulk of it – the Horn, Rantzau and Württemberg brigades – just 300 metres from the ford.[210]

---

202 Guthrie, *Batallas*, p.386.
203 Guthrie, *Batallas*, p.386.
204 De Vera, *Victoria sobre Norlinga*, p.188.
205 Guthrie, *Battles*, p.386.
206 The defeat of the Protestant army is described differently by Delbruck, who states that when Horn's troops were withdrawing, they intermingled with those of Bernard, who had yielded to the pressure of the Imperial advance. Bernard's troops were retreating towards the road to Ulm, causing the general confusion in the Protestant army, which was being skilfully exploited by Catholics (Delbruck, *Dawn of Modern Warfare*, p.211).
207 Guthrie, *Batallas*, p.386.
208 De Vera, *Victoria sobre Norlinga*, p.184.
209 Anonymous letter, *Sucesos de la Esdeveniments Successos 1634*, p.123.
210 Guthrie, *Batallas*, p.386.

THE BATTLE OF NÖRDLINGEN 1634

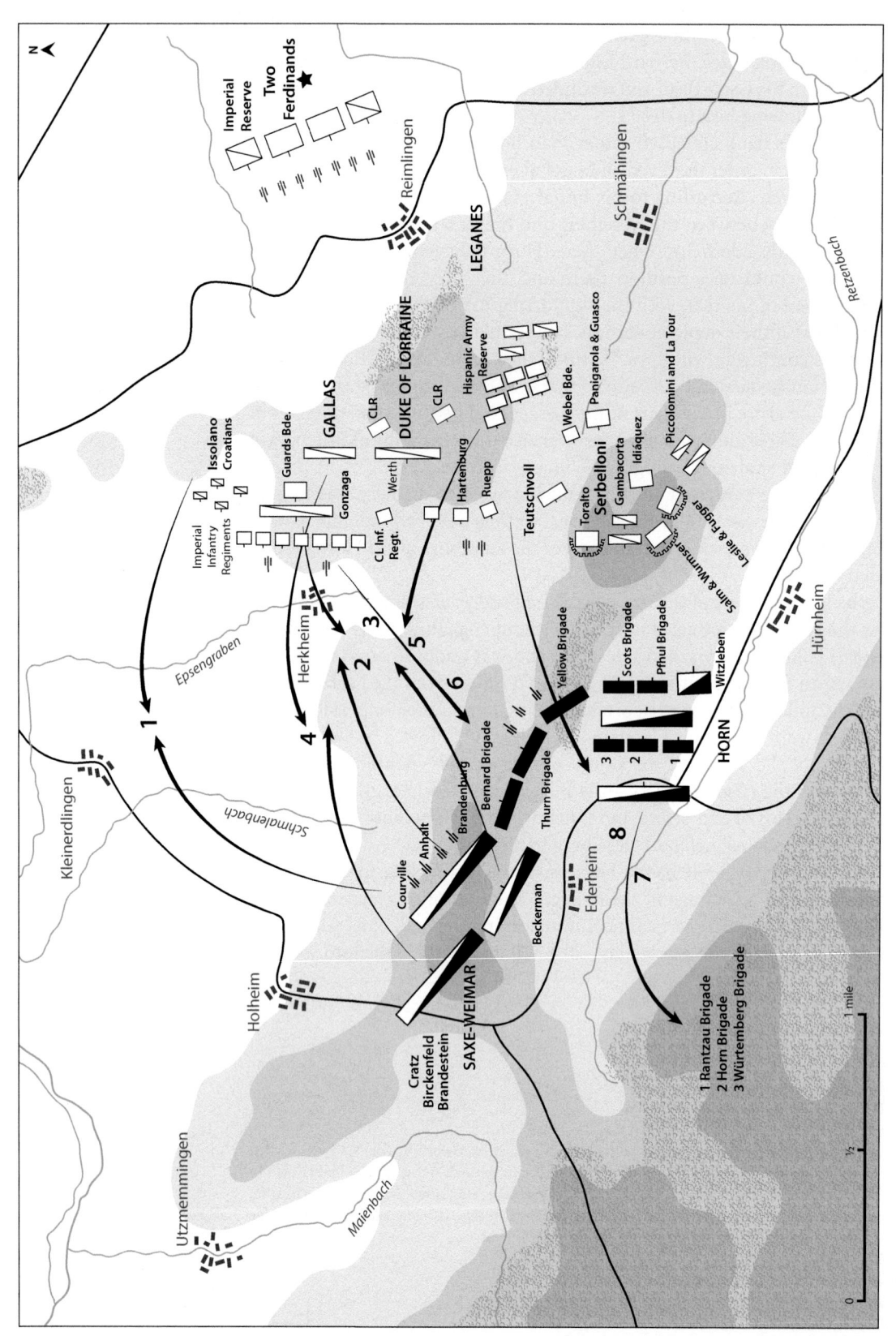

Map 6 The third phase of the battle (see Appendix II).

THE BATTLE

The human tide collided with Horn's column. Only Pfuhl and a few German companies had managed to cross the river and reach Ederheim. The Scots left the formation on their own initiative, crossed downstream and made their way to the forest for security.[211] Behind the Catholic riders came the musketeers of Fuenclara and the rest of the infantry, massacring the Protestants. Many Swedish and German soldiers threw their weapons down and cried for mercy, but many of them were cut down by the Catholic pursuers. Horn[212] and Cratz[213] were no doubt lucky to be recognised and taken prisoner.

Within minutes the Catholics had advanced their line, conquered the central hills and continued their advance, falling on Horn's column and destroying it. As the fighting ceased and the Catholic line carried on, so did both princes and their entourages. The Cardinal-Infante recognised the *maestres de campo* Idiáquez and Toralto, got off his horse and went to hug them, congratulating them on the courageous behaviour of their troops and the heroic defence of the hill.[214] Coming down from the Allbuch and heading for the plain, as they marched through the battlefield – sown with corpses and wounded – the two Ferdinands went on to speak to the fighting companies. It is said that King Ferdinand of Hungary exclaimed that with this victory they had already paid for the defeat of Breitenfeld.[215]

The slaughter of the Protestants continued for the rest of the day, through the night and into the next day.[216] Especially effective and cruel were the Croatian and Bavarian cavalry. The Croatians located the Protestant luggage

---

211 Guthrie, *Batallas*, p.386.
212 Horn was led before the two princes and the Cardinal-Infante embraced him when he was introduced to them. The Spanish prince recognised his courage and that of his men for having tried so many times to take the hill. The Swede thanked them and also commented on the courage and tenacity of the Catholic defenders (Mesa, *Nördlingen*, p.40).
213 Cratz was captured by a Croatian irregular captain called Fontana. The German officer negotiated with the Croatian to save his life in exchange for 30,000 *thalers* and giving him the command of a regiment, if the Croatian agreed to change of sides. As a sign of submission, Cratz gave his sword and pistols. On the way back to the Catholic line, a group of Swedish riders tried to free Cratz, but a squadron of Lorraine cavalry chased them off. (De Vera, *Victoria sobre Norlinga*, p.204). Lorraine had outstanding accounts with Cratz: years ago, the Duke of Lorraine had handed him up to 150,000 *thalers* so that Cratz could recruit an army to fight in defence of the Duchy of Lorraine, but Cratz changed sides and escaped with the Lorraine's money (Aedo, *Viaje del Infante-Cardenal*, p.143). After the battle, Cratz was be sent to Vienna, where he was tried for high treason and sentenced to death. On 26 March 1635, a day before his execution, he managed to escape from the prison disguised as a monk and rode to Silesia, but was captured by the Hussars of Count Stephan Pálffy, who dragged him back to Vienna, where he was beheaded July 6, 1635 (Landmann, *Kratz zu Scharffenstein*, pp.573–575).
214 Mesa, *Nördlingen*, p.42.
215 Rucker, *Eine strategisch-militärische Analyse*, p.15.
216 In 2006, in the course of an archaeological excavation on the battlefield, the mortal remains of seven individuals were found, north of the town of Ederheim and west of Hürnheim. Four of the bodies were aged between 16 and 19 and in two bodies it was clear that they had died from violent action, one of them with a large hole in the right parietal, caused by the impact of a gunshot bullet, presumably a pistol. Taking into account that the bodies were found away from the battlefield, the researchers concluded that these people were killed during the persecution that took place afterwards (Plum, *Die Bestattungen*).

THE BATTLE OF NÖRDLINGEN 1634

Battle of Nordlingen. This is the classic engraving of the battle, drawn by Mattaeus Merian. It gives us a fantastic overview of the battle, detailing the name and location of the units that fought. In the foreground, the motley defense of the Allbuch, with the three redoubts and the Hispanic units ready to intervene. In front, Horn's troops launch successive frontal assaults. More to the centre of the painting, we can see the fortified positions of the rest of the Spanish, Imperial and Catholic League units. Merian draws the Catholic troops in the classic formation of the 'tercio', while the Protestants form in Swedish brigades of three battalions of four companies each. In the centre of the painting is the battle of Herkheimerfeld Plain and to the right is the camp of the Imperial troops, perfectly depicted and protected by a parapet. In the distance, Merian also represents the fighting in the Rezen stream. (Theatrum Europaeum, period 1633, Edition 1670)

train in Neresheim, where they slaughtered the 2,000 *landvolk* guards who guarded it and pillaged their wagons.[217]

Aedo records that the Protestant Army escaped in small numbers in detachments, without order or any co-ordination and as a whole, the groups did not exceed 300 troops, making it easy for Catholic pursuers to catch them.[218]

In the swampy area behind the hills, many fugitives were halted, with the wetland coming up to their knees. In addition, the steep ascent to the other side slowed down their movements even further, so that they were easy targets for the Croatians who were chasing them.[219]

After touring the battlefield, the two princely cousins returned to their respective camps. In the Spanish camp, the wounded had been concentrated around the esplanade where the Cardinal-Infante had his luxurious tent. When he saw them lying there, Cardinal-Infante allowed the wounded to use his tent while he and his entourage went to some nearby houses where they rested and stayed for two days.[220]

The Cardinal-Infante ordered the Marquis of Leganés to make two payments to the surviving soldiers in recognition of their value and ordered his butler to give money to all the wounded soldiers and all those who presented him with war trophies from the enemy. All those gifts made the young prince's popularity and fame among his troops immense.[221]

---

217 Aedo, *Viaje del Infante-Cardenal*, p.144; Guthrie, *Batallas*, p.386.
218 Aedo, *Viaje del Infante-Cardenal*, p.144.
219 Aedo, *Viaje del Infante-Cardenal*, p.143.
220 Mesa, *Nördlingen*, p.42.
221 Mesa, *Nördlingen*, p.42.

Later that afternoon, the Duke of Lorraine returned with his troops, following their pursuit of the Protestant survivors. The Duke and his men went to pay their respects to the princes, telling them the actions they had taken, the officers captured and the ransom they could expect to obtain for them.[222]

The day after the battle, the King of Hungary and the Cardinal-Infante wrote letters to tell of the victory of Nördlingen, to Madrid, Vienna, Brussels and other capitals and the messengers departed with their triumphal letters exclaiming the victory. In Madrid the news was celebrated with a ringing of bells in all the churches and the *Te Deum* was sung in the Masses to give thanks to God for the victory. King Philip IV performed an official ceremony to receive 50 Protestant banners sent by his brother from Germany.[223]

---

222 Mesa, *Nördlingen*, p.42.
223 The Cardinal-Infante also sent two banners to Milan, in gratitude to the Lombard population for the treatment received during his stay in the city, the support given to their expedition and, in general, to the Hispanic Monarchy (Mesa, *Nördlingen*, p.43).

8

The Aftermath

The Swedish Army was devastated, and its German allies were also weakened in the extreme. As always, the various sources disagree on the number of casualties and prisoners, but the Heilbronn League lost about 13,000 to 15,000 men and the prisoners included Marshal Horn, Generals Cratz and Rostein, nine Colonels together with between 4,000 to 6,000 soldiers.[1] The dead numbered between 7,000 and 8,000,[2] and all artillery, supply train, 4,000 wagons, 450 Protestant flags[3] and 68 guns[4] were lost.

The Catholic Army recorded about 3,500 to 5,000 casualties of which there were 1,500 to 2,500 dead, including six Colonels[5] and 3,000 wounded; about 2,000 of whom were from the Hispanic Army. The Spanish chronicles recount the main personalities who fell, including the German Colonels Wurmser and Salm, the *maestre de campo* Paniguerola, Diego de Bustos, the Marquis de Rapalla, Captains Pedro Arias, Alonso de Noguerol, Juan Negrete and Pedro de Ulloa, Colonel Silvio Piccolomini (nephew of General Octavio Piccolomini) and General Villy of the Catholic League cavalry. As for the wounded, these included the governor of the Spanish cavalry Gerardo Gambacorta, the commissary general and commissioner of the cavalry of Naples, Álvaro de Quiñones, the *maestre de campo* Carlos Guasco and his sergeant major, Gualtero Gualteri, the *teniente de maestre campo* Tiberio

---

1 Of the prisoners of the protestant army, 1,494 of them enrolled in the Army of Bavaria (Spring, *Bavarian Army*, p.37). Aedo affirms that the Catholics captured about 4,000 Protestants, 'the more they enlisted into the service of the Emperor' (Aedo, *Viaje del Infante-Cardenal*, p.144). Poyntz reports that they also captured many wives of the Protestant Army officers and soldiers (Poyntz, *Relations*, p.113).
2 Guthrie, *Batallas*, p.387.
3 In particular, 457 flags and cornets: Imperialists claimed the capture of 280, Bavarians 125 and Spaniards captured 52 (Guthrie, *Batallas*, p.387).
4 The chronicles of the battle tell us that all the Swedish-German artillery was captured. In the relation to King Ferdinand, the figure of 42 pieces is mentioned, while the report of the Marquis of Leganés affirms four; Captain Poyntz indicates that about 50 were taken, and other chronicles speak of about 62, 70 and until 80. (Guthrie, *Battallas*, p.401). Apart from the natural trend to exaggerate the scale of the victory, the difference in the calculation of the lost pieces could be explained by the different appreciation about the types of the pieces: small brass cannons were perhaps not valued as artillery, while perhaps others only mentioned the biggest pieces (24 pounders and siege pieces).
5 Guthrie, *Batallas*, p.387.

THE AFTERMATH

The victory of Nördlingen, by Cornelius Schut (c1635). One of several paintings that were made to commemorate the Catholic victory. The two cousins are elated due to their military success. They wear a red sash, typical of the Habsburgs and the Hispanic Monarchy, as well as carrying general's batons. The painting presents clear allusions to divine help (the Virgin Mary and Jesus). On the ground are two dead enemy soldiers and a golden war flag, perhaps from one of Bernard of Saxe-Weimar's units. (Oudheidkundig Musseum van de Bijloke, 00711)

Brancaccio, Diego Manrique de Aguayo, Fernando de Heredia, Diomedes Garasa, Octavio Marqués, Tomás de Ávalos, Alejandro Campi and Lope de Ochoa de Oro.[6]

In the besieged Nördlingen, dismay spread when the news of the defeat of the Protestant army became known. The garrison surrendered on 7 September. They were able to save their lives, but abandoned weapons, flags and supplies, and the officers retained their swords, and set off for Frankfurt. The city was occupied by Imperial troops the next day, and on the 9 September the two Ferdinands made their entrance into the city.[7]

Bernard arrived at Ulm with only 10 of his men. The townspeople, knowing of their defeat, refused to help, out of fear of Imperial reprisals.[8] Bernard had to continue on his way to Frankfurt, regrouping his dispersed troops, including the survivors of the battle and the garrisons left in the Allied cities.[9] When he reviewed his demoralised regiments, he had approximately 12,000 troops.[10] But even with such considerable numbers, Nördlingen's Catholic victory could hardly be challenged. The echoes of the battle reverberated all over Germany and the Imperialists were able to capture many key cities in

---

6 Cánovas, *Estudios*, p.433; Aedo, *Viaje del Infante-Cardenal*, p.145.
7 Mesa, *Nördlingen*, p.45.
8 Aedo, *Viaje del Infante-Cardenal*, p.143.
9 The reinforcements that arrived with the Rhinegrave Otto Ludwig of Salm, had just found out the news, and returned by the way they came. (Aedo, *Viaje del Infante-Cardenal*, p.131).
10 Guthrie, *Batallas*, p.387.

THE BATTLE OF NÖRDLINGEN 1634

the Upper and Lower Palatinate and also in Württemberg, just by appearing outside of their walls.

Thus, after the surrender of Nördlingen, General Gallas dispatched several detachments to secure the submission of the major cities, including Nuremberg, Wurzburg, Heilbronn, Stuttgart, Mainz, Spire, Philipsburg and others.[11] In Spain, Prime Minister Olivares described the battle of Nördlingen as 'the greatest victory that has been seen in these times.'[12]

Returning to the battlefield, after victory at Nördlingen, the Cardinal-Infante planned with the King of Hungary a campaign to recapture the Swedish-German positions in the Danube and Rhine lands, but after a few weeks› marching, the Spanish advisers pressed Cardinal-Infante to continue to his main objective, which was to reach Flanders as if they remained in Germany during the winter the consequences could be as disastrous as a year earlier when illness, cold and hunger had led to the loss half of the army of the Duke of Feria.[13]

For this reason, the Hispanic Army changed the direction of its march and turned to the North. On 14 October it arrived in the environs of Cologne ready to cross the Rhine. The Cardinal-Infante took advantage the time he had to meet with representatives of the Rhine cities to secure their support for the Spanish cause. On 22 October, the Hispanic Army concentrated on Juliers, where the Cardinal-Infante met them. The next day the interim governor of Flanders, the Marquis of Aitona, arrived at the city, with an escort of 2,000 cavalrymen and all the main nobility of the Netherlands, to pay tribute to the Spanish prince and escort him to the Belgian capital.[14]

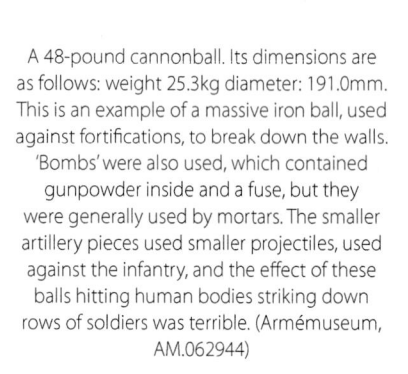

A 48-pound cannonball. Its dimensions are as follows: weight 25.3kg diameter: 191.0mm. This is an example of a massive iron ball, used against fortifications, to break down the walls. 'Bombs' were also used, which contained gunpowder inside and a fuse, but they were generally used by mortars. The smaller artillery pieces used smaller projectiles, used against the infantry, and the effect of these balls hitting human bodies striking down rows of soldiers was terrible. (Armémuseum, AM.062944)

---

11 Guthrie, *Batallas*, p.387.
12 Elliot, *El conde-duque de Olivares*, p.535.
13 Mesa, *Nördlingen*, p.46.
14 Mesa, *Nördlingen*, p.50.

The Cardinal-Infante entered Brussels on 4 November, assuming control of the government of the Spanish Netherlands. It would be the beginning of seven years of government accompanied by impressive military successes against the Netherlands and France. Olivares, a little bothered by how things had gone after the victory of Nördlingen, imagined that if the two Ferdinand cousins had continued working together, they could have driven the Swedes out of Germany, make Saxony a firm ally of the Empire, and finally free Alsace and Lorraine from the French. Olivares imagined that the Imperial troops could then be added to the war against Holland. But Olivares did not remember that he had instructed the Cardinal-Infante to reach Brussels as soon as possible. So, Olivares' imaginary plans were only a dream come from the euphoria of the victory at Nördlingen.[15]

With the distinction of Nördlingen behind him, the Spanish ambassador Oñate pressured Emperor Ferdinand II to sign the Alliance League treaty, but the Emperor again prevaricated on the matter. On 31 October 1634 the Emperor finally agreed to sign a limited military treaty with Spain, of a defensive and offensive nature, by which the Empire allowed an army supported by Spain to remain in Germany. Ferdinand II believed that it was best to reconcile the interests of the two Habsburg branches, although prioritising his own interest in defeating the assured that if the Empire was at peace, it would help Spain in its fight against the Netherlands and its new war against France.[16]

---

15 Elliot, *El conde-duque de Olivares*, p.535.
16 Elliot, *El conde-duque de Olivares*, p.536.

9

The Consequences

The Peace of Prague

With this military victory, Emperor Ferdinand II also launched a diplomatic offensive. The Imperial Catholic cause had not only triumphed on the battlefield, but it had destroyed the myth of Swedish invincibility and broken the Heilbronn League. In addition, it had eliminated the controversial figure of Wallenstein from the military and political scene. The moderate positions the Emperor displayed tended to help bring peace and both John George of Saxony and Duke George of Brunswick agreed to a cessation of hostilities.

Ferdinand of Habsburg, with the prestige he had gained on the battlefield, began discussions with many German princes. He first won over to his cause southern Germany, and then created the state of opinion necessary to establish the basis for a peace agreement. Germany had been at war for 16 years, with rampant epidemics and devastation, and all sides, military and civilian, were exhausted.

The Emperor's son seduced them by offering religious concessions, such as the suspension of the Edict of Restitution, and achieved a long-awaited peace. In November 1634 the Empire and Saxony signed a truce in Pirna. Saxony withdrew from the war in February 1635 and on 30 May the Peace of Prague was proclaimed, and although the Swedes rejected this it, many Protestant states accepted it, thereby agreeing to submit to Imperial authority.[1]

Certainly, Swedish power in southern Germany was gone. The garrisons to the south of the Main were abandoned and the Heilbronn League disintegrated,[2] and the Swedes retired to their bridgehead in Pomerania. Their 'German empire' fell like a house of cards, overthrown by the tornado of Nördlingen. Nobody remembered the Swedish victories of Frankfurt an der Oder, Werben, Breitenfeld, Lech, Munich and Lützen.[3]

1　Elliot, *El conde-duque de Olivares*, p.536.
2　Elliot, *El conde-duque de Olivares*, p.535.
3　Guthrie, *Batallas*, p.387.

Johann Georg I of Saxony, by Frans Luycx (1652). Although a Lutheran, the Elector initially supported Archduke Ferdinand on his way to the Imperial throne. However, realising that Ferdinand II now sought Catholic supremacy, he distanced himself. Finally, he allied with Sweden in 1631 against the Emperor. But the Imperial victory of Nördlingen motivated him to negotiate with the Catholics for an end to hostilities. When he signed the Peace of Prague, he promised to fight alongside the Imperialists against the Swedes and the French, in exchange for Upper and Lower Lusatia being handed over to him. Successive Swedish campaigns devastated the Elector's domains, which led to his military inactivity until the end of the war. The Treaty of Westphalia, signed in 1648, confirmed these territorial acquisitions agreed at the Peace of Prague. (Staatliche Kunstsammlungen Dresden, H0200)

Endless war

But Sweden, France and the United Provinces were not going to allow the Holy Roman Empire to control the kingdoms of Germany again. But Sweden was exhausted after four years of intense mobilisation of all its war efforts in Germany and could not sustain another sustained period of conflict. That is why France, forced by these new circumstances, decided to enter the conflict and declared war on Spain. Richelieu had delayed direct conflict with Spain as long as he could, but the Spanish victories provoked a French reaction.[4] Paris made the decision on 1 April 1635, but did not declare war until 19 May, after military agreements with Holland (8 February) and Sweden (28 April) had been signed.[5]

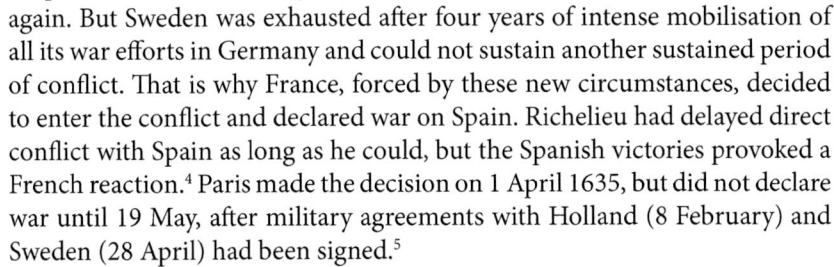

Bernard of Saxe-Weimar offered the services of his veteran army to France to continue his own private war against the Habsburgs. The Landgrave of Hesse-Kassel, William V, also took sides with France.[6]

As Guthrie states, 'the religious war has come to an end'.[7] Indeed, the peace between German Catholics and Protestants supposed that there was finally a political and religious understanding between the two communities. Until that time, each party had sought to annihilate the other, requesting the help of alleged foreign 'saviours' (namely the Spanish, Danish and Swedish) who, under religious pretexts also sought territorial gains. But after the Peace of Prague, the two faiths in Germany acted under Imperial protection, thus showing that what was underlying the conflict, and was now clearly manifesting itself, was the existence of two major political axes fighting for the continental control: the Spain-Austria-Bavaria-Saxony coalition, and France-Sweden-Holland-Hesse on the other.[8]

---

4   Elliot, *El Conde-Duque de Olivares*, p.536.
5   Elliot, *El Conde-Duque de Olivares*, p.538.
6   Guthrie, *Batallas*, p.388.
7   Guthrie, *Batallas*, p.387.
8   Guthrie, *Batallas*, p.388.

THE BATTLE OF NÖRDLINGEN 1634

Both sides had Catholics and Protestants in their ranks, so that, at least from 1635 onwards, the conflict could not be described simply as religious, or at least only religious, but as an inter-alliance conflict.

France ceased to be a 'spectator' of the conflict, giving the Swedes and Germans, generous subsidies, and decided to go to war. Richelieu feared that the Imperialists would now be extremely powerful, and that Spain could use their own scarce resources to launch an offensive to break the Dutch, as well as to reopen the traditional Spanish Road. So, Bernard of Saxe-Weimar and three French armies attacked Alsace, Flanders and Spain. In the north, Swedish Marshal Johan Banér returned to the offensive in 1636, attacking Saxony, without any pretence at defending the cause of Protestant Germany.[9]

The Empire was then again under siege, on the Swedish front in the East (Pomerania, Brandenburg, Saxony, Silesia, Bohemia) and the against French in the West (the Rhine and Bavaria). This terrible war was to continue for another decade.

---

9   Guthrie, *Batallas*, p.388.

10

Conclusion

Although the events of the 5 to 6 September may seem at first glance to be relatively well researched, a deeper analysis reveals that many facts are still unknown or incomplete.[1] Unlike other great battles in the Thirty Years' War, Nördlingen is little known. If Breitenfield is a turning point in the Catholic-Protestant struggle, with the emergence of the clear leadership of Sweden, Nördlingen is the complete opposite, and it has not yet been the subject of a focussed study.

The battle of Nördlingen does not appear in General J.F.C. Fuller's book 'The Decisive Battles of the Western World', although Breitenfeld and Lutzen do. The same is true of John Macdonald's book, 'Great Battlefields of the World' and Jeremy Black's book 'Illustrated Atlas of War.'[2] Why?

Maybe it was because they were fought between so few troops; 30,000 Catholics and 25,000 Protestants? At White Mountain (1620) 20,000 Protestants fought against 25,000 Catholics. At Höchst (1622) 17,000 Protestants battled against 26,000 Catholics. At Stadtlohn (1623) 15,000 Protestants fought against 25,000 Catholics. At Lutter (1626) both sides were equal at around 20,000 troops. At Breitenfeld (1631) 40,000 Protestants fought against 33,000 Catholics, and at Lutzen (1632) some 20,000 Protestants fought and won against 25,000 Catholics. We see that there is a great disparity in the forces present in these battles, where generally those with more troops were victorious, with the notable exception of Lutzen. Yet, despite Nördlingen following this general pattern, it has not received the consideration it deserves.

Or maybe it is because Nördlingen reveals a result that breaks the myths and clichés about the Art of War and the Military Revolution? In the words of Eduardo de Mesa:

> If the battle of Rocroi, lost by the Spaniards, is famous for its result, Nördlingen should also have been, but it was won by the Spaniards and, therefore, silenced, then and now.[3]

---

1 Hrncirik, *Spanier auf dem Albuch*, p.7.
2 Negredo, *Guerra*, p.188.
3 Mesa, *Nördlingen*, p.44.

THE BATTLE OF NÖRDLINGEN 1634

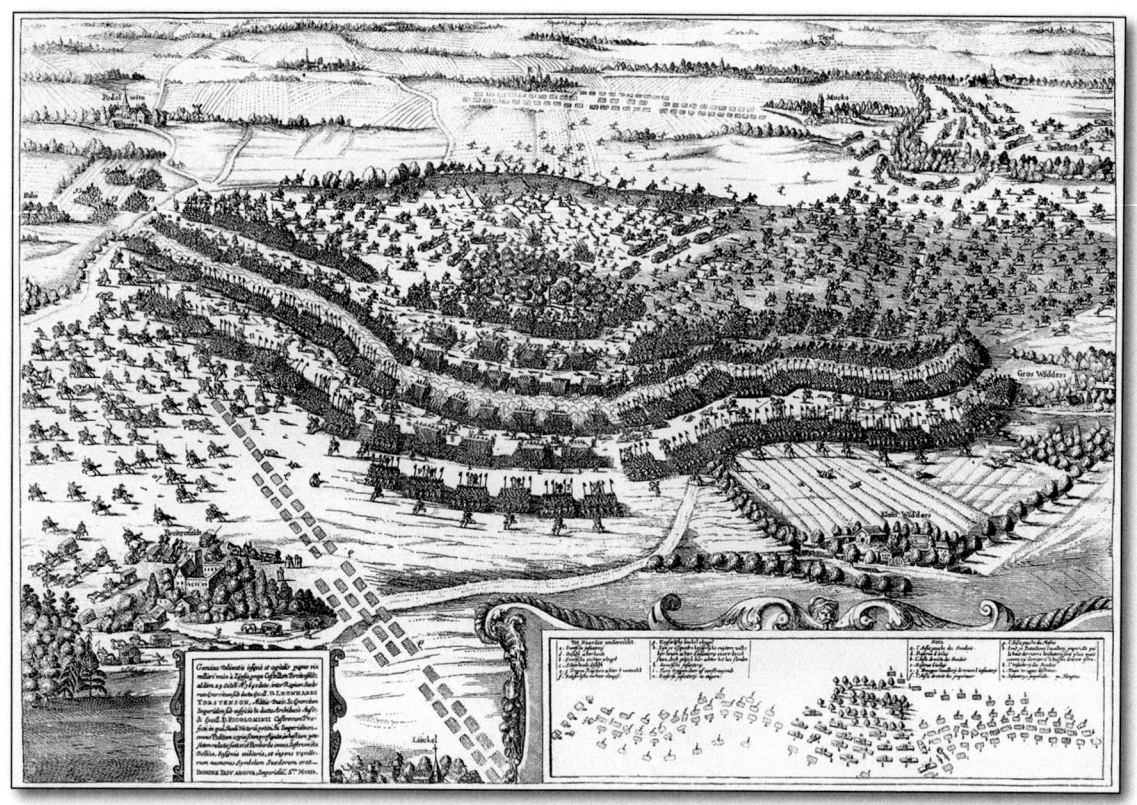

The Second Battle of Breitenfeld, also known as the First Battle of Leipzig, took place on 23 October 1642. This is a contemporary anonymous engraving. The Imperial army led by Archduke Leopold Wilhelm and Ottavio Piccolomini with 26,000 men (10,000 infantry, 16,000 cavalry and 46 guns). The Swedish army, under the orders of Lennart Torstensson, had 10,000 infantry, 10,000 cavalry and 70 guns. Despite their numerical inferiority, the Swedes won and the Catholics suffered 5,000 dead or wounded, and 4,500 soldiers and 46 guns were captured against the Swedish losses of 2,000 wounded and 2,000 killed. In this battle the superiority of the Swedish infantry and cavalry was evident. (Author's collection)

In my view, the widespread ignorance of the Battle of Nördlingen is due to two reasons. First, because it breaks the myth of Swedish invincibility and superiority, as with the exception of Alte Veste, Nördlingen was the only major battle in which a Swedish force was defeated, while in subsequent field battles such as Wittstock (1636), Chemnitz (1639), Breitenfeld (1642), Jankov (1645) and Second Nördlingen (1645), the Swedes were victorious over Imperial armies.

Secondly, Swedish tactics were overtaken by supposedly inferior Spanish tactics. All this would mean removing the orthodox approaches of the majority of thought of military history during the last decades. It would mean revising the concept of 'military revolution' presented by Roberts as well as the paradigm that the military reforms introduced by Gustavus II Adolphus would allow the Swedes to be victorious on the Imperialists and Bavarians in all confrontations. But on the only occasion the Swedes faced the 'decadent' Spaniards, the Spaniards emerged victorious, something difficult to reconcile if one considers that the Swedish brigades were superior in all tactics to the Spanish Tercios.

CONCLUSION

Our knowledge of the Spanish tactical systems at that time is still marked by many cliches and myths.[4] The latter manifests itself in the deliberate omission of the involvement of a Hispanic army in the forces of the Catholics. By way of an example, Delbruch and Wilson write about the battle of Nördlingen without mentioning at any time that Spaniards and Italians made up 40 percent of the Catholic troops, nor the participation of the Cardinal-Infante in the Imperial command structure. Even the strategic defence of the Albuch Hill is mentioned without even naming the Spanish, Walloon and Italian Tercios. Generally, Horn and Bernard's opponents are grouped under the broad designation 'Imperial' or 'Catholic'.

Delbruck hardly mentions the Spaniards, referring to the combined Imperial-Bavarian-Spanish army simply as 'Catholics',[5] and justifies the Protestant defeat because the Imperial-Bavarian union with the Spaniards totalled an army of more than 40,000 against 25,000 Swedish-Germans. For that reason, Delbruck wrote 'all the courage of the Swedes was in vain against the great superiority of the enemy'.[6]

Partly in the same vein as Delbruck, Rucker concludes that the Catholic army won not so much by its numerical superiority, but mainly because it soon understood the tactical importance of the hill of Albuch.[7] For that reason, the Catholic high command considered this combat to be like a defensive battle for the summit, as it was so tactically important. Horn stumbled along with his obsession of climbing the Albuch, as did Gustavus Adolphus two years earlier during the Battle of Alte Veste.[8] But whilst at Alte Veste Wallenstein's Catholic troops had a very well-fortified position, the Spaniards and Italians in the Albuch had resisted with only the benefit of improvised defences and in an exposed position.

Spanish participation during the Thirty Years War should not be forgotten. Undoubtedly, the contribution of the Hispanic Monarchy to its cousins in the Empire was decisive in sustaining the Catholic war effort, and this support already first manifested itself at the beginning of the conflict, as also did the support of Catholic Bavaria. The King of Spain helped the Emperor with money, but also with military advisors and for years the most experienced of the highest Imperial and Bavarian officers had served under the Spanish. Finally, Spain acted with direct intervention (for example, the Palatine Campaign), until it became fully involved in the Nördlingen campaign.

The analysis must be without prejudice, as Rucker says, the study of the Battle of Nördlingen and must begin from the following question: The victory was simply due to the numerical superiority of the Catholic troops

---

4 Hrncirik, *Spanier auf dem Albuch*, p.39.
5 Delbruck, *Dawn of modern warfare*, p.211.
6 Delbruck, *Dawn of Modern Warfare*, p.211. Rucker agrees that the Catholic army was 49,000 men strong (Rucker, *Die Entscheidungsschlacht bei Nördlingen*, p.11).
7 Rucker, *Die Entscheidungsschlacht bei Nördlingen*, p.15.
8 Mahr, Helmut: *Wallenstein vor Nürnberg 1632. Sein Lager bei Zirndorf und die Schlacht an der Alten Veste, dargestellt durch give Plan der Gebrüder Trexel 1634*. Degener, Neustadt, 1982; TREXE, Hans and Paulus: *Wallenstein'schen Lagers bei Zirndorf 1632. Nachzeichnung und Druck*, Nürnberg, 1932.

and the massive tactical errors committed by the Protestants, or was it the result of Spanish tactical superiority and effective use of terrain? [9]

At times, the commander-in-chief's strategic talent is decisive in understanding the development and outcome of a battle. However, it is sometimes extremely difficult to explain why a side sustains itself on the battlefield, when the battle remains undecided for many hours. What of the value of a unit that conquers a key position, or the tactical talent of a senior brigade commander who chooses the key moment to launch his soldiers into battle? At Nördlingen, a simple explanation might be that the Spaniards were simply entrenched, and the Swedes were not, but that is not enough. In the iconic Battle of White Mountain, the Catholics had to charge uphill against Bohemian redoubts, yet they defeated the Protestant army.

The explanation is both more complex and yet more direct. Traditionally, Central European historiography, both Anglo-Saxon and Germanic, has explained the Tercios' organisation and tactics as if they had maintained a structure similar to that of the Swiss or German *Landsknecht* pike blocks, that is its organisation remained unchanged for two centuries. This is because of the lack of access to Spanish sources, and the maintenance of certain stereotypes.

To assess whether the Swedish tactics were so superior to their enemies, or whether the tactics of the Spanish Tercios were so outdated and easily overcome, let us look at the axioms of this supposed superiority, the Swedish-Protestant organisation in small units, the firepower of its infantry deployed in three ranks, the effectiveness of the regimental cannons, and the cavalry charges favouring cold steel over firepower.

The Tercios maintained their name during the two centuries that they were operational, but their structure and tactics evolved over time. It is important to remember that the new Ordinances of 1632 unified the standard company type of the Spanish Tercios – 250 men, with 11 members of *prima plana*, 90 pikemen, 60 musketeers and 89 arquebusiers, to give them a standardisation and firepower that would allow them to continue to operate against the other European armies. The continuation of the pikemen should not be understood as a throwback to an archaic, wandering military liturgy, but as the realisation that on European battlefields the action of cavalry was a constant danger to infantrymen, and that the only sure remedy against those attacks was the constitution of a pike block that could repel the attacking cavalry, while the musketeers and arquebusiers continued firing at them, protected by the length of the pikes, or from inside the formation.

And it is necessary to remember the words of Brnardic:

> After the failure of the tercio system in the first battle of Breitenfeld (1631) (…) Spanish and Italian troops used in Nördlingen (1634) demonstrated that the tercio system could still compete with the innovative linear formation devised by Mauritius of Nassau and King Gustavus Adolphus of Sweden.[10]

---

9 Rucker, *Die Entscheidungsschlacht bei Nördlingen*, p.3
10 Brnardic, *Imperial Armies. Infantry*, p.22.

CONCLUSION

That is, despite the cliché that Swedish-Protestant units were more flexible and versatile due to their better relationship between soldiers and officers, this being possible because they operated in smaller units, somebody may wonder whether this view is sustainable or not, considering an analysis of the evolution of the battle, its participating units and the actions during battle.

The Spanish detachments of *mangas* could be as numerous or few as circumstances required. In addition, the officers-soldiers ratio was similar to that of the Swedish units. And finally, it is worth noting the presence of the 'reformed' officers, who enlisted and fought as common soldiers, but who when necessary exercised control over their companions.

One advantage of the Tercio over Dutch or Swedish linear formation was that the *escuadron* had complete defensive ability, changing its facing at any time, due to the depth of its ranks, as well as the flexibility and mobility of its *mangas* and *guarniciones* that allowed it to offer resistance in any direction.

But since the linear formations maintained a very wide frontage, the Spanish and Imperial military adapted the classic squadron, generally deeper and with a predominance of the pikes, to the new times of the seventeenth century. The Tercios used semi-linear formations, up to 12 rows deep, with a much broader frontage with musketeers and arquebusiers both to the front and on the flanks.[11]

Thus, the success of the Spanish infantry *escuadron* was due to excellent coordination between the various arms but was mainly due to strict discipline in combat and the enormous flexibility of the formations to adapt to any situation. Their officers also had the ability to organise small combat groups – the *mangas* – that allowed them to adapt to different combat situations.

Not many historians have considered the paradigm of the Spanish soldier and officers to be a *hidalgo* (gentleman) of the early modern age, clinging to his sword and unable to adapt to new times: a brave swordsman, but not a technician.[12]

But the Spaniards, after revolutionising military art in the late fifteenth century, with the combination of traditional infantry weapons – pikes and swords – with new portable firearms – as testified by Spanish victories in Italy since 1495, they did not remain stagnant in their organisation or in their mentality.

Indeed, like the Swedes and the Dutch, the Spaniards were also equally innovative and professional. They had strict standards formulated on the basis of experience, merits and technical knowledge, or in their deployment in small units. In short, the Spanish army was at least as advanced as its rivals.

If the key to the Military Revolution was the development of firepower capacity and efficiency and the deployment of small and effective units, the Spanish Army remained among the elite because it was just as innovative as its rivals.[13] Someone might propose that the Spaniards copied the Swedish innovations in order to better deal with them, but it would be a big mistake.

---

11 Brnardic, *Imperial Armies. Infantry*, p.22.
12 González De Leon, *Doctors of the Military Discipline*, p.85.
13 Parrott, *Strategy and Tactics*, p.227.

THE BATTLE OF NÖRDLINGEN 1634

'Great Assembly of the States-General in 1651, attributed to Bartholomeus van Bassen and Anthonie Palamedesz (c1651–1652). The Binnenhof is a building complex located in the city centre of The Hague, which houses the headquarters of the States-General of the Netherlands. The moment reflected in the picture, after the death of Stadholder William II, Prince of Orange (1650) is when the States-General convened a special assembly (1651) to decide on the appointment of another Stadholder. But the Provinces did not want it and the position was abolished. The large number of flags and banners hanging from the ceiling, belonging to the Monarchy of Spain, which are presented as a battle trophy are prominent. According to the sources, a large part of the flags was captured by Maurice of Nassau in the battles of Turnhout (1597) and Nieuwpoort (1600). The flags where the Spanish coat of arms appear are Tercio flags, while the smaller ones, with the Burgundian Cross, are company flags. To our left there is a flag with an armoured arm and a sword: surely it is a banner of German cavalry, in the service of Spain. Many damaged flags can be seen in the background, perhaps due to the passage of time or because of the harshness of the combat in which they were captured. (Rijksmuseum, SK-C–1350)

How could Hispanics copy Swedish tactics if both armies had never faced each other before?

Another element that would characterise alleged Swedish superiority would be its greater and faster firepower, thanks to the regimental cannons and its commanded volley fire from its ranks of musketeers. Certainly, that power existed, such as was demonstrated at the battle of Breitenfeld, but in 1634 and against the Spanish this was not decisive. The Spanish military manuals of that time already indicate that they knew several methods of fire, beyond the famous counter-march by ranks, and on the battlefield the arquebusiers and musketeers of the Hispanic Monarchy – Spanish, Italian, Walloon and Burgundian – were all able to keep up a steady, systematic, and accurate fire at the same level as their Swedish and German opponents.

CONCLUSION

With regard to regimental artillery, and in general to all Swedish-Protestant artillery, their use was lethal at certain times during the battle but was countered by the counter-fire of Catholic artillery, as well as the use of light pieces in support of infantry, both at Albuch and at Schonfeld. In addition, the proximity of the regimental guns to the fighting made them excessively vulnerable to attacks by Catholic cavalry and infantry.

Finally, the tactics of the Swedish cavalry who favoured the sabre charge as opposed to the caracole, or, in general, that the Swedish-Protestant cavalry was superior to the Catholics and especially to the Hispanics, is refuted by the subsequent clashes in the vicinity of the Albuch led by Gambacorta and Piccolomi, and in Herkheimerfeld Plain with the Duke of Lorraine and Werth.

And here we come to the crux of the matter. Were Spanish tactics so inferior to those of the Swedes and Germans? In view of recent research, it is certainly an old-fashioned stereotype to describe Spanish infantry and its tactics in the second half of the seventeenth century as outdated formations of pikemen, as opposed to a comparison with the 'modern' methods of the Dutch and Swedish. Obviously, if part of the historiography is simply based on pictorial conventions to represent battles, it is still believed that the Tercio was a monolithic block of up to 3,000 pikemen, but it should be remembered that it was merely an organisational or administrative unit, and that in battle the 'ad hoc' formation was the *escuadron*, with a variable central block of pikes, and with autonomous detachments of musketeers and arquebusiers.

Previous musters show that the Hispanic Tercios were no more than a thousand troops strong, with the exception of that of Idiáquez's, and the German regiments, at around 2,000 strength. The Tercios did not have, either before, during and after the combat 12 companies, nor did the companies number 250 men. This implies that the ratio of officers to soldiers was equal to or greater than that in Protestant armies.

Spanish military doctrine was also followed by its Italian, Burgundian and Walloon units, but not the German mercenary regiments, so at Nördlingen, as in the other battles in which Hispanic units participated, tactics were common to these nations. Pike blocks would be seven to 10 rows deep, while arquebusier and musketeer *mangas* were around five to seven ranks, deep, similar to the Swedes and Germans.

But the lack of any organisation in 'brigades' or 'battalions' was not a disadvantage in maintaining adequate firepower in a linear formation as the *mangas* provided this tactical solution precisely. The *mangas* acted independently on several occasions, like in the woods near the Heselberg, supporting the redoubts, and flanking the hill. They were such a flexible system that *mangas* could be operated individually[14] or from several different units.[15]

---

14 For example, when the Italian Tercio of Toralto was reinforced with a *manga* of 200 arquebusiers from the Italian Tercio of San Sivero, or when the arquebusiers detachment of Idiáquez's Tercio who came forward to recover the central redoubt.

15 The position of Escobar in the forest was reinforced with a *manga* of 200 Italian musketeers of the Tercio of Toralto and other 200 Burgundians. Another example of flexibility and

THE BATTLE OF NÖRDLINGEN 1634

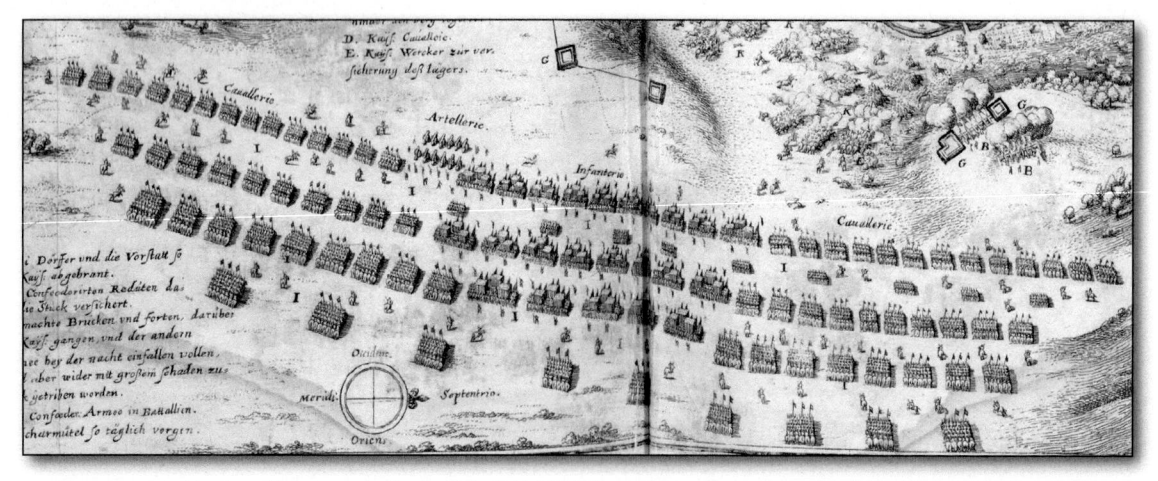

Deployment of the Swedish army at the Battle of Saalfeld, 1640. The Swedish allies, commanded by Field Marshal Johan Banér, appeared in front of the fortified encampment commanded by Archduke Leopold Wilhelm and General Ottavio Piccolomini. On several occasions, Banér deployed his army to tempt the Imperials into battle, to no avail. This situation dragged on for weeks, and disease and starvation took hold of the poor soldiers on both sides. Banérs own wife died and while he grieved and wept heavily, he did not grieve long. Considering that both armies combined total consisted of 130,000 people including accompanying civilians (half that number) and the war was conducted in an area well depleted from former campaigning it was hard, if not impossible, to find logistical support. Looking at the deployment of the Swedish formations, it can be seen that in this period the brigades were still formed in the shape of a T, with three battalions with the pikemen in the center and the musketeers around them. The infantry is deployed in three decreasing lines (10, eight and five brigades), with the flanks protected by the cavalry, deployed in four lines. In the middle of the deployment there are several detachments of musketeers, ready to intervene in support of the front line. The Imperial camp is drawn schematically but it is seen to have good defences and it stands to reason that Archduke Leopold Wilhelm would not want to venture out into a pitched battle. (*Theatrum Europaeum*, period 1638–1643, Edition 1648)

All this allowed the Hispanic army to adapt to the changing circumstances of the battle, unlike the more rigid Imperial army, for example, when it directed its units to support the Spaniards, they did so en masse (the Webel and Tieffembach brigades). If to this tactical flexibility we add that most of the Spanish, Italian, Walloon and Burgundian troops were veterans, then Hispanic superiority becomes more pronounced.

Unlike the Spaniards, in the Bavarian and Imperial armies, the pike formations were organised to a depth of seven to 10 ranks, with their musketeers on each flank of the formation. So, their units were wider than they were deep, similar to Protestant formations.

However, the Swedish brigades at Nördlingen differed from those at Lützen. Whereas, in the early years of the German adventure, the Swedes formed their brigades based on the classic three battalions. At the battle of Nördlingen the Protestant units deployed virtually as independent battalions. The pike blocks were escorted by musketeer formations of approximately the same size on both sides. This was due to the limited deployment options offered by the Nördlingen battlefield itself. The classic alignment of the

---

adaptability occurs when King Ferdinand requested the Cardinal-Infante to send a force of 1,000 Spanish foot soldiers to storm the city of Nördlingen: 100 Spaniards of the Tercio of Idiáquez, 100 Spaniards of the Tercio of Count of Fuenclara, 100 Neapolitans of the Tercio of the Prince of San Sivero, 100 Neapolitans of the Tercio of the Marquis of Torrecusa, 300 Germans of the regiment of Salm and others 300 of the regiment of Colonel Würmser.

CONCLUSION

wedge-shaped brigade was adequate for open terrain, for example, the Herkheimerfeld Plain, but succession of hills that had to be taken by Horn's troops caused prevented such deployment being carried out, and each of the infantry units acted as autonomous battalions.

From all this, it can be concluded that the supposed superiority of Swedish tactics over Spanish and Imperial ones did not manifest themselves at the Battle of Nördlingen.

Let us look at the key tactical decisions of the battle, their successes and mistakes.

On the Protestant side, despite the supposed tactical superiority of linear formation and increased firepower, due to fewer ranks, the approach and development of the battle was disappointing.

Globally, the first failure of the Protestant side was the poor intelligence on the size of the Catholic Army, especially of the Cardinal-Infante's forces. Swedish intelligence failed to identify the troops who marched from Italy, the episode between Bernard and *sargento mayor* Escobar, the misinformation provided by Venetian spies all testify to this. They also erred in gathering information on the features of the terrain and made the mistake of believing that the various hills formed a single mountain which confused the commands and demotivated the soldiers, who advanced through the tree-lined paths and repeatedly climbed up and down slopes, thinking that this would be the last.

If Nördlingen represented, on the Catholic side, good practice by its high command, it was also the worst example of Protestant commanders' behaviour. Enmity between the two general officers meant that they did not co-ordinate their actions, and Bernard remained inactive for many hours, with Horn wishing to launch frontal assaults on the Albuch. Everything that could go wrong, did so, and was as bad as could be.

In addition, the Protestant command underestimated the Catholic army entirely. The Swedes had not fought the Spaniards before and believed that their method of fighting would be like that of the Imperials and Bavarians, whom they had defeated successively. Bernard emphatically despised the Spanish troops, their number and their professionalism. Perhaps that is why the Protestants did not continue their advance after conquering Heselberg Hill, thinking that the next day, their rested troops would drag the Spaniards out at dawn. If they had understood the determination with which Escobar and his 500 men had defended the forest, they might have done better by continuing to press on at once, attacking the Albuch before their defences had been completed.

The Protestant army initially launched coordinated assaults, but as the battle for Albuch gained momentum, the chronicles indicate some increasing disorder. They managed to push out the Germans of Salm's and Würmser's regiments, but Protestant infantry and cavalry were not coordinated to repulse the Catholic counterattack. Bernard launched Cratz's squadrons without infantry battalions, and the magnitude of the lack of control and chaos came with the attack of Thurn's brigade without the support of the cavalry.

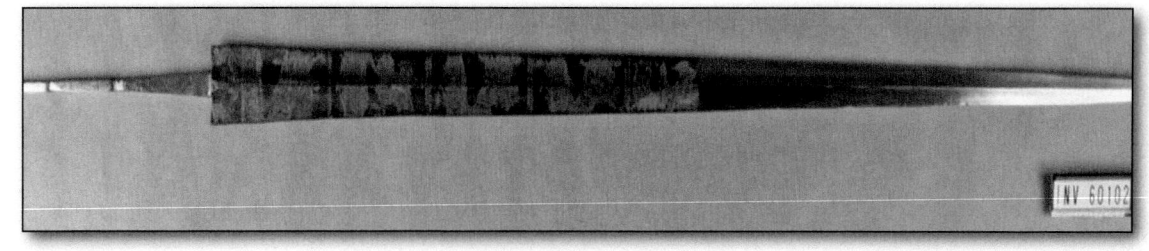

Infantry sword. The blade is double edged, it has on its upper part a gold engraving, which refers allegorically to the Catholic victory at Nördlingen. On one side of the blade there is an image of the battle, on the other side, the equestrian portraits of Ferdinand of Hungary, Maximilian of Bavaria and General Jean de Werth. It has been documented that it was manufactured by Peter Munich in the city of Solingen, in 1637–1648. (Armémuseum, AM.060102)

But to this lack of coordination, it is possible to add the successive and aggregated errors of the commanders of the Protestant Army, including Horn, Bernard, Cratz, Thurn, Morschauser and Witzleben. In Guthrie's words, 'too many good officers behaved with unusual incompetence; mere courage was not a substitute for dexterity'.[16]

Marshal Horn showed great stubbornness in his tactical approach to the development of the battle and the conquest of Albuch as a key position, confusing obstruction with determination. Lacking in strategic imagination the Swedish general was inflexible in launching frontal assaults of his infantry and cavalry on a fortified position, and as their forces diminished, the troops of the opponents were strengthened and, moreover, gained increased moral with the scent of victory.

But surely Horn's decision to launch unsuccessful frontal assaults may have been partly driven by his determination and, ultimately, courage, which he had been questioned about. During the war council on 4 September, Bernard himself had accused him of cowardice when he proposed the retirement of the army since they learnt of the union of the forces of the King of Hungary with those of the Cardinal-Infante. Now, on the battlefield, Horn was be determined to show the falsity of that unjust accusation, even at the expense of the lives of his soldiers.

Bernard didn't live up to his reputation either. His flank was idle during the first hours of the battle, with no sign of him diverting the attention of the Catholic commanders, who, in accordance with their designated plan, gradually sent reinforcements to bolster the defence of Albuch. Perhaps Bernard was kept in reserve waiting for Horn to do the dirty work of taking Albuch Hill and forcing a Catholic retreat, after which he could pursue the retreating enemy and take away the glory of victory or enter triumphantly into the streets of a relieved Nördlingen. But whatever the reason for his passiveness, it proved to be fatal to many of Horn's soldiers and decisive for the outcome of the battle.

Later, and surely aware of his mistake, Bernard launched his cavalry into a useless attack on the Herkheim Plain, engaging in his reserves, depleting them and later withdrawing, thereby as happened, exposing Horn's infantry to be surrounded in the Heselberg area.

And Thurn wasn't any better. When he got his chance, he moved toward his goal without coordinating his forces with Horn's cavalry and overlooked an enemy redoubt.

---

16 Guthrie, *Batallas*, p.387.

Also, the terrain did not help the Swedish tactics to enable them to succeed as in other battles. The deep forests and the narrowness of the pathways delayed the deployment of units. The lack of knowledge of the topography of the battlefield meant that the attacks slowed down and the rocky slope of the hill surely made keeping in good order difficult when ascending the Albuch. What if the combat had taken place on a plain and not on a stony hill? Would the outcome of the battle have changed? We will never know.

But not only did the outcome of the battle have an impact on the human and material disaster suffered by the Protestant army, but there was also a tremendous impact on the wider political and military arenas due to the loss of the Swedish army's reputation for invincibility. Indeed, Catholics had defeated them, but it was especially the Hispanic troops who triumphed, who had never even faced the Swedes in battle until that day.

Certainly, the battle was very intense and the Catholics, although acknowledging the importance of the Albuch from the beginning and planning its defence, with the constant sending of reinforcements, suffered much anguish due to the numerous attacks on the hill. In the words of Aedo:

> It was the most disputed and doubtful battle, since from the 5 in the morning it was fought with great efforts until the 12 a.m., being the battle in doubt until the 11 a.m. And even to two hours of day much lost on our part, and more lost was the late afternoon, that if the enemy had gone against the hill (Albuch) before attacking the forest (Heselberg) or had attacked the hill immediately to conquer the forest, they would also have conquered the mountain, which was not yet fortified enough. And that would have been its victory, forcing to retreat our armies with its artillery, and also forcing us to retreat to the plain. And so, it would have devastated our armies, at great risk to the Empire and the states of the Catholicism.[17]

Recognising the existing difficulties, the Catholic command led its forces throughout the battle successfully, preventing the enemy's movements and reacting appropriately.

On the Catholic side, success on the battlefield was largely based on recognising the importance of the Albuch Hill as the key position, and importance of the efforts to retain it.

Undoubtedly, the choice of Serbelloni and Gamassa as responsible for the fortification and placement of the batteries was of paramount importance. Both added experience and know-how in order to optimise defence. Archaeological work[18] reveals that the redoubts were located at the top of the hill, having at least one flank covered by a steep slope and providing each other with support. In Rucker's words, the Habsburgs' success in Nördlingen was not due to numerical superiority, which was a fact, but because they quickly understood the tactical importance of Albuch Hill and planned the battle as a 'defensive battle' for the hill.[19]

---

17 Aedo, *Viaje del Infante-Cardenal*, p.142.
18 Hrncirik, *Spanier auf dem Albuch*, pp.37–38.
19 Rucker, *Eine strategisch-militärische Analyse*, p.15.

THE BATTLE OF NÖRDLINGEN 1634

Detailed assault in Alte Veste. Wallenstein's army built a huge camp in the area of the present-day towns of the district of Zirndorf, Oberasbach and Stein, for which 13,000 trees were cut down to house 31,000 infantry, 12,000 cavalry, and 15,000 non-combatants, encamped there for 70 days. On 3 September 1632, the Swedish army advanced from Hardhöhe and at seven o'clock deployed between Unterfürberg and Dambachva. The assault began at nine o'clock on a 2.7km long battle line. The fighting was intense, but the Swedes were unable to break the entire Imperial line. There were 1,200 dead and 200 wounded on the Swedish side, and the number of officers killed was disproportionately high. The Imperial army mourned about 300 dead and 700 wounded. As the Swedes and Gustavus Adolphus had achieved nothing and lost their aura of invincibility, the battle was a one-off victory for Wallenstein. (*Theatrum Europaeum*, period 1629–1633, Edition 1646)

The sequence of staged reinforcements onto the hill was very successful throughout the battle. If at the battle of Alte Veste, the Imperial regiments had rotated in defence of the fortified positions, we see that at Nördlingen the Hispanic units were in constant action from the beginning, suffering huge losses. This could have led to their collapse, as indeed was the case with the Salm and Würmser regiments, but it was an exception.[20] In the defence of Albuch Hill, while the central nucleus of the Tercios or regiments resisted, the sending of several *mangas* from other units – like the German *kampfgruppe* of World War II – to counter the Protestant attacks which were

---

20 The Würmser regiment was mostly made up of newly recruited soldiers, whose first combat experience was the devastating attack of Horn's infantry, causing its withdrawal twice. Salm's regiment had experience, but the withdrawal of soldiers from the nearly Würmser regiment surely also caused panic to be involved and also prompted its abrupt withdrawal.

CONCLUSION

materialising on the hill, and they later gained momentum by sending whole Tercios, they showed a high degree of professionalism in their commanders, officers, and soldiers. Thus, the continuous sending of *mangas* of arquebusiers and musketeers, both to support the defence and to advance to attack the Protestant units on the flank, was successful.

The Catholic command was constantly informed of events happening along the battlefield, thanks to the presence of liaison officers, such as Captain Manuel Sanchez de Guevara. This allowed them to register the movements of the enemy, the state of their defences and the morale of their army, and to be able to make the most informed decisions. In addition, this ensured full cavalry and infantry cooperation, as in times of conflict over the Albuch, the repeated charges of the Gambacorta's and Piccolomini's riders relieved the pressure on the infantry in the redoubts, and to the north, the charges by Lorraine and Werth were supported by infantry.

The experience and value of senior officers, such as the Duke of Lorraine, Gambacorta, Piccolomini, Werth, Idiáquez, Toralto was decisive in detecting and seizing the right momentum to advance, attack, support other units, and react to enemy movements quickly.

It is also possible to highlight the individual initiative shown by the common officers and non-commissioned officers, who with their leadership and personal example dragged their units into battle. Thus, *sargento mayor* Escobar, who on several occasions left the protection of the forest to support the Catholic cavalry with his fire, or other examples like that of *sargento mayor* Diego de Bustos and Captains Francisco de Aragon, Diego de Contreras and Lope Ochoa de Oro, who led the *mangas* that regained the central redoubt on Albuch position.

However, the Albuch's defences had their weaknesses. First, it was a poor decision to place the Salm and Würmser regiments in one of the redoubts, rather than to have placed the Idiáquez or Italian Tercios there from the beginning. However, the success of the Protestants in capturing the redoubt was short lived, as Idiáquez's Tercio recaptured the position and drove off the worn out the Swedish and German units.

Second, the Catholic command erred in not allocating more resources for the fortification of the hill, leaving most of the infantry unprotected outside the redoubts, which were mere parapets and trenches, instead of a full fortified position.

Furthermore, insufficient pieces of artillery were allocated for defence in that sector, as if they had been present in greater numbers the Protestant attacks would have been stopped at the foot of the hill.

So, the Battle of Nördlingen, sometimes described as a battle between 'Swedes' and 'Spaniards', but in fact was less Swedish and Spanish than in other fighting in the Thirty Years' War. It was the only clash between troops using Swedish or Spanish tactics, with the result that the former was overcome by the later.

Colour Plates

Plate 1 Spanish arquebusier and *Sargento Mayor* Escobar

This Spanish arquebusier (1.1) is loading his weapon, as it appears in Jacob de Gheyn's famous book, the military manual "The Exercise of Armes", with its 117 engravings. The arquebusier wears a high crowned felt hat, red doublet and breeches of the same colour - the colour red was the hallmark of the Hispanic Monarchy. The shirt collar worn on the outside of his doublet in the fashion known as "cuello a la valona" (literally, "collar to the Walloon"). He carries a sword with bowl guard, a dagger, concealed by his clothing, and a gunpowder flask as well as various lengths of match for his arquebus. He does not carry the classic bandolier or collar of charges. Like all musketeers, he has no armour, to have better mobility and to move quickly around the battlefield, although some were known to wear a morion or sallet helmet. The thickest and least refined powder was carried in the main flask, which served to charge the bullet, loaded via the muzzle of the musket. The finest and most refined powder was carried in the smaller flask, which was used to prime the arquebuses and muskets, and was ignited by the match cord after which the weapon was called.

"*Sargento Mayor*" Escobar (1.2) wears a wide-brimmed hat decorated with pheasant feathers. Being a high-ranking officer, his clothing is much more expensive and of better quality than that of the soldier. The lace collar ("a la Valona") of his shirt is very elaborate. He has fine clothing, a light blue suit, quality white hose and leather shoes. Under his suit he wears a yellow doublet. Officers, as gentlemen, clothed themselves at their own expense, and this outfit is the result of his own choice of fashion. As a Spanish senior officer, he also wears a red scarf and a breast plate as protection and carries a rapier.

Plate 2 Italian musketeer and pikeman, in the defence of the redoubts of Albuch Hill

The Italian and Walloon soldiers, (called *Tercios de Naciones*) of the Spanish Armies were hardly distinguishable by their uniform from their Spanish comrades. In this case, the musketeer (2.1) wears a wide-brimmed hat, and carries a musket, with a long, lit match, knotted around the wrist, and a simple rapier. As protection, as much against the weather as for his person, he wears a reinforced buff leather coat, called in Spanish "*coleto*" or "*búfala*" (water buffalo) because the leather of this beast was highly valued for its resistance. On his back we see a flask of gunpowder and a large bag (snapsack) in which he would carry his food, any spare clothing he may have along with his personal belongings. In the background of the image there is another musketeer, protected by a small parapet, giving an idea of how basic the fortification of the redoubts on the hill was during the battle.

The pikeman (2.2) wears full body armour, which protects his chest and thighs. In the Tercios, pikemen were known as "*coseletes*" (corselets), after the name of the armour. He wears a tall, wide-winged morion with a smooth crest that ends in a pointed back. These morions, in the next decade, would evolve into smoother and more rounded shapes. He also carries a simple sword. To distinguish themselves in combat, the soldiers of the Spanish armies endeavoured to wore red clothing, or they would sew field signs, such as ribbons or a red Burgundian Cross onto their clothing; in this case the pikeman is wearing his on his right breast, but we don't see it. He wears thick leather gloves to protect his hands from possible injuries, since he would be likely to be a file leader in the front ranks of the pike "*escuadron*" and therefore very vulnerable to wounds caused by the enemy pikes. In the background we see the parapet of one of the redoubts that defended the Albuch hill.

Plate 3 German cuirassier and Croatian trooper

The cuirassier (3.1) is wearing full three-quarter armour, protecting his body from head to knee. He has two wheellock pistols and a straight cavalry sword, of the type "*epee wallone*" (Walloon sword), from Spanish Low Countries: its characteristics were the knucklebow formed by extending a quillon upwards to the pommel, and pierced side guards braced by rings. To distinguish himself as fighting with the Spanish Imperialist forces, he wears a red scarf.

Like the Hungarian Hussar raised for early Protestant armies, the Croats (3.2) were raised from along the frontier with the Ottoman Empire. Best suited for scouting and skirmishing duties, the Croatian cavalry were usually deployed on the flanks of the army. This trooper wears the fur-trimmed cap with a feather, a characteristic neck garment called a "*cravat*". He has been issued with a pair of wheellock pistols and a "*kilij*", a type of one-handed, single-edged and moderately curved scimitar, which originated from the Ottoman Empire. The *kilij* first became popular with the Balkan nations and the Hungarian cavalry. In the background we see a comrade from the same regiment who carries a characteristic sharp-pointed war-hammer for use against armoured opponents.

Plate 4 Bavarian Officer and Imperial Musketeer, prior to the attack on Lachberg Hill

The officer (4.1) wears an eye catching, but somewhat old-fashioned ruff. Like many officers, this captain is armed with a partizan, as a distinctive weapon denoting rank, but not used in combat. The blue scarf, worn over his shoulder and across his chest distinguishes him as an officer of the Catholic League. He has shaved except for a moustache and goatee beard, following contemporary fashion. With the entry of France into the war, a different style of fashion was introduced; longer hair, more pronounced moustaches and breeches that reached slightly above the knees.

The Imperial musketeer (4.2) wears a blue coloured woollen jacket with raw edges (unhemmed). Instead of wearing the classic wide hat of the time, he wears a Montero, a cap with a spherical crown and pulldown flaps to protect the ears and neck in cold weather. His weapon is a matchlock musket, and he carries the match tied to his wrist. The musket is a modern type which is much lighter than those made previously, so he does not need a musket rest. His sword is simple and unadorned. In the background we see how his company is forming by division, with the pikemen in the centre and the two divisions of musketeers flanking them. Beside him, a sergeant armed with a halberd is commanding the company.

Plate 5 Swedish cavalry trooper

The trooper who wears the characteristic Swedish wide-brimmed and low hat, called a "*Schwedenhut*", carries a sabre for combat along with a wheellock pistol. He wears a blue scarf over a protective and warm buff coat, and a back and breast plate. When mounted, the upper part of his high riding boots was pulled up to protect the top of his legs and thighs. Behind us we observe his troop awaiting orders. Alongside them is a division of commanded musketeers. These were a tactical innovation devised by King Gustavus Adolphus, which gave firepower support to the cavalry units.

Plate 6 Swedish musketeer

This Swedish musketeer carries as a principal weapon a matchlock musket. It is of a modern design and is light enough not to need a musket rest. Whilst some units might have snaphaunce or flintlock weapons, most of the Protestant forces present at the battle would have been issued with the less sophisticated but still effective (when used en-masse) such as a heavy Dutch 10-bore matchlock musket. He carries a typical, plain "Swedish-style" rapier. He wears a brown doublet and breeches, a russet colour associated the hardships of military life, and on top of it a blue cassock, a garment that was used to give some uniformity to infantry formations

COLOUR PLATES

Plate 7 German Infantry at the Allbuch Hill redoubt

The German soldier (7.1) tries to defend himself, fighting with his weapon as a club, since he has run out of ammunition. He wears a morion helmet to protect himself from blows to the head. His sword is old, with a simple protective loop on the hilt.

This musketeer (7.2), who waves his hat as a sign of victory, seems poorly dressed. His breeches are ragged and patched with the remains of other garments. His doublet is also torn. He is one of the German veterans of Count Salm's regiment, who had served in the 1633-1634 campaign with the Army of Alsace, under the orders of the Duke of Feria. These veterans spent winter in harsh conditions, and when they were recovering, they marched to join the Cardinal-Infante's forces. He carries a musket, a plain straight sword, along with various pieces of equipment needed in the service of his musket. It was not uncommon to see soldiers from all armies during this era looting the dead and wounded, not necessarily just of the enemy in the search for better clothing and equipment.

Plate 8 The Cardinal-Infante

The young Fernando, Cardinal-Infante of Spain, is portrayed here riding a large Andalusian, a horse breed popular amongst Spanish nobility. He wears a black wide-brimmed hat, with a pheasant or ostrich feather tinted red, the symbolic colour of the armies fighting for the Spanish Crown.

Like all Spanish Habsburgs, he was blond and pale-skinned, with blue eyes. Since the early seventeenth century it was customary to be clean shaven, although by the 1590's the fashion for growing a goatee had begun. As for the moustache, King Felipe III in around 1600 began the custom of curling the tips of the moustache upwards, using wax. Towards the 1630's, Spanish high-ranking nobility began to grow their hair longer, leaving a falling lock in front of their ears.

He wears an exquisite white collar made of linen or other fine fabrics that became fashionable in Spain at the beginning of the seventeenth century. By the start of the seventeenth century, ruffs were falling out of fashion in Western Europe, in favour of wing collars and falling bands.

The Cardinal-Infante bears the symbols of a Spanish general: a general's red scarf, made of silk and with gold trim, and the general's baton, called a *"bengala"*. For protection he has blackened body-armour with leather gloves. This full suit of armour was proofed to stop bullets fired from a modest distance.

Appendix I

Battlefield Photograph locations by Daniel Staberg

Location A
Photo A.1
Photo taken from the Riegelberg area, looking northwest. The left flank of Bernhard de Saxe-Weimar's army corps would deploy close to this position. In the distance can be seen, from left to right, the city of Nördlingen, with the "Daniel" tower of the Church of St. George standing out, 90m high. A little closer is the municipality of Kleinerdlingen, and a little further behind, the wooded hills of Galgenberg, Staffelberg and Adlenberg. The little town on the right is Herkheim.

Photo A.2
In this photo the terrain behind Herkheim can be seen in more detail: the current Reimlinger cliff, and from there and along the entire ridge, towards the forest on the right, the Imperial troops of Gallas would deploy. Thus, from left to right, the Croats of Issolano's cavalry were deployed near Reimlinger, then the rest of the Imperial units of Gallas with Billehe and Werth's Cavalry in front of the Staffelsberg and Adlerberg in a line stretching to Herkheim. On the hill above Herkheim, the infantry of Gallas, Lorena and some of Leganes' troops would be visible as well as along the ridge. On the hills behind the battle line was the the sprawling Imperial-Spanish camp. Bernhard of Saxe-Weimar's Protestant cavalry squadrons would have been hidden from view by the line of trees in the middle of the photo.

Location B
Photo B.1
From the town of Hürnheim a road leads us to the top of Albuch. The assaults by Horn's brigades came from the left, heading for the summit. The battlefield memorial is visible next to the tree.

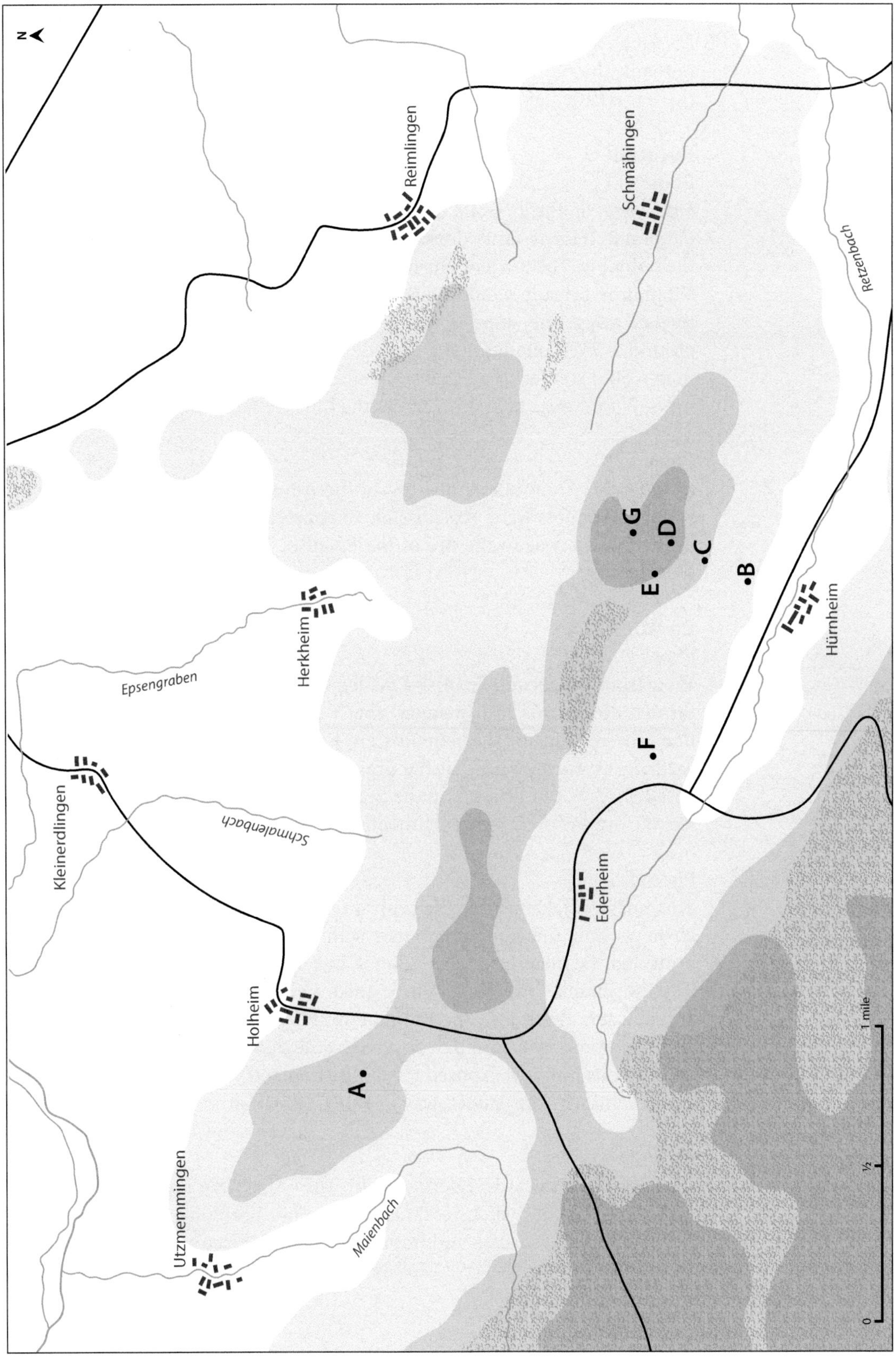

APPENDIX I

Map 7 Photo locations.

Photo B.2
Looking east it is possible to see the area which saw the Swedish attempt to outflank the redoubts with cavalry. The attack was easily beaten back and there was little fighting in that sector for the rest of the battle.

Location C
Photo C.1
Side view of the bottom of the Albuch, looking west. Throughout this panorama, Horn's units deployed to launch their unsuccessful assaults on the redoubts. The town of Hürnheim was on the left, not in this photograph. Vitzthum's brigade would have been closest to the camera with the Scots further away. The slope is not particularly steep but it is long, while the ground is even enough for a brigade to advance without disorder, but the men would still feel the exhausting effort of going up hill with muskets and pikes. Numerous craters run across the hill, probably from cannonballs.

Photo C.2
A wide view from almost the top of the Albuch, just in front of where the Spanish redoubts were. It is possible to appreciate how exposed the advance of the Swedes was to the fire of the Spanish. The town that can be seen is Hürnheim.

Location D
Photo D.1
View from the second Spanish line, located behind the redoubts. Here they formed the Tercios and "mangas" that were to reinforce the main defensive line. The remains of the redoubts are barely perceptible. The traces of the earthworks are so faint that the grass effectively hides them from view. At best a shadow can be seen on the ground or it would be possible to actually feel the outline of the entrenchment if the field was walked.

Photo D.2
This image is taken inside the central redoubt looking down on Hürnheim. It shows how the slope combined with the raised earthwork would have protected the men inside the redoubt, but not those on the firing step, from Swedish infantry fire. From the Spanish point of view, the musketeers and arquebusiers defending the redoubt would have had a wide field of fire, although some areas would be covered by the slight unevenness of the terrain. It is obvious just how exposed the Swedish infantry was as they advanced up the hill and why the Albuch was a strategic position.

Photo D.3
Looking west towards Ederheim. In 1634 this was the position of the northern redoubt, which researchers have not been able to find any trace. Beyond that, the Spanish and Imperial cavalry of Piccolomini and the rest of Spanish Tercios would have deployed.

Location E
Photo E.1
Looking south and showing the shallow depression between the middle and northern redoubts. The Swedish cavalry attacked here in the last stages of the battle only to be repulsed. Hürnheim and Ederheim are visible, although in 1634 they were much smaller and the panorama would be different.

Location F
Photo F.1
This photo is taken in the northern Redoubt area, looking to the West with Ederheim just visible. This is probably the general area where Thurn's brigade advanced from the Heselberg only to be halted and defeated by the Spanish counterattack. The modern-day woodland hides the Heselberg from view and covers a good part of this section of the battlefield.

Photo F.2
The hill and fields behind Herkheim was the scene of Bernhard of Saxe-Weimar's failed cavalry attack late in the battle, with the Imperial counter-attack coming down the slope and pushing the Protestants back to the ground just outside the right edge of the photo.

Location G
Photo G.1
This image is taken from the Battlefield Memorial looking towards the central redoubt and "Otto Rehlen's" hut. This is roughly where the southern redoubt, held by Leslie and Fugger's units, was located but again traces of the defences have eroded over time and are invisible.

Photo G.2
Erected in 1896, in the shape of a pyramid, this commemorative monolith atop Albuch Hill commemorates the battle. It was built by the Verschönerungsverein Nördlingen (VVN). A replica of the engraving of the battle by Matthäus Merian was attached to the memorial stone in 2009.

Appendix II

Battle Maps Key and Phases

Map 4 Phase 1-page 139

1. The 3 cavalry squadrons under the command of Lieutenant Colonel Witzleben charge towards the Southern redoubt, intending to outflank the Spanish defences. Despite the enemy fire, Witzleben was not intimidated and ordered his disordered and tired troopers to deploy from column into line and charge against the Catholic positions. However, his advance was cut short when La Tour and Alberg's cavalry regiments charged into his flank.
2. The Scottish and Pfhul brigades had to advance unprotected from enemy fire in the final part of their attack on the three Catholic redoubts. The Scots from the northwest and the Germans from the southwest.
3. The pressure put on by the Protestants forced the German regiments of Salm and Wurmser to withdraw. Serbelloni ordered a counterattack with the Gambacorta cavalry regiment, who charged against the Scottish and Pfhul brigades then in the central redoubt. The force of the Spanish counterattack pushed the Protestant infantry out of the earthworks and withdraw.
4. Marshal Horn ordered that his second line to advance and attack Toralto's redoubt. The assault was formed of a large cavalry squadron, along with the Horn and Rantzau infantry brigades. He also oversaw the reorganisation and reinforcement of the exhausted Pfuhl and Scottish brigades.
5. While the fighting was taking place at the Toralto Neapolitan redoubt, the Swedish-Germans launched a new, fierce cavalry assault that caused the Wurmser and Salm regiments to collapse again, and they fled. Serbelloni ordered that the 1,800 Spaniards of the Idiáquez Tercio recover the lost position. The Protestants launched a furious counterattack to try to regain their lost position.
6. General Serbelloni, worried that the defenders of the Albuch might end up succumbing to losses and exhaustion, gradually sent the reserves of the Italian Tercios of Paniguerola and Guasco. Over the next few hours, the defenders of the redoubts were constantly reinforced by *mangas* from other *Tercios*.

7   Marshal Horn launches various infantry and cavalry attacks against the redoubts; but each fails, due to increasing losses in men and growing shortages of ammunition.

Map 5 Phase 2-page 151

1   The Marquis of Leganés ordered the Tercios defending the Albuch to be reinforced by 1,000 musketeers, and that the Tercios of Guasco and Paniguerola advanced from the Schonfeld Hill and approached the forest rising at the foot of the Heselberg, with the mission to open fire on the enemy units that were advancing through that part of the battlefield.
2   Waiting for Bernard's reinforcement, Horn again sent his cavalry to attack, but was repelled again by Catholic troopers.
3   Thurn's brigade marched from Bernard's flank to Horn's position. On his march from Heselberg to the south, Thurn saw the fort defended by Toralto's tercio, and he decided to attack the position. But throughout the march, the brigade received fire simultaneously from both flanks. Despite this, General Thurn insisted on maintaining the assault.
4   Horn concentrated all his available cavalry, between 3,500-4,000 men, and moves them as a body between Heselberg and Albuch. The Protestant cavalry engaged in a battle against the 1,830 of Gambacorta's and the 1,200 of Piccolomini's troopers. However, despite their numbers, Protestants gave ground to Catholic cavalry and retired. Thurn's infantry was left alone and isolated again.
5   The Spaniards of Idiáquez Tercio charges against Thurn's brigade and then the Swedes are forced to retreat to Heselberg Hill.
6   Albuch's defenders are reinforced by Torrecusa's arquebusiers and the Spanish line advance down the hill and extend their defensive perimeter.

Map 6 Phase 3- page 156

1   Taupadel's Dragons led a flanking attempt on their left the Catholic right flank, on the town of Kleinerdlingen, but were repulsed by the Issolano's Croatian light cavalry.
2   Bernard's 2,000 troopers make a bold and aggressive advance, threateningly breaking into the Herkheimerfeld Plain. However, in the vicinity of the village of Herkheim, where the advanced Imperial infantry companies had deployed, supported by several groups of Croat cavalry, the Protestant cavalry was stopped.
3   Gallas ordered the counterattack of his own cavalry. Gonzaga and Werth's Catholic troops attacked Bernard's mounted units. The cavalry clash was very intense, but the greater number of Catholics led to Bernard's cavalry being defeated.
4   Bernard ordered up his reserve echelon into the battle charge to rescue them; Cratz took command of these 7 squads. But upon seeing Cratz's movement, General Gallas brought up the Imperial Cavalry Reserve,

5. Bernard then sent his last 5 reserve squadrons. The Catholics sent more regiments to support Gonzaga and Werth's cavalry. At the same time the Marquis of Leganés sent 400 musketeers from the tercio of the Count of Fuenclara to support the advance of the Catholic cavalry.

6. The general Catholic attack overwhelms Bernard's brigade and the Protestant's defensive line. The Protestant troops start to retreat in disorder.

7. Marshal Horn orders the withdrawal of his army. The survivors of Pfuhl's brigade lead the vanguard, with the Swedish artillery was located immediately afterwards. The rest of the survivors of the Horn's forces covered the retreat.

8. As the Horn column was almost reaching Ederheim, about to cross the Rezen stream, Bavarian cuirassiers appeared riding from the Lachberg and Heselberg, followed by Gambacorta's troopers and other imperial cavalry units, as well as some Croatians, followed by 400 Spanish musketeers of the tercio of the Count of Fuenclara. They are in turn followed by the reserve of the Hispanic army. Horn's cavalry barely resisted, before being scattered. Taking advantage of their speed, the Catholic cavalry captured artillery and cut off the Protestant column. The battle was over, and the massacre of the fugitives began.

Bibliography

Aberg, A: 'The Swedish Army from Lützen to Narva', in *Sweden's age of greatness, 1632–1718*. Macmillan, London, 1973.

Aedo Y Gallart, Diego de: *El memorable y glorioso viaje del Infante Cardenal de Fernando de Austria*. Ivan Cnobbart, Antwerp, 1635.

Albi De La Cuesta, Julio: *De Pavía a Rocroi: los tercios de infantería española en los siglos XVI y XVII*. Desperta Ferro Ediciones, Madrid, 2017.

Albi De La Cuesta, Julio: *Entre Nördlingen y Honnecourt: los tercios españoles del Cardenal-Infante I (1632–1636)*. Almena, Madrid, 2015.

Aldea Vaquero, Quintín: *España en Europa en el siglo XVII. Correspondencia de Saavedra Fajardo. Tomo II: La tragedia del Imperio: Wallenstein, 1634*. CSIC, Madrid, 2008.

Aldea Vaquero, Quintín: *España en Europa en el siglo XVII. Correspondencia de Saavedra Fajardo. Tomo III: El cardenal Infante en el imposible camino de Flandes, 1633–1634*. CSIC, Madrid, 2008.

Allen, Paul C.: *Felipe III y la Pax hispánica, 1598–1621*. Alianza Editorial, Madrid, 2001.

Almirante, José: *Diccionario militar. Etimológico, histórico, tecnológico*. Imprenta del depósito de Guerra, Madrid, 1869.

Álvarez-Coca González, María Jesús: 'La concesión de hábitos de caballeros de las Ordenes Militares procedimiento y reflejo documental (s. XVI-XIX)' in *Cuadernos de historia moderna*, 14, 1993, p.277-298.

Andersson, Ingvar: *A History of Sweden*. Praeger, New York, 1956.

Andújar Castillo, Francisco: *Ejércitos y Militares en la Época Moderna*. Síntesis, Madrid, 1999.

Anónimo: *Relación de sucesos de 1634*. Biblioteca Nacional de España, 1635.

Arroyo Martín, Francisco: 'El marqués de Leganés. Apuntes biográficos', in *Espacio, Tiempo y Forma*, Serie IV, Historia Moderna, 15, 2002, p.145-185.

Asch, Ronald G.: *The Thirty Years War. The Holy Roman Empire and Europe, 1618–1648*. Macmillan, Houndmills, Basingstoke, 1997.

Bagi, Zoltán Péter: 'The Life of Soldiers during the Long Turkish War (1593–1606)' in *The Hungarian Historical Review*, Vol. 4, 2, Cultures of Christian–Islamic Wars in Europe (1450–1800) 2015, p.384-417.

Beladiez Navarro, Emilio: *España y el Sacro Imperio Romano Germánico. Wallenstein (1583–1634)*. Editorial Prensa Española, Madrid, 1967.

Bierther, Kathrin: 'Piccolomini, Ottavio', in *Neue Deutsche Biographie* (NDB). Band 20, Duncker & Humblot, Berlin, 2001, p.408-410.

Black, Jeremy: *A Military Revolution? Military Change and European Society 1550–1800 (Studies in European History)*. Red Globe Press, Basingstoke, 1991.

Black, Jeremy: *The Cambridge Illustrated Atlas of Warfare: Renaissance to Revolution, 1492–1792*. Cambridge University Press, Cambridge, 1996.

Bonney, Richard: *The Thirty Years' War 1618–1648*. Essential Histories 29. Osprey, Oxford, 2002.

Borreguero, Beltrán: Cristina: *La guerra de los Treinta años 1618–1648: Europa ante el abismo*. La Esfera de los Libros, Madrid, 2018.

Bourdeu, Etienne: 'Hombres y dinero. La ayuda española al emperador', in *Desperta Ferro. Historia Moderna*, 60, 2019, p.28-31.

Bracewell, C. W.: *The Uskoks of Senj: Piracy, Banditry, and Holy War in the Sixteenth-Century Adriatic*. Cornell University Press, New York, 1992.

Brightwell, Peter: 'The Spanish Origins of the Thirty Years' War', in *European Studies Review,* 9, 1979, p.409-431.

Brightwell, Peter: 'Spain and Bohemia: The Decision to Intervene, 1619', in *European Studies Review,* 12, 1982a, p.117–141.

Brightwell, Peter: 'Spain, Bohemia and Europe, 1619–1621', in *European Studies Review,* 12, 1982b, p.371-399

Brnardic, Vladimir: *Imperial Armies of the Thirty Years' War (1). Infantry and Artillery.* Men-at-Arms 457. Osprey, Oxford, 2009.

Brnardic, Vladimir: *Imperial Armies of the Thirty Years' War (2). Cavalry.* Men-at-Arms 462. Osprey, Oxford, 2010.

Brzezinski, Richard: *The Army of Gustavus Adolphus (1). Infantry.* Men-at-Arms 235. Osprey, Oxford, 1991.

Brzezinski, Richard: *The Army of Gustavus Adolphus (2). Cavalry.* Men-at-Arms 262. Osprey, Oxford, 1993.

Brzezinski, Richard: *Lützen 1632: Climax of the Thirty Years' War.* Campaign 68. Osprey, Oxford, 2001.

Caimi, Ricardo: *La Guerra de Friuli.* Libreia Editrice Goriziana, Gorizia, 2007.

Calvo, María del Carmen: 'España y la Guerra de los Treinta Años en el quinquenio 1630–1635' in *Saitabi,* 20, 1970, p.161–179.

Cánovas Del Castillo, Antonio: *Estudios del reinado de Felipe IV.* Vol. II. Pérez Dubrull, Madrid, 1889.

Cañete, Hugo A.: *Los Tercios de Flandes en Alemania: la Guerra del Palatinado (1620–1623).* Platea, Barcelona, 2014.

Carrasco Martínez, Adolfo: 'Guerra y virtud nobiliaria en el Barroco. Las Noblezas de la Monarquía Hispánica frente al fenómeno bélico (1598–1659)', in García Hernán, Enrique y Maffi, Davide (eds.): *Guerra y sociedad en la Monarquía Hispánica. Política, estrategia y cultura en la Europa Moderna (1500–1700).* Laberinto, Madrid, 2006, Vol. II, p.135–162.

Chudoba, Bohdan: *España y el Imperio.* Rialp, Madrid, 1963.

Claramunt Soto, Alex: *Farnesio. La ocasión perdida de los Tercios.* HRM Ediciones, Zaragoza, 2016.

Clonard, Conde de: *Historia orgánica de las armas de infantería y caballería españolas desde la creación del ejército permanente hasta el día.* Imprenta D.B. González, Madrid, 1851-62, Vol. IV.

Croxton, Derek: 'The Prosperity of Arms Is Never Continual: Military Intelligence, Surprise, and Diplomacy in 1640s Germany', in *The Journal of Military History,* 64, 4 (Oct 1, 2000), p.981–1003.

De La Rocha, Carlos y Cañete, Hugo A: *El Ejército de Alsacia. Intervención española en el Alto Rin (1633/34).* Sátrapa Ediciones, Zaragoza, 2010.

De Vera, Juan Antonio: *La Vitoria, que tuvieron sobre Norlinga la Magestad de Fernando III, Rey de Vngria, y el Serenisimo Infante de España Don Fernando.* Juan Bautista Malatesta, Milan, 1638.

Delbrück, Hans: *History of the Art of War 4. The Dawn of Modern Warfare.* University of Nebraska Press, Lincoln, 1990.

Dotzauer, Winfried: *Die deutschen Reichskreise in der Verfassung des alten Reiches und ihr Eigenleben. 1500–1806.* Wissenschaftliche Buchgesellschaft, Darmstadt, 1989.

Eguiluz, Martín de: *Discurso y regla militar.* Pedro Bellero, Antwerp, 1595.

Engerisser, Peter: *Von Kronach nach Nördlingen. Der Dreißigjährige Krieg in Franken, Schwaben und der Oberpfalz 1631–1635.* Verlag H. Späthling, Weißenstadt, 2005.

Engerisser, Peter y Hrncirik, Pavel: *Nördlingen 1634. Die Schlacht bei Nördlingen. Wendepunkt des Dreißigjährigen Krieges.* Verlag H. Späthling, Weißenstadt, 2009.

Elliot, J.H.: *El conde-duque de Olivares.* Grijalbo Mondadori, Barcelona, 1990.

Eltis, David: *Military Revolution in Sixteenth Century.* Barnes Noble Books, New York, 1998.

Esteban Ribas, Alberto Raúl: *La batalla de Fleurus, 1622.* Almena, Madrid, 2013.

Esteban Ribas, Alberto Raúl: *La batalla de Tuttlingen, 1643.* Almena, Madrid, 2014.

Finkel, Caroline: *The Administration of Warfare: The Ottoman Military Campaigns in Hungary, 1593–1606.* VWGÖ, Vienna, 1988.

Fredholm Von Essen, Michael: *The Lion from the North. The Swedish Army during the Thirty Years War (1618–1632).* Helion, Warwick, 2020.

Fredholm Von Essen, Michael: *The Lion from the North. The Swedish Army during the Thirty Years War (1632–1648).* Helion, Warwick, 2020.

Frost, Robert I.: *The Northern Wars. War, State and Society in North-eastern Europe 1558–1721.* Routledge, New York, 2000.

BIBLIOGRAPHY

Fulaine, Jean-Charles: *Le Duc Charles IV de Lorraine et son armée: 1624-1675*. Editions Serpenoise, Woippy, 1997.

Fuller, J. F. C.: *The Decisive Battles of the Western World and Their Influence Upon History (480 B.C. - 1757)*. SPA Books Ltd, London, 1993.

García, Bernardo José: 'Felipe II y la Guerra de Flandes en una década decisiva (1589-1598)', en Campos Y Fernández De Sevilla, F. J. (ed.): *Felipe II y su época. Actas del Simposium II*. Estudios Superiores del Escorial, San Lorenzo del Escorial, 1998.

García, Bernardo José (ed.): *Tiempo de paces: La Pax Hispanica y la Tregua de los Doce Años*. Fundación Carlos de Amberes, Madrid, 2009.

García Hernán, David: *La cultura de la guerra y el teatro del siglo de oro*. Sílex Ediciones, Madrid, 2006.

García Hernán, Enrique y Maffi, Davide (eds.): *Guerra y sociedad en la Monarquía Hispánica. Política, estrategia y cultura en la Europa Moderna (1500-1700)*. Laberinto, Madrid, 2006.

Giménez Martín, Juan: *Tercios de Flandes*. Falcata Ibérica, Barcelona, 1991.

Gindely, Antonín: *History of the Thirty years' War*. Putnam's Sons, New York, 1884.

Gonzalez Cuerva, Ruben: *Baltasar de Zúñiga, una encrucijada de la monarquía hispana (1561-1622)*. Síntesis, Madrid, 2012.

González De León, Fernando: 'Doctors of the Military Discipline: Technical Expertise and the Paradigm of the Spanish Soldier in the Early Modern Period', in *The Sixteenth Century Journal*, 27, 1 (summer, 1996), p.61-85.

González De León, Fernando: *The Road to Rocroi: Class, Culture and Command in the Spanish Army of Flanders, 1567-1659*. Brill Academic, Leiden, 2008.

Guthrie, William P.: *Batallas de la Guerra de los Treinta Años. De la Montaña Blanca a Nördlingen, 1618-1635*. Ediciones Platea, Málaga, 2016.

Hallwich, Hermann: 'Gallas, Matthias Graf von', in *Allgemeine Deutsche Biographie*: (ADB). Volumen 8, Duncker & Humblot, Leipzig, 1878, p.320-331.

Hengerer, Mark: *Kaiser Ferdinand III (1608-1657): Eine Biographie*. Böhlau Verlag, Vienna, 2012.

Houben, Birgit: 'La casa del Cardenal Infante don Fernando de Austria (1620-1641', in Martínez Millán, José y Hortal Muñoz, José Eloy (coord.): *La corte de Felipe IV (1621-1665): reconfiguración de la Monarquía católica,* Vol. 3. Polifemo, Madrid, 2015, p.1679-1705.

Hrncirik, Pavel: *Spanier auf dem Albuch, Ein Beitrag zur Geschichte der Schlacht bei Nördlingen im Jahre 1634*. Shaker Verlag, Aachen, 2007.

Jacob, Karl: *Von Lützen nach Nördlingen. Ein Beitrag zur Geschichte des Dreissigjährigen Kriegs in Süddeutschland in den Jahren 1633 und 1634*. Van Hauten, Strasbourg, 1904.

Jimenez Candil, Justino: *Don Juan del Águila. Caballero español y maestre de campo general de Felipe II*. Ayuntamiento de El Barraco, El Barraco, 2009.

Jiménez Estrella, Antonio y Andújar Castillo, Francisco (Eds.): *Los Nervios de la guerra. Estudios sociales sobre el Ejército de la Monarquía Hispánica (s. XVI - XVIII): nuevas perspectivas*. Comares, Granada, 2007.

Landmann, Carl von: 'Kratz zu Scharffenstein, Johann Philipp Graf', in *Allgemeine Deutsche Biographie* (ADB), 4, Duncker & Humblot, Leipzig, 1876, p.573-575.

Livet, Georges: *La Guerra de los Treinta Años*. Davinci Continental, Barcelona, 2008.

Londoño, Sancho: *Discurso sobre la forma de reduzir la disciplina militar a mejor y antiguo estado*. Luís Sánchez, Madrid, 1593.

Lynn, John A.: *Giant of the Grand Siècle. The French Army 1610-1715*. Cambridge University Press, Cambridge, 1997.

Macdonald, John: *Great Battlefields of the World*. Hungry Minds, Foster City, 1988.

Maffi, Davide: *En defensa del Imperio. Los ejércitos de Felipe IV y la guerra por la hegemonía europea (1635-1659)*. Actas, Madrid, 2014.

Mahr, Helmut: *Wallenstein vor Nürnberg 1632. Sein Lager bei Zirndorf und die Schlacht an der Alten Veste, dargestellt durch den Plan der Gebrüder Trexel 1634*. Degener, Neustadt, 1982.

Martín Sanz, Francisco: *La política internacional de Felipe IV*. Editorial Libros en Red, 2003.

Martínez Aragón, Lucio y FIOR, Michela: *El Conde de Fuentes de Valdepero y el Fuerte de Fuentes en el Camino Español*. Glyphos Publicaciones, Valladolid, 2015.

Martínez Gómez, Pablo: *El ejercito español en la Guerra de los Treinta años*. Almena, Madrid, 2006.

Martínez Laínez, Fernando: *Una pica en Flandes. La epopeya del Camino Español*. EDAF, Madrid, 2007.

Martínez Laínez, Fernando y Sánchez De Toca, José María de: *Tercios de España. La infantería legandaria*. EDAF, Madrid, 2006.

Martínez Ruiz, Enrique: *Los soldados del Rey. Los ejércitos de la Monarquía Hispánica (1480–1700)*. Actas, Madrid, 2008.

Mears, John A.: 'The Thirty Years' War, the 'General Crisis,' and the Origins of a Standing Professional Army in the Habsburg monarchy', in *Central European History*, 21-2, 1988.

Mendoza, Bernardino de: *Comentarios de don Bernardino de Mendoça de lo sucedido en las guerras de los Payses Baxos*. Pedro Madrigal, Madrid, 1592.

Merian, Matthäus: *Theatrum Europaeum, 1646–1738*. (https://en.wikipedia.org/wiki/Theatrum_Europaeum)

Merlin, Pierpaolo y Ieva, Frédéric: *Monferrato 1613, La vigilia di una crisi europea*. Viella, Roma, 2016.

Mesa, Eduardo de: *Nördlingen 1634. Victoria decisiva de los tercios*. Almena, Madrid, 2003.

Mesa Gallego, Eduardo de: 'Innovaciones militares en la Monarquía hispánica durante el siglo XVI. Origen y desarrollo' in García Hernán, Enrique y Maffi, Davide (coord.): *Guerra y sociedad en la monarquía hispánica: política, estrategia y cultura en la Europa moderna (1500–1700)*. CSIC, Madrid, 2006, p.537-552.

Mesa Gallego, Eduardo de: *La pacificación de Flandes: Spínola y las campañas de Frisia (1604–1609)*. Ministerio de Defensa, Madrid, 2009.

Montes, Diego: *Instrucción y regimiento de guerra*. Jorge Coci, Zaragoza, 1537.

Moreno Casado, J.: 'Las Ordenanzas de Alejandro Farnesio, de 1587' in *Anuario de historia del derecho español*, 31, 1961, p.431-458.

Mortimer, Geoff: *Wallenstein. The Enigma of the Thirty Years War*. Palgrave Macmillan, New York, 2010.

Mugnai, Bruno y Flaherty, Christopher: *Der Lange Türkenkrieg (1593–1606): The long Turkish War*. Soldiershop, Bergamo, 2014-2015.

Navarro Méndez, Joaquín: 'La instrucción de 1536 u Ordenanza de Génova (la génesis de los Tercios)' in *Revista Ejército*, 827, March 2010, p.108–110.

Negredo Del Cerro, F: *La Guerra de los Treinta Años. Una visión desde la monarquia hispánica*. Síntesis, Madrid, 2016.

Nider, Valentina: 'La Relación verdadera sobre el hecho de los Uscoques de Emanuel de Tordesillas y el Mundo caduco de Francisco de Quevedo', in *La Perinola*, 18, 2014, p.143–159.

Notario López, Ignacio&Iván: *The Spanish Tercios, 1536–1704*. Men-at-Arms 481. Osprey, Oxford, 2012.

Pagès, Georges: *La Guerre de Trente Ans: 1618–1648*. Payot, Paris, 1991.

Palencia, C.: *El Cardenal Infante Don Fernando de Austria*. Speech delivered at the opening of the course of the Royal Academy of Fine Arts and Historical Sciences of Toledo. Toledo, 1946.

Paoletti, Ciro: 'L'Italia e il Cammino di Fiandra', in Congresso internazionale 'Le armi del sovrano. Eserciti e flotte da Lepanto alla Rivoluzione Francese, 1571–1789', Roma, Archivio di Stato, 2001.

Parker, Geoffrey: *La Revolución militar. Las innovaciones militares y el apogeo de Occidente, 1500–1800*. Crítica, Barcelona, 1990.

Parker, Geoffrey: *Los soldados europeos entre 1550 y 1650*. Ediciones Akal, Madrid, 1990.

Parker, Geoffrey: *La Guerra de los Treinta Años*. Editorial Antonio Machado, Madrid, 2004.

Parker, Geoffrey: *El ejército de Flandes y el Camino Español 1567–1659*. Alianza Editorial, Madrid, 2006.

Parrott, David: 'Strategy and Tactics in the Thirty Years War: The Military Revolution,' in Rodgers, Clifford (ed.): *The Military Revolution Debate Readings on The Military Transformation of Early Modern Europe*. Westview Press, Boulder, 1995.

Pérez Preciado, José Juan: *El marqués de Leganés y las artes*. Thesis. Universidad Complutense de Madrid, Madrid, 2010.

Picouet, Pierre: *The Armies of Phillip IV of Spain (1621–1665)*. Helion, Warwick, 2019.

Polišenský, Josef V.: *The Thirty Years' War*. New English Library, London, 1974.

Portugués, Joseph Antonio: *Colección General de Ordenanzas militares*. Imprenta de Antonio Martín, Madrid, 1764.

Poyntz, Sidney: *A true relation of these German Warres*. Camden Society, 1908.

Priorato, Galliazo Gualdo: *Historia delle guerre di Ferdinando II e Ferdinando III, imperatori e del re Filippo IV di Spagna Contro Gostavo Adolfo re di Suetia, e Luigi XIII, re di Francia*. Giacomo Monti, Bolognia, 1641.

Puddu, Raffaele: *El soldado gentilhombre*. Argos Vergara, Barcelona, 1984.

Puig, Rogelio: 'El cardenal-infante don Fernando de Austria, evocación militar de una gran figura histórica', in *Saitabi: revista de la Facultat de Geografia i Història*, 8, 35-38, 1950–1951, p.66-71.

BIBLIOGRAPHY

Polišenský, Josef V.: *The Thirty Years' War*. Batsford, London, 1971.
Quatrefages, René: *Los tercios*. Ediciones Ejercito, Madrid, 1983.
Quatrefages, René: *La revolución militar moderna: el crisol español*. Ministerio de Defensa, Madrid, 1996.
Quesada Sanz, Fernando: 'Los mitos de Rocroi', in *La aventura de la Historia*, 97 (november 2006), Arlanza Ediciones, Madrid.
Reberski De Baricevic, Z.: 'El duque de Osuna y los uscoques de Seña', in *Cuadernos de Historia de España*, XLV-XLVI, 1967, p.45-46 and p.300-351.
Rebitsch, Robert: *Matthias Gallas (1588–1647). Generalleutnant des Kaisers zur Zeit des Dreißigjährigen Krieges. Eine militärische Biographie*. Aschendorff Verlag, Münster, 2006.
Redlich, Fritz: *The Germany Military Enterpriser and his Workforce*. Franz Steiner, Wiesbaden, 1964.
Ribot, Luis (coord.): *Historia Militar de España. Edad Moderna II. Escenario europeo*. Ministerio de Defensa, Madrid, 2013.
Roberts, Michael: *Gustavus Adolphus, A History of Sweden 1611–1632*. Longman, London, 1953–1958.
Roberts, Michael: *The Military Revolution 1560–1660*. M. Boyd, Belfast, 1956.
Roberts, Michael: 'The political objectives of Gustavus Adolphus in Germany', in *Transactions of the Royal Historical Society*, 7, 1957, p.19 – 46.
Roberts, Michael: *Essays in Swedish History*. Weidenfeld Nicolson, London, 1967.
Roberts, Michael: *Sweden as a great power 1611–1697*. St. Martin's Press, London, 1968.
Roberts, Michael: *Gustavus Adolphus and the Rise of Sweden*. English Universities Press, London, 1973.
Roberts, Michael: *The Swedish imperial experience 1560–1718*. Cambridge University Press, Cambridge, 1984.
Rodenas Vilar, Rafael: *La política europea de España durante la Guerra de los Treinta Años (1624–1630)*. CSIC, Madrid, 1967.
Rodríguez Hernández, Antonio José: *España, Flandes y la Guerra de Devolución (1667–1668). Guerra, reclutamiento y movilización para el mantenimiento de los Países Bajos españoles*. Ministerio de Defensa, Madrid, 2007.
Rodríguez Hernández, Antonio José: *Los Tambores de Marte. El Reclutamiento en Castilla durante la segunda mitad del siglo XVII (1648–1700)*. Universidad de Valladolid, Valladolid, 2011.
Rodríguez Hernández, Antonio José: *Breve historia de los Tercios de Flandes*. Nowtilus, Madrid, 2015.
Rodríguez Hernández, Antonio José y Mesa Gallego, Eduardo de: 'Del Gran Capitán a los Tercios: La herencia de Gonzalo Fernández de Córdoba en los ejércitos de los Austrias (siglos XVI y XVII)', in *Revista de Historia Militar*, II extraordinario de 2015, p.143-188.
Rogers, Clifford J. (ed.): *The Military Revolution Debate Readings on The Military Transformation of Early Modern Europe*. Westview Press, Boulder, 1995.
Rucker, Christian: *Die Entscheidungsschlacht bei Nördlingen im Schwedischen Krieg (1630–1635)*. Grin Verlag, 2011.
Ruiz Ibáñez, J. J.: *Laberintos de hegemonía. La presencia militar de la Monarquía Hispánica en Francia a finales del siglo XVI*. Universidad de Valladolid, Valladolid, 2012.
Sánchez, Jorge: *El Camino Español. Un viaje por la ruta de los Tercios de Flandes*. Editorial Dilema, Madrid, 2014.
Schiller, Friedrich: *The history of the thirty years' war in Germany*. A. L. Burt, New York, 1897.
Spring, Laurence: *The Bavarian Army During the Thirty Years War, 1618-1648: The Backbone of the Catholic League*. Helion, Warwick, 2017.
Spring, Laurence: *In the Emperor's service. Wallenstein's Army, 1625–1634*. Helion, Warwick, 2019.
Struck, Walter: *Die Schlacht bei Nördlingen im Jahre 1634, Ein Beitrag zur Geschichte des Dreißigjährigen Krieges*. Universität Berlin, 1893.
Taylor, Francis L.: *The Art of War in Italy, 1494–1529*. Cambridge University Press, Cambridge, 1921.
Thompson, I.A.A.: *Guerra y decadencia. Gobierno y administración en la España de los Austrias, 1560-1620*. Crítica, Barcelona, 1981.
Thompson, I.A.A.: 'Milicia, sociedad y estado en la España Moderna', in Vaca Lorenzo, Ángel (ed.): *La Guerra en la Historia*. Universidad de Salamanca, Salamanca, 1999.
Thompson, I.A.A.: 'Consideraciones sobre el papel de la nobleza como recurso militar e la España Moderna', in Jiménez Estrella, Antonio y Andujar Castillo, Francisco (eds.): *Los Nervios de la guerra. Estudios sociales sobre el Ejército de la Monarquía Hispánica (s. XVI - XVIII): nuevas perspectivas*. Comares, Granada, 2007.

Todesco, A.: *Gli Uscocchi,* Casalvelino Scalo, Galzerano, 1982.

Tordesillas, E.: *Relación verdadera de lo que ha passado entre la Serenísima República de Venecia, y el Serenísimo Archiduque Ferdinando, sobre el hecho de los Uscoques súbditos de su Alteza: y las razones que por las partes se alegan, y lo sucedido en la guerra. Y entre el señor Duque de Saboya, y el señor don Pedro de Toledo.* Juan Sanchez, Madrid, 1616.

Trexe, Hans y Paulus: *Plan des Wallenstein'schen Lagers bei Zirndorf 1632.* Nachzeichnung und Druck, Nürnberg, 1932.

Vázquez De Prada, Valentín: *Felipe II y Francia (1559–1598). Política, religión y razón de Estado.* Eunsa, Pamplona, 2004.

Van Creveld, Martin: *Supplying War: Logistics from Wallenstein to Patton.* Cambridge University Press, Cambridge, 2004.

Van Nimwegen, Olaf: *The Dutch Army and the Military Revolutions 1588–1688.* Boydell, Woodbridge, 2010.

Van Der Essen, Alfred: *Le Cardinal-Infant et la politique européenne de l'Espagne (1609–1641).* Brussels, 1944.

Van Der Hoeven, Marco (ed.): *Exercise of Arms. Warfare in the Netherlands (1568–1648).* Brill, Leiden, 1997.

Vigato, Mauro: 'La Guerra Veneto-Archiducale de Gradisca (1615–1617)', in *Rivista della Società Filologica Friulana 'Graziadio I. Ascoli',* LXX, 1994.

Wedgwood, Cicely Veronica: *The Thirty Years War.* Review of Books, New York, 2005.

Weyhe-Eimke, Arnold von: *Octavio Piccolomini als Herzog von Amalfi.* Steinhauser & Korb, Pilsen, 1871.

Wilson, Peter H.: *Europe's Tragedy: A History of the Thirty Years War.* Penguin UK, London, 2009.